Asian Women in Transition

Asian Women in Transition

Sylvia A. Chipp

and

Justin J. Green

Editors

The Pennsylvania State University Press

University Park and London

This book is dedicated to

Dr. Marguerite J. Fisher
Professor Emeritus
Syracuse University

in appreciation of her inspiration and guidance.

"The Japanese Woman: Evolving Views of Life and Role," by Susan J. Pharr, appears in slightly different form in Lewis Austin, ed., *Japan: The Paradox of Progress,* New Haven: Yale University Press, 1976. Copyright © 1976 by Yale University.

"Women in the People's Republic of China," by Kay Ann Johnson, appears in slightly different form in Joan I. Roberts, ed., *Beyond Intellectual Sexism: A New Woman, A New Reality,* New York: Longman, 1976.

Library of Congress Cataloging in Publication Data

Main entry under title:

Asian women in transition.

1. Women—Asia—Addresses, essays, lectures.
I. Chipp, Sylvia A. II. Green, Justin J.
HQ1726.A84   301.41'2'095   79-20517
ISBN 0-271-00251-4 cloth
ISBN 0-271-00257-3 paper

Contents

Preface

This book provides a view of Asian women based on field research that goes beyond mere reading of government documents and the like. It is hoped that this book will be useful especially to those making comparative studies of women around the world as well as to those attempting to gain a broader understanding of Asia. Although we have not imposed a theoretical framework, a good many of the chapters address themselves either directly or indirectly to the issues raised in the introduction.

The arrangement of this volume is essentially a geographical one: East Asia, Southeast Asia, and South Asia. It is exceedingly difficult to generalize about Asia: there is so much diversity in terms of political and economic systems, cultural and religious beliefs and practices. We hope this geographical division will further meaningful analysis and comparisons.

We would like to take the opportunity to express our appreciation to the contributors to this volume for their role in its creation. Our thanks also to those too numerous to list for their long hours of typing, reading, and advising. Special thanks and appreciation go to understanding families and friends who cheered us on. Last, but not least, we would like to thank the staff of the Pennsylvania State University Press for their role in bringing this volume to fruition.

About the Contributors

Sylvia A. Chipp is Associate Professor of Political Science at Northeastern Oklahoma State University. She is the author of a number of articles on Pakistani women.

Stephen A. Douglas is Associate Professor of Political Science at the University of Illinois, Urbana. He is the author of numerous works on Southeast Asia, including *Student Activism and Political Socialization in Indonesia.*

Justin J. Green is Associate Professor of Political Science at Villanova University. He is executive secretary of the Philippine Studies Association and editor of the *Philippine Studies Newsletter.* He has published articles on a wide variety of topics in a broad assortment of social-science journals.

Rounaq Jahan is Professor of Political Science at Dacca University, Bangladesh. She is the author of a number of books and articles including *Pakistan: Failure in National Integration, Political Participation in Bangladesh,* and *Women in Bangladesh.* She is on the editorial boards of *Alternative, Asian Survey,* and *Asian Political Thought.*

Kay Ann Johnson is Assistant Professor of Asian Studies and Political Science in the School of Social Science, Hampshire College. She is the author of *Feminism and Socialist Revolution in China: The Politics of Family Reform and Women's Rights,* and she recently visited North China gathering research materials for a village study.

Joyce K. Kallgren teaches Political Science with an emphasis on the People's Republic of China at the University of California, Davis. She also serves as Vice-Chair of the Center for Chinese Studies at Berkeley.

Manjulika Koshal is Assistant Professor of Business Administration in the Department of Administrative Sciences at Ohio University. She has published several articles and presented papers at a number of professional meetings.

Gail Minault is Assistant Professor of History at the University of Texas, Austin. She served with the U.S. Information Service in Pakistan, and has lived and done research in India, 1967–71 and 1976–77. Her book *The Khilafat Movement: Religious Symbolism and Political Mobilization in India, 1911–1924* is forthcoming.

Susan J. Pharr is Assistant Professor and Associate Chairperson of Political Science, University of Wisconsin-Madison. She was formerly Staff Associate at the Social Science Research Council in New York. She is the author of a number of articles relating to gender roles and political behavior, and has just completed a book entitled *Political Women in Japan*.

Heather Strange is Associate Professor of Anthropology at University College, Rutgers—The State University of New Jersey. During 1977–78 she was a Fulbright Exchange Lecturer in the Department of Malay Studies and the Southeast Asia Program, University of Malaya, in Kuala Lumpur, Malaysia.

Ann R. Willner is Professor of Political Science at the University of Kansas. She served as an adviser to the Indonesian government and has published a number of monographs and articles on developing countries and on charismatic political leadership.

Introduction

Women's Changing Roles and Status

The growing consciousness that women have rarely if ever received justice is a worldwide phenomenon. In the past, attention has been paid primarily to women in the modernized nations. Increasingly since the late 1950s, through the efforts of the United Nations in conjunction with organized women's groups all over the world, the spotlight has focused on women's roles and status in the developing countries. This new emphasis is particularly true of Asia, where according to many observers the activities of women and their social positions are in a state of flux both in well-developed Japan and in the less-developed societies.

The International Women's Year Conference in Mexico City, in June of 1975, intensified the interest in, and consciousness of, the role and status of women in developing countries. This conference, however, was in part the result of earlier efforts to delineate the problems of women in developing countries. In the earliest of these efforts, in the late 1940s, Eleanor Roosevelt and others induced the United Nations, in its Declaration of Human Rights, to show a serious concern for the worldwide status of women.

Approximately one decade later, in 1957, the United Nations sponsored one of the first official conferences dealing with the status of women. This seminar, held in Bangkok, Thailand, dealt with the "Civic Responsibilities and Increased Participation of Asian Women in Public Life." In the following year the International Institute of Differing Civilizations met to discuss "Women's Role in the Development of Tropical and Subtropical Countries." Several years later, in December of 1966, the Philippines was the scene of yet another conference sponsored by the United Nations, which met to propose "Measures Required for the Advancement of Women with Special Reference to the Establishment of a Long-Term Program."

The scholarly community has demonstrated its interest in Asian women with its own series of smaller conferences, with frequent panels at scholarly meetings, and by developing a growing number of courses at universities and colleges, large and small, that focus on Asian women. These conferences and other events have crystallized for many the economic, sociological, and political fact that most women the world over have been relegated to their own separate "women's world," and while they have often been powerful in that realm, for the most part they have been excluded—at high cost to their societies—from the mainstream of economic and political power as well as from the decision-making process. Herbert Feldman (1967), observing Pakistan in the middle 1960s, was acutely aware of the problem when he noted that "it has long since been proved that any nation which fails to utilize its women-power to the best advantage simply divests itself of half of its human assets, in both physical and intellectual terms.[1] This observation, particularly as applied to the Asian societies with which we are concerned here, leads inevitably to a discussion of roles and relationships and their consequences for the status of women.

Barbara Watson (1976) offers us simple definitions of role and status on which to build our discussion. She defines a *role* as a "bundle of expected behaviors and attributes," and *status* as the "prestige accorded to the social category which typifies or does these things."[2] Thus one's *role* is what one does and may be ascribed, assumed, or achieved. One's *status* is, by this definition, what one is perceived to be.

The impression of most observers is that women's role and status are in a state of flux in Asian societies. The question raised by this observation is: What are the economic, social, political, ideological, and religious factors that are or will be affecting the process of role and status changes? The chapters in this book attempt to shed some light on these factors.

As indicated above, there is some evidence over the years of concern on the part of international organizations and national governments for the relative economic and political status of women in their respective societies. This concern, however, has rarely gone beyond the rather superficial level of government commissions, international conferences, and United Nations documents. These efforts have accomplished little toward introducing changes in practice, or for that matter, changes in thought.

Similarly, at the academic level there is a paucity of role and status theory that might contribute to an understanding of the change process. The literature suggests that there are several ways of studying the status and roles of women: life cycles; economic, political, ritual, and marital events; or the relationship of female roles to society as a whole, in several contexts—the growth of nationalism, the modernization process, economic growth, and the stability of the system. The lack of theoretical framework may be due to the facts that the necessary data are not readily available and that what information is available is often subjective and therefore not easily categorized into theoretical frameworks.

Several social scientists have registered concern about the relative invisibility of women in social science studies. Rosaldo and Lamphere (1974) note a lack of interest in women in conventional anthropology which they feel has led to "distorted and impoverished ethnographic accounts." The anthropological literature, they charge, "tells us relatively little about women, and provides almost no theoretical apparatus for understanding or describing culture from a woman's point of view."[3]

Bullough (1973) noted a similar problem in the field of history (which records the past subjugation of women). He suggests that because history has been written by men from the masculine perspective it causes particular problems: "Unfortunately we do not know how most women in the past regarded themselves or their role."[4] The *Ms. Magazine* series on the "Lost Women in History," which appeared during the American Bicentennial, was not merely an attempt to be clever. In the developing countries this scarcity of historical material on women is magnified.

Pescatello (1973) discusses at length the neglect of women in the social sciences and urges that this situation be rectified:

> As women and men are quite different, their historical roles have usually been divergent; "different" in our Western democratic mode of thought should not mean "unequal," but it has often been translated as such. It is particularly to rectify any note of inferiority or inequality—male or female—that studies of women should be undertaken and conducted according to criteria devised to deal with the difference between the sexes, in their roles and their achievements.[5]

Joan Roberts (1976) notes a continued bias against women resulting from an essentially masculine world view. She asks, "If the masculist God of religious belief is dead, as publicly proclaimed, why are women subjected to a new masculist God of science from whom they obtain no greater justice?"[6]

Though there would appear to be rather widespread agreement concerning the relative invisibility of women, or at best the generally restrictive treatment of women in social-science studies, there are indications of disagreement as to the actual portrayal of women's role and status.

Roberts discusses status in the context of women's inferiority in a man-made and male-dominated world. Although most roles are re-

served for men and roles serve to limit choices, change here is at least
theoretically possible. A thornier question is whether changes in
women's roles will really change their status very much. *Role* would
seem to be far more flexible than *status.* One can choose his or her role
within certain limits, but status is not usually a matter of individual
choice.

Is status, then, so intangible as to defy a theoretical framework? At
the practical level, as Kay Ann Johnson tells us in her chapter on
China, even a society consciously attempting to change female status
through expanding available roles may have only limited success.

Although the concerns of anthropologists, sociologists, and political
scientists differ, most social scientists perceive status, authority,
leadership, and elites as concepts that are closely related to each other
and are ultimately linked to power. Power is usually defined function-
ally, as the ability to control the choices made in any given decision-
making process. Thus people of high status are more likely to get
their way in such a situation. If the social scientist accepts this notion,
then he or she must decide which areas to examine for evidence of
differential status. For example, it is probably safe to assume that if we
were to examine only the institutional political arena in Asia, we
would find few females of high status and would therefore conclude
that women have little to say about important decisions. In other
areas, however, women may play more important roles.

From another perspective, Roberts associates role and status with
physical and economic power. She argues that to "create new cultural
images of women is to form a new image of power." She explains:

To re-think the male-female bond is to restructure the meaning of force in
all human endeavors. The inequity between women and men ultimately
resides in one fact, differential physical strength. This difference, exaggerated by socialization for strength in men and weakness in women, is the
basic source of social inequality in all human relationships, the prototype of
all subsequent forms of humiliation. It is muscle rather than mind that has
too often governed the fate of women and their children. This fact is one
that men and women try to avoid. However, the central and unavoidable
issue is the capacity and willingness to exert physical force in order to
impose one's will over another. A change in the relation of women to men
will require a radical reassessment of force and realignment of power.

Physical strength is often translated into the capacity to accumulate
resources, which as substitutes for personal prowess, serve the same purpose: to impose the primacy of one's desires and to obtain special privilege.
In this translation, women themselves have become a form of property. A
lucky combination of genes or a sheer accident of birth has allowed a few
women a brief but false sense of control. For the many, their condition as

chattel has been the concrete historical reality. It is money and not morality that has too often determined the lives of women and their children.

As in the past, men now control most institutional sources of money. The ability and desire to exert economic force as a substitute for brawn is the crucial issue. Since conflicting political theories are largely based on forms of economic control, a change in the status of women, who are one form of money, will necessitate a dramatic reordering of social priorities and a drastic redefinition of authority.[7]

From a slightly different perspective, Rosaldo notes that although women may be important, powerful, and influential, "relative to men of their age and social status, women everywhere lack generally recognized and culturally valued authority." She then proposes a structural model that "relates recurrent aspects of psychology and cultural social organization to an opposition between the 'domestic' orientation of women and the extra-domestic or 'public' ties that, in most societies, are primarily available to men."[8]

Rosaldo argues that women "lead lives that appear to be irrelevant to the formal articulation of social order." The woman's status is thus derived from her "biological functions, and in particular from the sexual or biological ties to particular men." Arguing that *man* is equated with culture and *woman* with nature, she sees woman as having an ascribed status: she is naturally what she is. Rosaldo notes that "purity and pollution are ideas that apply primarily to women, who must either deny their physical bodies or circumscribe their dangerous sexuality," and she continues:

> Now I would suggest that women in many societies will be seen as something "anomalous." Insofar as men, in their institutionalized relations of kinship, politics, and so on, define the public order, women are their opposite. Where men are classified in terms of ranked, institutional positions, women are simply women and their activities, interests, and differences receive only idiosyncratic note. Where male activities are justified and rationalized by a fine societal classification, by a system of norms acknowledging their different pursuits, women are classified together and their particular goals are ignored. From the point of view of the larger social system, they are seen as deviants or manipulators: because systems of social classification rarely make room for their interests, they are not publicly understood.[9]

Sanday (1974) makes a similar distinction between the public and domestic spheres in terms of the concepts of power, authority, respect, and reverence. But she emphasizes that respect and reverence are necessary for high status and defines female status in terms of "(1) the degree to which females have authority and/or power in the domestic and/or public domains; and (2) the degree to which females are accorded deferential treatment and are respected and revered in the domestic and/or public domains."[10]

It is important to note, however, that these social-science concepts are rather narrow in their perspective. Important decisions are made in areas normally not considered part of the public domain. But to attempt a study of power of women in the home and as "keepers of the tradition" is actually to attempt the unobservable and unresearchable. Further, if in Asia one were to study only the female elites (leaders, or educated modern women), one might be left with many false impressions garnered from the Western veneer of these "split-level societies."

It is necessary but understandably difficult to examine the roles and status of women cross-culturally. The barriers placed in the way of the researcher are many and varied. Survey research techniques prove to be somewhat sterile, and language presents important barriers to communication. Cultural norms, politeness toward the interviewer, who is, after all, an outsider, and the necessity of "saving face" (especially among the upper-class elites) are noteworthy concerns for the social scientist attempting research in such a sensitive subject area.

Barbara Ward (1963) deals with the concepts of role and status in the context of transitional societies. Her argument, stated simply, is that a female's status is a result of the social roles assigned to her by her culture. She notes that "as far as the sociological understanding of personal relationships is concerned, we believe that analysis in terms of new changing social roles is one of the keys."[11] Thus Ward is interested not only in roles as a source of status, but also in changing roles as a source of changing status. She discusses the emancipation of women—in terms of the franchise, office-holding, level of political awareness, and the ability to engage in activities outside the home—as resulting from four different factors. These factors show inter-relationships rather than cause and effect and can thus be said to be acausal.

The first consists of "common modern factors," by which Ward means modern medical measures, better communication, urbanization, new economic opportunities, and modern education. The second factor is sociologically defined as the relative role freedom provided by the traditional family form. The third factor is historical; for example, the extent to which women participated in the anticolonial struggle. The last is ideological, specifically the tolerance of the dominant religion for change.

But is it really clear that modern factors such as communication, urbanization, and new economic and educational opportunities necessarily lead to changing roles and status? In certain cases modern education, expanding economic roles, or participation in the anticolonial struggle can freeze women in inferior status positions and at times even drive them further down the status ladder. In fact, these modern outcomes are probably as much the result of changing roles as they are the cause of them. The other three factors in role openness—the traditional family form, historical accident, and religion—would seem to be better candidates for examination than these modern factors. We can illustrate this point by looking at the comparative effects of Asian religions on the status of women here. The other factors, family form and historical accident, will be considered later.

Unlike Western societies, which generally pride themselves on being secular, many Asian societies are essentially religious societies where virtually everything is explained in religious terms, whether it be Islam or Maoism. As noted by the individual authors of the chapters in this book, the influence of Islam, Hinduism, Buddhism, the teachings of Chairman Mao, or Catholicism can be seen in varying degrees throughout Asia; however, their impact has not been uniform, nor has it always been negative.

The tendency of the Westerner is to view innovation, social change, and modernization as rather impossible in countries "steeped in ancient religious traditions." Further, if culture is defined as a way of life and religion as a way of looking at life, one can speculate that quite different things should be happening in countries espousing the more or less "otherwordliness" of Hinduism and Buddhism and in those espousing a more pragmatic system of beliefs such as Maoism or the all-encompassing religiosity of Islam. Donald Smith (1970), exploring the interrelationships of traditional religions, political development, and the complex phenomenon of secularization, noted that religious factors have played and continue to play a positive role in certain aspects of political development, particularly in terms of religious legitimation of change.[12] Let us take a brief look at the major religions with which we are concerned: Hinduism, Islam, Catholicism, and the secular faith of modern China and successor to Confucianism called Maoism.

It can be argued that Hinduism is actually a collection of many diverse religions, that is, a loose unit of a wide variety of sects, local cults, and regional practices. Probably the most basic beliefs of any Hindu are rebirth, karma, and dharma. The doctrine of rebirth involves every living being in an eternal process of birth, death, and rebirth. Karma ("the law of cause and effect") provides the "reward" or "punishment" in the next life for the deeds performed in this life.

The concept of dharma constitutes an individual's duty, responsibilities, and behavioral expectations for all aspects of life and is
usually dependent on caste status.

Caste and class are intermingled in a Hindu society where there
have been outside influences, particularly from the West. Class, by
universal definition, refers to social status, which may be either
attained (for instance, by the acquisition of economic or political
power) or ascribed (for instance, by the accident of birth into a family
or ethnic group). Caste is a phenomenon unique to certain religions,
primarily Hinduism, and is more rigid than class because of its
religious sanction. Strictly applied, a caste system perpetuates by
birthright every individual's communal affiliation and thereby his or
her entire life style including form of worship, occupation, and
marriage partner. In India, the introduction by the British of modern
forms of political, economic, and military organization has superim-
posed Western class onto traditional Hindu caste.

Within this framework of beliefs, it is difficult to achieve many of
the major changes deemed necessary for a modernization of society
unless the changes are explainable in religious terms or unless a
separation of society and religion occurs. For example, it took a
Western-educated Jawaharlal Nehru to obtain such women's-rights
legislation as the Hindu Code Bill. It is no coincidence that one of the
few women leaders in Asia, Indira Gandhi, was Nehru's daughter.

Unlike Hinduism, Islam is a religion involving congregational worship. There would seem to be a far greater unity here, although there
are slight regional and national variations in customs and practices. As
Smith points out, "The most fundamental affirmation of Islam as a
system of belief and social organization is indeed that no man's life is
independent of God's awesome sovereignty."[13]

The Five Pillars of Islam spell out the basic religious obligations of
the faithful. The first involves the recitation of the Islamic creed:
"There is no god but Allah, and Muhammad is His Prophet." The
second pillar involves the ceremonial recitation of certain prayers five
times daily while facing in the direction of Mecca. The third pillar is
observance of Ramadan, a month of fasting in which no food or drink
may be taken during the day. The fourth pillar involves the giving of
alms according to Islamic law. The fifth pillar, haj, is the pilgrimage to
Mecca which is required at least once in their lifetime of all Muslims
who are physically and financially able to make the trip.

The Qur'an, which is the word of God as revealed to Muhammad,[14]
and the Sunnah, which records what Muhammad said and did in
regard to certain religious questions, form the basic source of Islamic
law. According to these sources, everything that happens is attributed

to the unchangeable decrees of Allah. The ulama, men learned in Islamic law, are the primary instruments by which the traditions are passed on. They bitterly condemn such modernist interpretations as those embodied in the changes in the status of women and in the institution of polygamy legislated by the Pakistan National Assembly in the Muslim Family Laws. The modernist, through the principles of *ijma* ("consensus") and *ijtihad* ("private judgment"), argues that such changes can be made in Islamic law through properly elected legislative bodies rather than through reliance solely on the interpretation of the ulama.

The centralized ecclesiastical organization lacking in Islam and Hinduism is evident in the authoritarian structure of the Roman Catholic Church, which was strongly resistant to change until Vatican II, the second Vatican Council of the early 1960s. Organized on a strictly authoritarian basis, the Church has both legislative and judicial powers, with supreme authority vested in the Pope as the vicar of Christ and the visible head of the Church. Bishops are appointed by the Pope and administer their respective dioceses through directives from the Pope and the prescriptions of canon law. The parish priest is directly responsible to his bishop.

The most telling feature of Catholicism resides in its doctrine of the infallibility of the Pope and in the sacramental system by which the Church mediates divine grace to men. Through its court system, the Church decides matters of morality and applies penalties, the ultimate penalty being excommunication.

In the early days of the Church there was no attempt to separate Church and state. A reading of the 300 years of Spanish rule in the Philippines is a case in point. It was not until the recent leadership of Pope John XXIII and Vatican Council II that the Catholic Church seemed to come to grips with the modern world. Professor Smith summarizes:

> First, there is the ethical doctrine of religious freedom as a human right, which stands in clear although unacknowledged contradiction to previous Catholic teaching. Secondly, there is a new concept of the basis of church-state relations: "The role and competence of the Church being what it is, she must in no way be confused with the political community, nor bound to any political system." Thirdly, there is acceptance of the basic idea of the welfare state and the necessity of increased governmental intervention in social and economic affairs. Fourthly, there is acceptance of the ideological and religious pluralism of the modern world: the modest claim put forth is that the Church can make its contribution on the basis of dialogue with the world.[15]

While not officially classified as a religion, Maoism may be viewed essentially as the new "transcendent belief" of China, with achieve-ment of the good of society as its ultimate goal. Women are expected to share in working toward this goal. In fact they are directed by Mao to hold up their half of the sky. Mao made the improvement of the social, economic, and political status of women a specific goal of the Revolution, although the achievement of this goal has been somewhat uneven.

The doctrines of Mao's New Democracy tend to be rigid and aggressive, but at the same time pragmatic and meant to instill nationalist pride in its people. The unitary patriarchal family of Confucianism has been extended to the nation. (See the introduction to Part I for a further discussion of Confucianism.) Here is an apparent translation of practical political and economic goals into "religious" (or philosophical) terms acceptable to the people.

It is interesting to note, however, that in spite of the very visible successes of the Chinese Revolution the other nations of Asia, while occasionally accepting Chinese aid, maintain their neutrality and view with suspicion the Chinese government.

When we examine the effects of these religions on the status of women in Asia, we see that though religion has been important its influence varies according to the total cultural climate in each society. One key cultural variable, for instance, is the kinship system (as is noted in the introductions to Parts II and III). Thus Islam has limited female status to a greater extent in South Asia, where it is tied to a patriarchal family system, than it has in Indonesia, where the effects of a bilateral kinship system still persist and where historically the state and church have been poorly integrated. The current problems of Iran, though complex, appear to be in part an example of how a modernizing government can be threatened by the forces of Islamic religion. A significant aspect of the shah's modernization program consisted of greater freedom for women. If this reform comprises one of the objections of the Muslim leaders, then a possible conclusion is that women may have special difficulty in achieving true equality in societies where Islam is strong, where the patriarchal family exists, and where church and state are closely integrated.

The role of Catholicism in limiting the status of Philippine women is less clear. Here bilateral kinship ties, combined during the twentieth century with an open American educational system, have tended to overcome any tendency of the Church to depreciate the status of women. One residual influence of Catholicism in the Philippines consists of negative attitudes toward family planning and population control. Although such attitudes affect the development of the whole society, they obviously place a heavier burden on women than on men.

The effects of Hinduism on Indian women vary according to their caste and class. In general, the higher the caste or class of an Indian woman, the less her role and status are diminished by religious tradition. The complex relationships between modern class and traditional caste, as observed earlier, affect all members of Indian society so profoundly that their particular impact on women is hard to discern.

In summation: Institutions both worldwide and local have begun to examine and advance the status of women in Asia. For both scholars and planners, however, explanatory theories and reformatory devices remain inadequate. Nonetheless, as the contributors to this book demonstrate, women in Asia—sometimes deliberately, more often circumstantially, usually slowly, and mostly in fits and starts—are moving into new roles and have begun to climb the status ladder.

Notes

1. Herbert Feldman, *Revolution in Pakistan* (New York: Oxford University Press, 1967), p. 150.

2. Barbara Bellow Watson, ed., *Womens' Studies: The Social Realities* (New York: Harper's College Press, 1976), p. 61.

3. Michelle Zimbalist Rosaldo and Louise Lamphere, eds., *Woman, Culture and Society* (Stanford: Stanford University Press, 1974), pp. v–vii.

4. Vern L. Bullough, *The Subordinate Sex: A History of Attitudes toward Women* (Urbana: University of Illinois Press, 1973).

5. Ann Pescatello, ed., *Female and Male in Latin America: Essays* (Pittsburgh: University of Pittsburgh Press, 1976), p. xii.

6. Joan I. Roberts, ed., *Beyond Intellectual Sexism: A New Woman, A New Reality* (New York: Longman, 1976), p. 6.

7. Roberts, p. 15.

8. Michelle Zimbalist Rosaldo, "Women, Culture and Society: A Theoretical Overview," in Rosaldo and Lamphere, pp. 17–18.

9. Ibid., pp. 30–32.

10. Peggy R. Sanday, "Female Status in the Public Domain," in Rosaldo and Lamphere, p. 191.

11. Barbara E. Ward, *Women in the New Asia: The Changing Roles of Men and Women in South and Southeast Asia* (Paris: UNESCO, 1963), p. 3.

12. Donald Eugene Smith, *Religion and Political Development.* (Boston: Little, Brown, 1970).

13. Ibid., p. 45.

14. The spelling *Muhammad* is preferred over numerous variants for the Prophet's name. When namesakes use other spellings, this book respects their preferences. In this book *Muslim* is preferred over *Moslem, Qu'ran* over *Koran.* However, the word *parda* is rendered by English writers variously as *parda, pardah, purda, purder, purdow,* and perhaps in other spellings according to their hearing of the various foreign languages. In this book Gail Minault uses *parda;* Sylvia Chipp uses *purdah.*

15. Smith, pp. 55–56.

I East Asia

In examining the relative status of women in any society we must deal with the real status of women measured along some power continuum as opposed to the ideal status prescribed for women by cultural norms. In East Asia, as compared to South and Southeast Asia, the real status of women is somewhat higher than the ideal. The roots of this paradox are many and complex and vary from nation to nation. We do not expect to unravel them here. Rather, our goal is to suggest some of the possible reasons for this phenomenon.

At the ideal level, Chinese women were victims of the Confucian social order and its fixed interaction patterns that placed emphasis on a male-oriented hierarchy. The extent to which Chinese women participated in the society's economic life emanated from the Confucian values and supported them. In many parts of China, though not all, women rarely participated in labor outside the home. The custom of foot binding, where it was practiced, precluded women from playing a role in agricultural production. The marital and domicile customs of the Confucian-decreed patriarchal family excluded women from the economic arena and also served to deprive women of the external support system that might have decreased their dependence on males. The very same Confucian system, however, in decreeing partible inheritance, provided women with a resource for expanding their status. The fact that all sons were entitled to equal shares of the family patrimony allowed wives some room for manipulation, at least where the ideal family existed. In this environment, wives who established close personal influential relationships with their husbands were in a position to manipulate the sources of conflict between brothers. If they were successful in dividing the extended family either psychologically or physically (by division of land, walling off part of the home, or the like), they were often able to gain some measure of status and some control over their own lives.

When we turn to the Japanese women we see that, unlike the Chinese women, they have always participated in agricultural activities, at least at the village level. Looking at Japanese belief systems, we note that neither Shinto nor most of the popular forms of Japanese Buddhism take a particularly hostile position on the status of women. How then do we account for the ideal Japanese woman's being one who defers to the male in all things? It would seem that in Japan, as in China, the woman's inferior status stems from the patriarchal family. But in Japan, where primogeniture rather than partibility was the inheritance pattern, there was nothing to mitigate the status-smothering effect of an all-encompassing patriarchy.

In Japan, the patriarchal family in its present form became the norm during the long and bitter years of Japanese feudalism. The code of Bushido developed and regulated the total behavior of the Japanese during this time. This code, designed in part to imitate Confucian values and in part to ensure perpetuation of a family's name and inheritance under the almost anarchical conditions of the feudalistic centuries, became the basis for ideal Japanese behavior and placed Japanese women at the lowest status level in Japanese life. The Tokugawa regime, which brought order and stability to Japan at the conclusion of the feudal period, attempted to preserve its power position by freezing the social order as it had found it. One result was to stabilize the *ideal* social order as decreed by Bushido. Thus the Japanese woman was left at the bottom of the *ideal* social hierarchy during a period in which, despite the regime's attempt to prevent it, many other changes took place. In the real order, however, women in Japan were rarely as far down the social ladder as Bushido prescribed. In many parts of Japan, particularly in the more isolated mountain villages, Japanese women continued to make an important contribution to the economic life of the family. In these places the higher pre-feudal status of Japanese women tended to persist. One has only to recall Embree's description of female behavior in his classic study of Suye Mura to find support for this view. Further, the Japanese custom of male adoption, which allowed a family with no sons of its own to adopt a young man who would both marry their daughter(s) and carry on the family's name, often operated to allow a Japanese father to keep a well-loved and bright daughter at home and in a meaningful decision-making position.

None of the preceding discussion is meant to indicate that either Chinese or Japanese women, past or present, were at similar status levels or even that status levels can be located and compared accurately across cultures. Rather, we wish to stress that what Japanese and Chinese women had in common, though for different reasons, was that their real status was higher than their ideal status.

It should be noted that we have excluded Korea from this discussion only becaue we were unable to obtain a chapter on Korea for this book. The real status of Korean women, though they too labor under the burden of the Confucian system, also tends to be higher than the ideal. Particularly in the last decade the pressures of rapid economic growth have enabled Korean women to occupy new roles and gain higher status.

In the first contribution in this volume, Joyce Kallgren examines the changing economic and political climate in Asian urban areas and suggests that the changes have important implications for female roles. She remains unconvinced, however, that "women's liberation" is either a goal or a meaningful term for most women in Asian cities. Women's participation in the political process, beyond voting, is extremely limited. Their participation in the industrialization process remains at very low levels.

Kay Ann Johnson examines both the rewards and the handicaps imposed on women in the new China, a society consciously attempting to bring about revolutionary changes in female status and roles. The "liberation" that has occurred has not been consistent, and Johnson finds this not surprising given the long history of Chinese women's second-class status.

Susan Pharr describes the gradual economic, political, and social emancipation of Japanese women in a setting characterized by slow-paced revolutionary change. She sees the Japanese woman—whether she be the Neotraditionalist, the New Woman, or the Radical Egalitarian—in a state of flux searching for her self-identity and trying various roles.

1   Women in Asian Cities, Their Political and Economic Roles: Research Problems and Strategies

Joyce K. Kallgren

Is women's position becoming better or worse as society changes? Some planners, policy advocates, and scholars who believe they know the answer to this question proceed to develop social programs for the Third World. Others, less certain, look at current data and research prior to initiating policies. In the past decade, research has made clear that development planning often has resulted in special difficulties for women in the transition from an agricultural society to an industrial one.[1] Where initially the study of development and urbanization rested on data based on such terms as "employed workers," "heads of households," and "gross national product" (all of which were most commonly assumed to be men or to be based on men's actions), in recent years the limitations that such terms and their definitions have imposed upon programs have made scholars and practitioners more thoughtful and flexible in their analysis of urbanization and social planning. It is still difficult, however, to develop strategies that take appropriate account both of the conditions that affect the lives and work of women and also of the different political and economic forces that shape, influence, and ultimately change the various societies of Asia.

This chapter will sketch some of the general dimensions of urbanization and social forces that affect women in Asian societies; it will illustrate some of the ongoing problems for the scholar, as well as the planner; and it will suggest some research strategies that may be useful in assessing further the status of women and the avenues for effective change. Since the emphasis is on the Asian Third World, Japan is excluded. The assumption made here is that cities most often feel the consequences of modernization policies and strategies sooner than rural areas, hence serve as a useful test of the implications of certain policies. Obviously policies directed at the countryside have to be excluded from such an assumption. It is also important, argues Hanna Papanek, to be careful in the use of such terms as "status of women." "This is particularly important for studies of urban women where status differences between families as well as broader class differences are such crucial distinguishing variables."[2]

For the observer committed to effecting the kind of social change that will enhance women's participation in the economic and political life of the Asian nations, some anomalies are to be observed in the cities of Asia. For example, many of the middle-class women in Hong Kong, graduates of prestigious middle schools in the colony and married to rising business executives, possess the necessary training and education for successful careers in business or politics. Yet they refrain from seeking such careers or withdraw after a relatively short time to more traditional endeavors. In social gatherings they exhibit considerable conservatism, often withdrawing from conversations concerning political or social problems. These women have counterparts in other cities in Asia.[3]

Do women who might be expected to constitute the cutting edge for broader participation in the economic and political life of their community undertake that task? Do the women of Asia seek a broadened set of alternatives for themselves and their children, and do they seek to achieve those alternatives? Students of women's participation have come to recognize that

> important changes in woman's work occur in connection with broad shifts in the economy and society or when an individual or family moves into another class . . . because upward social mobility into the middle class is accompanied by a withdrawal of women from the paid labor force in many societies . . . this pattern is often considered the norm for all classes.[4]

Some women see their education not as a training ground for productive careers outside the home but rather as a means for living the "good life" as married women without the complexities of employment. On the other hand, it is clear that for poor women such options or choices do not exist. Differences based in class exist among women as well as men.

In studying the roles of women in cities, it is essential to recognize that those being studied differ in their perception of appropriate roles and are by no means of one view with respect to all goals and alternatives.

This observation with respect to diversity based upon class has a counterpart in the assumptions of those studying the problem. As individuals have painfully learned, a scholar's assumption that a topic is relevant or a planner's assumption that a policy choice is obvious is often not shared by those being studied or by those who are the subject of a proposed policy. Some of the policies that have evoked the most intense and sustained argument in the United States are seen in another setting as less important or are even rejected on the grounds of relevance. The political question of the status and condition of women is, in part, one of those questions. For example, the 1971 *Asian Student,* a weekly newspaper of the Asian Foundation, selected for its essay competition the topic "Asian Society and the Women's Liberation Movement." In discussing the chosen topic, the editor commented:

> The things women demand and agitate for vary with the various countries depending upon the traditions, customs, cultures, laws and philosophies, religions and other factors involved. Essentially they ask for equal status and opportunities with men, politically, economically, socially, educationally and in other respects.

The editor then suggested possible approaches and issues to be considered by the prospective contestants, and concluded with this observation:

> You don't need to side with everything the women's liberation movement stands for, or even with the movement itself. The subject as it is worded does not imply that you should. You may want to justify some of the traditions, customs, religious tenets, ethical ideas, and other things that advocates of women's liberation are attacking as discriminatory of the fair sex. You may even deplore the movement as detrimental to Asian society and culture . . . The nature of the subject gives wide latitude of treatment . . . You may inject even some humor or satire to drive home your point.

The choice of the essay topic was an indication of the presumed popular appeal of the problem—often referred to as "women's liberation"—to Asian students. The tenor of the instructions, indeed some of the language (for instance, "the fair sex"), raises questions about the seriousness with which the editor viewed the topic.

Despite some doubt on the part of Asian students about the importance of the topic, there is ample evidence of its significance in the eyes of governments and scholars. The 1975 United Nations International Women's Year Conference (held in Mexico City) focused worldwide attention on the need for "intensified action to insure the full integration of women in the development process."[5] A number of interdisciplinary professional associations, such as the Association for Asian Studies, together with specific professional groups, routinely report at their national meetings or in their professional journals on important questions of research and policy that influence or alter the roles of women in Asia.

In looking at these research results and even more at the planning efforts, it is important to keep in mind the very different perspectives and ideological assumptions that men and women bring to such work. As the Mexico City Conference also demonstrated, many women adopt a class interpretation to explain their problems. They see nationalism as the effective instrument for the social change necessary to combat imperialism and neocolonialism. For these women, national goals rank higher than those associated with the development of broader choices and options for themselves. There is still a deep hostility to women's participation in politics and some aspects of the economy, as is clearly implied in the language and literature of the attacks on three major women political leaders recently defeated in Asia (in India, Sri Lanka, and the People's Republic of China).

Thus research on the role of women in Asia generally and in its cities particularly presents formidable problems. There is the obvious difficulty of drawing general conclusions from the widely differing circumstances in which women find themselves in the nations of Asia, indeed even among the various ethnic subgroups within Asian nations. There is division among women with respect to change and the appropriate role of women. There is the problem of the means for the measurement of change, even of the perception of change. Given the relatively recent achievement of independence by many Asian nations and the modest industrial development that has occurred, has sufficient time elapsed to measure change? If differences do not appear, this may mean that relatively little change has occurred. However, it may also mean that the important changes under way are simply too subtle for detection. With these caveats in mind, the question now turns to the context in which the role of women in Asia should be viewed.

The Setting

The very great impact of traditional cultural values on the role of women in Asia is a given fact that is familiar to many and consequently will not be dwelt on here. The differences between Muslim and non-Muslim societies and the varying effects of Buddhism and Christianity are reflected in the data now available. Kinship patterns, religious prescription, marital law, and other kinds of customs play an obvious role. The required seclusion of women and their lack of freedom of movement even in such matters as marketing clearly retard more open and more varied activities for women in some societies. Although many of the legal barriers surrounding inheritance rights and divorce have been eliminated or weakened, the values and customs from which they derive are naturally declining more slowly. Furthermore, some of these limitations on freedom in certain circumstances do provide a measure of security for women—for example, the opposition to divorce in the Philippines.

The achievement of national independence throughout Asia has had an important impact on traditional values and thus on the role of women, but this factor should not be overemphasized. For most countries, the winning of independence represented a high-water mark of national unity but at best only a partial social revolution. The unified coalitions of forces that won the nationalist struggle frequently did not develop social goals beyond independence except in the broadest terms, such as adequate national defense and economic development.

Economic development is taking place, although slowly and unequally. The Asian nations remain largely agricultural, though urbanization is a reality, as witness not only the cities of Hong Kong and Singapore but also the rapid growth of such metropolitan centers as Jakarta, Bangkok, Taipei, Saigon, Seoul, and Delhi. Industrialization, though proceeding from an extremely modest base, is producing a broadening array of kinds of paid employment with consequent need and opportunity for the development of new skills.

For urban populations, the development of skills rests primarily on access to education. While overall educational gains have been made, it remains a fact that in most areas of Asia the educational system has been biased against women. Though real efforts have been made to modify this bias, the strongly entrenched attitudes, fortified by religion, have been hard to overcome. Furthermore, the winning of independence did not work any miracles in Asian societies. For many of them, the existing educational institutions are part of a larger institutional system that is marked by strong social stratification. This social stratification, rather than simply the level of investment in education, is at the heart of limitations in educational opportunity for many Asian citizens, particularly women.

Urbanization is having its effects upon the institution of the family, as will be indicated in more detail in the section on Economic Roles for Women. The move from an agricultural setting to a metropolitan setting often produces a smaller family circle. This tendency subjects the family in the cities of Asia to certain hazards in exchange for the better economic opportunities its members *may* find there. There is no question but that much of Asia lacks the social programs needed to replace the traditional supportive services of the extended family. So long as the nuclear family remains healthy, the children are reasonably well spaced, and resources for support are adequate, city life may indeed be exciting and richer in opportunities, but if illness strikes, or if the children occur too closely, or if regular income fails, the social costs for all family members may be great. They will be particularly acute for the women.

In the context of the modern social, political, and economic development of Asia, three questions of obvious relevance should be kept in mind: First, have roles and opportunities for development and participation increased for the population as a whole? Second, to what degree have women been able to share in these increased roles and opportunities? Third, and finally and more speculatively, does it seem likely that the years ahead will bring an acceleration of those patterns generally favorable to broader participation by women in their societies?

Women and Politics in Asia

As United Nations studies have shown, there have been important changes in the political rights of women in Asia.[6] These changes suggest the possibility of an expanded political role. In Thailand, the right of women to vote was granted in 1932. Now, with few exceptions, women throughout the world have the right to vote. In some of the countries of Asia, this right preceded independence. In Burma, prior to independence, certain categories of women were granted voting rights in 1922; universal suffrage came in 1935, and the right was reconfirmed in the constitution upon the achievement of independence in 1947. In the Philippines, the United States colonial administration stressed the joint rights of men and women. It may be argued that voting rights were circumscribed or without meaning in the preindependence period, but at the least the suffrage, whatever the reality of options, was not granted or restricted on the basis of sex.

The more common experience has been that the right to vote has come with the achievement of independence. The demand for voting rights for men and women has often been a part of the nationalist appeal. Such has been the case in Indonesia, Vietnam, and Malaysia. In China, the nationalist struggle embodied more than a colonial versus nationalist clash. The organizational unity embodied in the nationalist fight became a mechanism for social mobilization embracing both men and women, though it may not be used for that purpose after independence.

The adoption of a constitution by the new state is a symbolic act of faith that affirms social, economic, and political goals. The rights recognized in the constitution are those that have been denied, limited, or seen as meaningless prior to independence. One has only to witness the apathy which greets voter registration in Hong Kong, still a British crown colony, to realize the practical consequence for voting behavior of the achievement of independence.

The right to vote may open the door to a wide range of activities beyond that of casting a ballot, such as the development of political programs and slogans, the recruitment of candidates and supporters for an election, and in some countries, the development of political choices and alternatives.

In trying to assess the level of political activity and the interest of women, it is important to recognize that political activity may be restricted or circumscribed for citizens in general and thus for women. Asia has a number of effectively one-party states, states where political opposition and/or effective political organization are limited. A single-party state may minimize political divisions or proscribe discussion of divisive issues at the same time that it enhances ritual political participation. In the single- and multiparty states of Asia, where difficult economic constraints constantly impinge on individual lives, political participation and action may well be seen as the appropriate or sole means for engendering effective political and social changes. In this setting the political party may become the agency of protest, whether effective or impotent.

If the difficulties can be linked to remnants of colonial power, imperialist ventures, or other targets of agreed upon social opprobrium, the political organization mobilizes sentiments and activities on behalf of the nationalist government. Such policies, incidentally, distract from internal stresses and weaknesses of the current leadership. When problems cannot be successfully externalized, because the economic and cultural clashes are too clearly an internal matter, a single-party or a multiparty system may effect elaborate compromises and coalitions within and among the ruling elites so that they are able to govern. In these cases, effective political participation by the general citizenry is often nonexistent. If eventually political organizations are banned, then action or opposition may become criminal and finally rebellious. Even acknowledging these restraints on general activity and participation, such simple criteria as election to office and participation in the decision-making process demonstrate that women in Asia lag behind, though the extent of that lag varies among nations.

Participation requires freedom of movement, possession of skills of leadership, usually a minimum level of education, and, in general, "political awareness." While overall data on the position of women are limited, it is clear that the results reported in the early 1960s still obtain.[7] In 1963 Barbara Ward attempted to characterize women's emancipation in Burma, India, Pakistan, Singapore, Thailand, Cambodia, Sri Lanka (Ceylon), Indonesia, Laos, the Federation of Malaya, the Philippines and Vietnam. She did not include Korea, the People's Republic of China, or Taiwan. She found emancipation lagging—women had relatively little part in social and economic, even in personal, decision making. Since she wrote, many of the circumstances that occasioned her initial judgment have been moderated. In the socialist countries, Marxism has injected politics into daily life and requires a high degree of participation and awareness. But in the other independent states there is still substantial limitation on the freedom to engage in activities outside the home and there are few indications of "relatively many women in political office." Except where seats in government are either formally or informally provided, rates of achievement of political office by women are low.

Because women usually have less freedom of movement, have rarely been called upon to exercise leadership in their societies, and usually have less education than men of the same age, they enter into politics with a distinct handicap. Even when looking at the urban settings, where one might expect a higher educational standard, female participation, let alone leadership, is limited. Two exceptions outside the socialist bloc must be noted: participation of women is more common in Indonesia, partly in consequence of the nationalist struggle, and in the Philippines, where the role of women has been less restricted.

Within the socialist states, as noted above, there is a much higher emphasis upon outward political participation (putting aside the issue of its effectiveness) and a heightened sense of political awareness. Even in these states, in the People's Republic of China, for example, almost thirty years after the Communists' coming to power, there is explicit recognition that women lag with respect to political leadership and participation.[8]

It is productive, however, to move outside the more narrowly defined boundaries of political participation and consider activity in the so-called voluntary associations. These groups are only tangentially related to politics but are potentially a training ground, and in their programs frequently are allied with desired national policies. For example, in urban areas it is possible to look at the kinds of activities and skills represented in the programs and functions of organizations such as welfare agencies, schools, and consumer cooperatives that form organizations to support specific activities. In addition, there are associations established to promote or prevent certain social activities or types of conduct.

These organizations, which often emerge in the process of urbanization and industrialization, have in common the idea that purposive social action is possible and appropriate. It is, of course, true that the idea of social betterment often generates a multitude of ineffective groups, but the development of a membership does manifest an important change in the relation of an individual to the social order. Furthermore, the organization, planning, and implementation of the activities of these groups offer steps toward the acquisition and practice of skills for political organizations—the ability to lead, to initiate activities, to recruit members, and similar traits. Thus middle-school charitable fund-raising activities, often observed in Hong Kong, may provide the confidence and know-how that can be transferred into other programs in adult years and ultimately merge into the activities of political parties. There is not a great deal of published research on these activities. Lenore Manderson's work on the Women's Section of the United Malay National Organization provides important insights into women's activities.[9] "Mothers' Clubs and Family Planning in Korea," published in Seoul by the Seoul National University School of Public Health in 1974, reports on the work of Park Hyung Jong and others, who were studying these quasigovernmental organizations that focused upon specific programs yet also served to meet other needs of Korean women.[10]

That there are serious methodological considerations in the study of voluntary associations in Asia is acknowledged. Emphasis often tends to be placed upon formal organizations that have such specific characteristics as regular recruitment procedures and membership lists. This focus may serve to exclude less structured but perhaps equally purposive organizations or activities, namely, the informal networks that emerge to meet special needs in a city neighborhood. In addition, there are obvious problems in analyzing the characteristics of those who join and lead these voluntary groups.

Frequently the person engaged in these activities is least likely to be the one needing the development of skills or the reinforcement provided by success. This latter problem is an important one. Some practical examples of this self-selection may be observed in the early years of the People's Republic of China when the urban street committees (which have many similarities to the organizations discussed here) found their leaders being constantly co-opted into other activities or organizations. Those street committees became the arena where activists were identified. Today a similar role is played by the National Women's Federation.[11]

In Asia one barrier, economic in nature, is a sharp restriction on the potential effectiveness of these informal organizations in recruitment and training. For those on the lowest rung of the economic ladder, both men and women, the demands of securing and maintaining a livelihood are often so pressing as to preclude other activities. Though the barrier may be somewhat less prominent in the socialist countries (with their integration of political activity and economic life), it remains important in all societies.

Other aspects of activity and participation in the political process might be examined and almost certainly form an important part of any effort to appraise the role of women. How many positions in government, elective or appointive, are held by women? Do governmental politics treat men and women equally for salaries and perquisites? What are the possibilities for reward for men and women within the existing political structures?

Government positions are often highly prized. Since there is usually an oversupply of middle-school and university graduates, and since the structure of educational opportunities is frequently skewed against women, the conservatism of a culture might be expected to play an important role in restricting the likelihood of governmental appointment and long-run success. Research on this problem would profit from longitudinal studies, periodic resurvey of the careers of selected women political and governmental figures, together with continued review of bureaucratic personnel policy.

Though problems of political participation occur in both city and countryside, the confluence of urbanization, increased communication, and technical innovation have made the urban area an interesting setting for the study of political rights and their exercise.

Economic Roles for Women

A number of the considerations that make analysis difficult with respect to political participation of women also apply in the field of economics. Industrialization and urbanization are themselves complex phenomena, and when these are combined with the specific national decisions with respect to the role of government, the goals for various sectors, and the desired rate of change, analysis is challenging and difficult. These decisions all have consequences with respect to the development of increased opportunities of employment for men and women, the speed and direction of education and training, and other related matters. In addition, there are the ongoing complex sociological factors that encourage or retard opportunities for women. Against this backdrop of issues stands the difficulty in establishing statistical bench marks in order to demonstrate the existence and direction of change.

Both in the field of traditional agriculture and in that of labor utilization outside of traditional agriculture there is a problem of reliable statistical data. Macrodata seem to be reported largely as percents. For example, Gunnar Myrdal provides some estimates for women's participation in the labor market in some selected Asian cities.[12] With respect to women in the labor force in Singapore as a percent of the total female population, he reports that Indians constituted 3.5 percent, Malays 5.2 percent, and Chinese 14.1 percent, with an overall 12.3 percent of women in the labor force. The figures are somewhat higher when calculated as percents of the female population aged between 18 and 59 years. Here he reports that Indian women constituted 7.3 percent, Malay women 11.2 percent, and Chinese women 25.4 percent, with an average of 22.7 percent. Myrdal also reports two additional figures. He estimates 14.5 percent of the women in the total female population were in the labor force in Rangoon, 22 percent of the female population aged between 18 and 59 years.

Additional data are available in Barbara Ward's work.[13] She provides some percent data for the female labor force in agriculture, industry, and services, for India, the Federation of Malaya, Pakistan, the Philippines, and Thailand. The data show the overwhelming agricultural nature of the societies, except in the Philippines where only 44 percent of the female labor force is estimated to be in the agricultural sector, 23 percent in industry, and 33 percent in service. This distribution reflects the somewhat more developed nature of the Philippine economy as well as the more open quality of the Philippine society in terms of opportunities for paid employment for women. In addition Ward provides some data (percent of total) on the distribution of the female labor force by status, divided between (a) those who are employers and/or work on their own account, and (b) those who are unpaid family workers and/or are employees. Here Ward reports that the percent of women who are employers and/or work on their own account in India is 26 percent, in the Federation of Malaya 29 percent, in Pakistan 83 percent, and in the Philippines 11 percent. Those who are unpaid family workers in India are 60 percent, in the Federation of Malaya 23 percent, in Pakistan 2 percent, and in the Philippines 60 percent; those who are employees in India are 14 percent, in the Federation of Malaya 48 percent, in Pakistan 15 percent, and in the Philippines 29 percent. Though these data are general, and queries can be raised with respect to the definition of terms, the overall picture represented here has been generally supported in studies of the last decade.[14]

It is important to keep in mind certain aspects of such data. First, much of the work for women the world over—that is, unpaid housework and the care and rearing of children—is excluded from most statistics of economic activity. There is increasing awareness of the consequences of excluding this important component in a societal output, and some effort must be made to take account of this aspect of societal productivity. On the other hand, how to integrate these facts in the data and planning of development programs remains a problem. A second aspect of such data that must be kept in mind is the need to recognize that a high proportion of women employed is, not unexpectedly, in agriculture as compared to industry. A third aspect is that a number of important qualifications must be made with respect to the fields of agriculture, industry, and service as found in each society.

The number of women who are employers on their own tends to be low the world around. The reason for this fact, though, may differ among societies, depending upon the degree of urbanization, industrialization, and development. In many industrialized societies, the important factors are the high rate of manufacturing and the high degree of organization in the service industries. Both of these factors tend to limit the opportunities for the independence of women. In less industrialized societies other forces are at work. In Burma, Thailand, the Philippines, and Indonesia, for example, a large number of women are classified as employers not in industry but in agriculture. Among those engaged in certain aspects of trade and commerce, many are similarly classified, as in Burma and Thailand, where women have important roles in the economic life of the country. In reviewing these data, therefore, it is important to keep in mind that none of these situations result from industrialization. These are not new occupations. Furthermore, many of those classified as employees are not in industry, but are domestic servants, which also is not a new occupation. Thus only a very small percentage of women have entered into new kinds of employment.

Nonetheless, the absolute numbers are growing and there can be no doubt of their significance. Furthermore, in the urban sector certain professions show a higher increase in their rate of growth, especially in terms of the number of women involved. Among these, for example, is education at the primary and secondary level. In virtually all countries of Asia women serve as teachers, overwhelmingly at the primary level and to a lesser extent at the secondary level. The tendency is striking in the Philippines but is also quite pronounced in China and other countries of Southeast Asia. Nursing and aspects of the health professions, both in the cities and the countryside, are often employers of women. It must, unfortunately, also be recognized that "women's professions" are often beset by problems of low status, low salaries, and sometimes quite limited training requirements.

The relationship of skill to employment opportunities is important and relevant. Throughout much of Asia, one avenue of work for women is often at the lowest skilled (though backbreaking) level of construction. Because of labor surplus and low skill demands, these jobs are often poorly paid, with minimal organization to provide for improvement in pay, working conditions, and other aspects of employment. In general, the avenues of employment for women are frequently few in number and low in status. There are exceptions, such as the textile industry, where women participate in large numbers.

Why is this so? Though the picture is a fragmented one, there are aspects of the industrial process as it has emerged in the cities of Asia that contribute to the difficulties of women. Professor Shigeru Ishikawa, in his study *Economic Development in Asian Perspectives,* sets out to discuss some of the difficulties of development. Though he addresses a number of problems, several are particularly important to the topic at hand. Ishikawa notes:

> (1) The specific initial conditions tend to make the establishment of the intermediate and, even more, capital-goods branches of manufacturing more urgent, but at the same time more difficult. (2) The special initial conditions tend to make the scarcity of capital in the course of economic development more acute. (3) The special initial conditions tend to make the problem of surplus labor more serious, a tendency which occurs partly from the initial conditions related to the existing surplus of labor and the rapid increase of population, but it tends to be accelerated by the tendency in which those industrial branches with high capital-labor ratios require a greater share of the given amount of investable capital in the economy.[15]

The implications should be made clear. Even if industrialization should accelerate, Ishikawa argued, the technological qualities of present-day borrowing between nations will make more likely those industries that require high capital investment and relatively small numbers of highly skilled workers in order to compete. Consequently, the competitive labor situation for women is not likely to brighten in terms of the availability of jobs.

There is another facet to the Ishikawa analysis, namely, certain qualities of the industrial process as they impinge upon women. The problem is well known and is aptly stated by Wilbur Moore: "The outstanding characteristic of factory work is the extent to which the timing and sequence of events is regulated by the machine."[16] Especially for women who enter the more modern sector of the economy, the scheduling and regulation of machines pose important problems in completing tasks at home, as well as for the care and rearing of children (virtually everywhere the major responsibility of women). In the Asian setting, this problem is heightened by the fact that virtually all women marry.[17] Though the age of marriage may, in some cases, be rising, and despite the important efforts in some countries to lower fertility rates, a woman cannot consider the option of an unmarried career as can be done in the West. The problems of family tasks and child care are pressing for those who work, and contribute to the number of women who withdraw from the labor force or do not seek employment.

Within the modern sector of the economy, there have been sporadic efforts to develop more services or amenities for women, such as crèches, nurseries, and the like. These are likely to be offered where there may be a labor shortage or where efforts are made to restrict migration to the city and to induce the unemployed urban resident to seek employment. The difficulty is that these services raise the cost of employment of women and hence, on a cost basis, make the employment of men more attractive. The competitive position of women, particularly if there is equal pay for equal work, is thus worsened if the costs of maternity leaves and crèches are born by the employer. Regulations designed to check the worst abuses in the employment of women have not operated to their economic advantage. Protective legislation (as appears to have been the case in some Western nations) may tend to promote the displacement of women by men. Padimini Sengupta in an early 1960 work suggests that the percent of women employed in factories might have been higher one or two decades earlier.[18] There is fragmentary evidence of this type of problem in revolutionary China in the 1970s. The difficulty is understandable. If legislation forbids working women on the night shift, then there cannot be rotation throughout all the shifts by all workers and there will be understandable dissatisfaction among the men who may be forced to work permanently on the late night shift. Sengupta comments that such a policy can lead to the displacement of women. It may well lead to the employment only of unmarried women. Others who have written in the 20 years since her work have recognized the validity of her observations.[19]

In addition to the issue of industrial investment, labor discipline, and the problem of uneven application of legislative provisions, there is the underlying factor of social desires. The achievement of economic improvement may well lead to a woman's withdrawal from the economic marketplace as an indicator of improved social position.[20]

Even as one looks at the difficulties implicit in the broadening of women's opportunities for industrial employment, opportunities are in slow decline, often with very considerable effort to minimize the social and economic consequence, in the cottage sector of industrial activity in Asia. This sector is characterized by the use of productive techniques based upon manual skills and indigenous and often outmoded equipment, and by an organization form represented by the household enterprises aiming mainly at maintaining the livelihood of the family and maximizing its welfare.[21] This sector does not involve new roles for women in the urban setting.

The cottage-type industry of which Ishikawa wrote, in a somewhat altered form and attached to an economic unit other than the family, may be found in the People's Republic of China, where the production team or brigade in the countryside or the factory run by the neighborhood street committee in the city employs women at modest rates that permit them to achieve or maintain a level of economic independence and status. In the countryside these units often employ men, in the cities more frequently women. Parish reports a relatively gloomy picture with respect to effecting changed roles for women. Though his reference is to rural China, it is also to a relatively wealthy province and might have been expected to serve as an advanced area.[22]

The point of this analysis has not been to deny certain changes in the development process but to suggest that a more thoughtful look may be necessary at how the phenomena of urban development are characterized and the likely consequences for women of living in the burgeoning cities of Asia. There is a growing body of scholarly work arguing that urbanization and development often result in a decline in the status and roles of women. The argument is that the status and roles protected and reinforced in the countryside by important and necessary tasks are lost in the move to the city and not replaced by other attributes.[23]

The facts of urban living and physical separation from the place of work may produce changes other than those that seem at first glance to be likely. Even if the economic position of women is not markedly improved, their authority in the family may increase, if only in response to the absence of the father; but in transitional periods, the outcomes can be mixed.[24]

When production is no longer a family affair, the mother's duties may be reduced so that she will have greater independence of movement and disposition of time but her position as a wife may be lowered because many of her traditional economic and social functions are lost. Greater freedom and alternative opportunities for independent employment offer possibilities for those willing and able to undertake such employment. But the transition period in an urban setting is likely to be one of heightened insecurity until the problems of employment and status are resolved.

Research Strategies

Salaff and Merkle in a 1970 article concluded that "when conditions which oppress women can be attributed to exploitative traditional economic structures, then revolutionary efforts to change the economic system will also liberate women." But they go on to say, when analyzing why the postrevolutionary regimes in the Soviet Union and China have not been willing or able to make the effort required to liberate women, "In both cases attempts to change the status of women were eventually blocked when they became too costly in terms either of direct economic costs such as child care and household services or political resistance and disruption resulting from attempts to change the family or bring women into production." They believe that the outcome in China and the Soviet Union has been "clearly a system in which individual women are elevated as symbols of the fulfillment of revolutionary promises rather than substantial commitment to end the oppression of women as a class." They conclude, "Without a power base, the demands of women are met only when their liberation was beneficial to the political and economic interests of the revolutionary regime."[25]

The Salaff and Merkle observations about China have some usefulness in looking at the political and economic roles of women in all of Asia. To be sure, most of Asia is not revolutionary. Most of the leadership of Asian countries does not attach priority to the social liberation implicit in the women's liberation language of American society. But even a cursory look at women in the cities of Asia shows change. Legal and substantive change in the position of women has occurred, though the degree and rate varies and, in many cases, is quite modest. If Salaff and Merkle are correct in suggesting that "women's liberation" has a better chance of occurring in advanced industrial societies, then to what degree is it true that this "liberation" is also more likely to occur first in urban settings where industrialization and its attendant changes are likely to be initially experienced?

Detailing and measuring the change that does exist requires considerable ingenuity and thought in devising useful and effective measurement tools and in making maximum use of the input or research already completed or under way. First steps have been taken in the compilation and publication of annotated bibliographies cited in note 6 to this chapter. Since the number of people trained both linguistically and in the social sciences is likely to be limited, it is essential to continue the wide distribution of materials that has been facilitated in large measure by the Overseas Development Council and the United Nations. This work could be a useful supplement with more attention to the integration of available data as currently reflected in the *Handbook of International Data on Women.*[26] Though it is customary for social scientists to deplore the lack of data as a preliminary to every project report, it is essential to make maximum use of available data, reports, and statistics despite their limitations.[27]

There is little research on the political roles of women. This fact reflects the realities of political life and processes in a number of Asian countries; politics remains, by and large, the domain of men. It also reflects the fact that ongoing research in Asia, both urban and rural, draws primarily upon the work of sociologists, anthropologists, and economists but on that of only a few political scientists. Some political emphasis is necessary, and the role of elites and the importance of leadership must rank high.

To a great degree, the political achievements of Asian women have been illustrated by the "star system," that is, by the individual stories of women who somehow acquire the special training and opportunities that made it possible for them to participate in political, academic, or economic life in their countries. They were frequently from upper- or upper-middle-class families with intellectual backgrounds, and they have often shown remarkable persistence in the face of substantial handicaps and obstacles. Their activities, at least initially, are often on the fringe of accepted social roles.[28]

Political biographies, together with intranational and international analysis of female leadership, would provide the opportunity for some cross-comparisons and possibly for the discovery of special circumstances and/or characteristics that seem to mark successful political candidates. Middle-level survey projects focusing upon women in elected or appointed positions and using basic socioeconomic data might well provide some benchmark data for ongoing or periodic resurvey analysis.[29] This kind of research literature is of importance because of the need for generational analysis.

From where will the next generation of leadership come? As political and economic barriers slowly lower, is there an emerging new elite to give direction and drive to such expanded opportunities as exist for women? Are there middle- and upper-class women in Asian cities committed to using their skills and their relative economic security to pursue leadership options? Will their plans lead them into the economic sphere and why? One recurring theme in recent research has been the emphasis on the importance of support by parents, peers, workmates, and society with respect to certain tasks. Analysis of the sources of support would shed light on the likely directions of the emerging young leaders, however limited in number they might be, and provide some insight into their possible success.[30]

Recently conferences and program developers have recognized the limitations of past measurements of economic progress and the need to develop, incorporate, or apply existing means to chronicle the contributions and roles of minorities (most often defined as the poor and women) into the national planning effort. One research technique that might prove useful in Asia, as it has proven elsewhere, is the trial use of the time-budget series in the urban setting, in order to document the hours of nonremunerative work of many women and the tasks of the poor and of women that often are not visibly recorded in more formal statistical systems. Such studies would permit cross-comparisons among differing economic systems and provide benchmarks for documenting change in life patterns occasioned by increased rates of industrialization and development as well as class changes for segments of women in specific professions or tasks. In addition, good observations might be achieved through the use of photographs together with participant analysis of the meaning of the photographs to provide some useful comparative insight into the multiple roles played by men and women as they move into and live in the city.[31]

The problems confronting most of the countries of Asia are so numerous and so intractable that there seems little likelihood that "women's liberation" will be ranked high in the assignment of priorities, either by men or by women. Furthermore, some problems implicit in development and modernization as well as in the role of women are intricate, and upon occasion so subtle that they are difficult to measure. Students of politics and economics recognize that certain policies, virtually universally supported in a society, have a disproportionate positive effect on women. Programs with respect to child and maternal health care, public health and sanitation, even education, benefit women. Until such time as change in the role of women receives greater emphasis or until industrialization seems to encourage new options, useful interim remedies and policies may be provided by more thoughtful research into maximizing the congruences of policies that impact positively upon women and by more careful research to investigate the numerous myths about women's participation in the labor forces of the cities.

Notes

1. Ester Boserup, *Women's Role in Economic Development* (New York: St. Martin's Press, 1970) is a careful scholarly account of the transition process, using a wide range of data from experiences in various countries of the Third World.

2. "Women in Cities: Problems and Perspectives," in *Women and National Development: The Complexities of Change*, edited by the Wellesley Editorial Committee (Chicago: University of Chicago Press, 1977, p. 56). Hereinafter referred to as *The Wellesley Conference*.

3. Norma Diamond, "The Middle Class Family Model in Taiwan: Woman's Place Is in the Home," *Asian Survey* 13, no. 9 (September 1973): 853–872.

4. Hanna Papanek, "Development Planning," in *The Wellesley Conference*, p. 18.

5. Carolyn M. Elliott, "Theories of Development," in *The Wellesley Conference*, p. 4. Point 14 of the Introduction to the "Report of the World Conference of the International Women's Year."

6. Recent annotated bibliographies show the important role played by the United Nations and its Committees in terms of the support of research and publications of findings on the topic of the status and role of women. See Myra Buvinic, *Women and World Development: An Annotated Bibliography* (Washington, D.C.: Overseas Development Council, 1976) and May Rihani, *Development as if Women Mattered: An Annotated Bibliography with a Third World Focus* (Washington, D.C.: Overseas Development Council Occasional Paper No. 10, 1978).

7. Barbara E. Ward, *Women in The New Asia: The Changing Social Roles of Men and Women in South and Southeast Asia* (Paris: UNESCO, 1963), pp. 69–70, has a detailed chart which is summarized here. In general, it still remains an accurate appraisal.

8. In the fall of 1978 the Women's Federation of the People's Republic of China held its first national meeting in 21 years. The reports of the meeting, including the major speeches, return to this theme of the need for greater participation by women. See *Peking Review* 21, no. 39 (29 September 1978): 5–12.

9. Lenore Manderson, "The Shaping of the Kaum Ibu" (Women's Section) of the United Malay National Organization, in *The Wellesley Conference*, pp. 210–228.

10. Other reports include: Lee Sea Baick, "Village Based Family Planning in Korea: The Case of the Mother's Club," paper presented at the Conference Workshop on Non-Formal Education and the Rural Poor, Kellogg Center, Michigan State University, East Lansing, 26 September–3 October 1976. Also see Planned Parenthood Federation of Korea, *Family Planning through Non-Family Planning Organizations: A Significant Experience in Korea* (Seoul: Planned Parenthood Federation of Korea, June 1975).

11. Mass organizations, a familiar term for students of Communist societies, have traditionally served this role of mobilizing public support and identifying potential leaders. The topic is discussed in James Townsend, *Politics in China* (Boston: Little, Brown, 1974), esp. pp. 100–104.

12. Gunnar Myrdal, *Asian Drama: An Inquiry into the Poverty of Nations* (New York: Pantheon, 1968), 2:1133.

13. Ward, p. 46.

14. Boserup's volume has some supplemental data, though not all the sources seem to be more current than the earlier published Ward figures. See especially pp. 176–177. Page 188 discusses the Southeast Asian pattern. Also see Cheng Sick-hwa, "Singapore Women's Legal Status, Education Attainment, and Employment Patterns," *Asian Survey* 17, no. 4 (April 1977): 358–374.

15. Shigeru Ishikawa, *Economic Development in Asian Perspective*. Economic Research Series No. 8, Institute of Economic Research, Hitotsubashi University (Tokyo: Kinokuniya Bookstore Co., 1967), p. 384.

16. Wilbur Moore, "Industrialization and Social Change," in *Industrialization and Society*, ed. Bert F. Hoselitz and W. E. Moore (New York: Humanities Press, 1963), 304 pp.

17. Myrdal, p. 1432. Note the comparison to Sweden.

18. Padimini Sengupta, *Women Workers of India* (Bombay, 1960).

19. Boserup accepts much of Sengupta's argument. Nadia H. Youssef, "Women in

Development: Urban Life and Labor," in *Women and World Development,* ed. Irene Tinker and Michele Bo Bramsen (Washington, D.C.: Overseas Development Council, 1976), pp. 70–77, especially p. 72, also concludes that Sengupta was correct.

20. This is the import of the Diamond article cited above. See also Elizabeth Johnson, "Women and Childbearing in Kwan Mun Hao Village: A Study of Social Change," in *Women in Chinese Society,* ed. Margery Wolf and Roxanne Witke (Stanford: Stanford University Press, 1975).

21. Ishikawa, p. 407.

22. William L. Parish and Martin King Whyte, *Village and Family Life in Contemporary China* (Chicago: University of Chicago Press, 1978), pp. 235–249. See especially their chart on p. 319, quite useful in explaining the changes that they believe have occurred primarily through normative or governmental pressures.

23. Irene Tinker, "The Adverse Impact of Development on Women," in Tinker and Bramsen, pp. 22–34.

24. James Watson in his analysis of a village in the New Territories of Hong Kong, where fathers migrated to England for long periods of time, returning only occasionally to see their families, reported on the problems of discipline and control that developed when grandparents and women attempted to fill the role originally played by the absent males. Though the Hong Kong experience is undoubtedly atypical, there certainly are changes growing out of the daily absence of the father. James L. Watson, *Emigration and the Chinese Lineage: The 'Mans' in Hong Kong and London* (Berkeley: University of California Press, 1975).

25. Janet Salaff and Judith Merkle, "Women in Revolution: The Lessons of the Soviet Union and China," *Berkeley Journal of Sociology,* Summer 1970, pp. 189–190.

26. E. Boulding, et al. *Handbook of International Data on Women* (New York: Halsted Press, 1976).

27. Hanna Papanek, "Development Planning," in *The Wellesley Conference,* p. 18.

28. Much of the Ward volume is devoted to personal accounts. Recent books draw more widely for their personal accounts, including a broader spectrum of women in terms of class and educational backgrounds. See especially Perdita Huston, *Third World Women Speak Out: Interviews in Six Developing Countries* (Washington, D.C.: Overseas Development Council, 1978).

29. Justin J. Green, "The High Status of Filipinas: Myth or Reality? Or the Problem of Finding a Chameleon in a Rain Forest with only a Microscope or Telescope for Tools," paper presented at the 27th Annual Meeting of the Association for Asian Studies, San Francisco, Calif., 1975. Mimeo. Green discusses the difficulties in the Filipina context of this research.

30. External support and its importance are discussed in Everett M. Rogers, Park Hyung Jong, Chung Kyung Kyoon, Lee See Baick, William S. Puppa, and Brenda A. Doe, "A New Work Analysis of the Diffusion of Family Planning Innovations over Time in Korean Villages: The Role of the Mother's Clubs," paper presented at the Annual Meeting of the Population Association of America, Seattle, Wash., 1975. For a summary of this paper see Item 339 in *Women and World Development: An Annotated Bibliography.* See also Janet Salaff, "Effect of the Rate of Change in Hong Kong on the Demographic Performance of Women," paper presented to the Symposium on Social and Political Change, The Role of Women, jointly sponsored by the University of California, Santa Barbara and the Center for the Study of Democratic Institutions, Santa Barbara, Calif., 1974. Mimeo.

31. Ximena Bunster, "Talking Pictures: Field Method and Visual Mode," in *The Wellesley Conference,* pp, 278-294.

2 The Japanese Woman: Evolving Views of Life and Role

*Susan J. Pharr**

A young editor of a women's magazine was recalling her senior year several years before in a private coed university in Tokyo.[1] "A strange thing happened once," she remarked. "One day I was sitting in the dorm talking with several of my classmates about the future. I mentioned that I would soon start looking for a serious job in publishing to begin after graduation. As I talked, gradually I realized that they were all staring at me. As it turned out, they were girls who were planning to marry as soon as possible after college. But the funny thing was, I had never realized . . . I had always assumed that we all felt the same way about things. . . ."

In today's Japan, and especially among younger generations of postwar women, there is much disagreement on the question of how women should conduct their lives. Even young women of the same socioeconomic and geographical background may have highly divergent attitudes toward education, marriage, and work. Women, as in the case of the editor, are sometimes brought up short, astonished to find that their perspectives may be quite at odds with those of their friends and other contemporaries.

Based on interviews with 100 young Japanese women, this chapter explores these different views of woman's role and suggests how they may change over the coming decade. The term "woman's role" specifically refers to the wife-mother role traditionally allocated to women in most societies of the world today. At issue in most contemporary analyses, and in the lives of my respondents, is the question of how the domestic role should be combined with other roles (worker, student, citizen, and so on) that a woman may play in her lifetime and, indeed, whether the homemaker role itself should continue to be so

*This chapter appears in a different form in Lewis Austin, ed., *Japan: The Paradox of Progress*, New Haven: Yale University Press, 1976. Copyright Yale University.

assigned to women on the basis of sex. Three views of woman's role to be described here represent differing answers to this question in terms of the life experiences and attitudes of 100 women.

The interviews for the study were conducted in 1971–72 in Tokyo and the Kyoto-Osaka area from a sample of women in the age range from 18 to 33 who had grown up and attended school entirely under the new order instituted since the end of World War II. In keeping with the purpose of a larger study for which the data were originally gathered, all the women chosen to be interviewed were participating in political activities ranging from political parties to the citizen's movement.[2] The informants represented many political interests and ideologies. At one end of the spectrum were women stuffing envelopes and pouring tea at the headquarters of the Liberal Democratic Party, the conservative party in power, only because their father or husband was running for office on the LDP ticket. At the other were a few student radicals in hiding from the police. Most of the informants, in their ideological convictions and in the amount of time they gave to politics, fell somewhere between the two extremes.

The three general viewpoints that emerged from interviews will be described more fully later, but briefly they are as follows. First, there was a *Neotraditional* view. Proponents of this view hold that the wife-mother role is primary in a woman's life and that, in general, all other life activities should be subordinated to it. Aspects of the view, as expressed by young women today, distinguish it from a still more traditional ideology of woman's role current before the war, but its links to the past are strong. A second view, espoused by those I call *New Women*, represents a subtle but fundamental change from the Neotraditional perspective. New Women accept the traditional assumption that the domestic role should be central to their lives as women, but, in what is a major change in attitude, they hold at the same time that women should be able to engage in numerous other activities not relating to the homemaker role. Finally, there was a *Radical Egalitarian* view. Radical Egalitarians not only believe that adult women should feel free to play many roles simultaneously, but challenge the very basis of contemporary social arrangements by rejecting traditional patterns of sex-role allocation that have made it woman's duty to maintain the home.

These ideologies come to light in interviews with young Japanese women, but it is clear that the three views are in competition in a number of countries today.[3] Nations differ, however, according to how the three ideologies rank in relation to one another. In a society at any moment in history, one view generally prevails over the others in the degree of acceptance accorded it.[4] Among the sample for this particular study, the New Woman's view predominated. Of the sample, 60 percent were New Women, with the remaining 40 percent divided equally between Neotraditionalists and Radical Egalitarians. But it is clear that a sample made up of women active in political causes is to some extent a special group. In society at large, the degree of support for each view is obviously quite different. Data from background interviews with women who were not active in politics, and findings of numerous writers, suggest that the Neotraditionalists hold the view that has widest acceptance among young Japanese women today. The New Woman's view is a variant pattern in the population at large, tolerated but denied full social approbation by a great many people. Finally, the Radical Egalitarian view is highly marginal, going far beyond what most Japanese men and women can even understand, much less accept. It might be pointed out that the views of virtually all young women to some extent reflect the high degree of social change characteristic of the postwar period. Certain beliefs of even Neotraditional women today were seen as either variant or deviant for much of Japanese history prior to 1945.

The Traditional View of Woman's Role

All three of the views discovered in interviews with young postwar women grew out of definitions of woman's role in force during earlier periods of Japanese history. In prewar society and before, certainly for all of recorded history, the great majority of people held that women were intended for one major role in life, that of wife and mother. Behind this belief were certain interrelated assumptions. Men and women were seen as essentially different beings. Though each was acknowledged to have special talents and abilities, men were deemed superior in most areas of endeavor. They were therefore entitled to many rights not shared by women, and by the same token, had certain duties and responsibilities women were thought incapable of assuming.

Men led, made decisions, and provided for the basic unit of society, the family. Women often contributed their labors on behalf of the family, but it was widely understood that a married woman's work plans were subject to her husband's approval, and were secondary to his own plans as the main provider. A man answered to society for a household that bore his name. It was an orderly chain of authority. Woman answered to man, and man to society.

These assumptions, taken together, constituted the traditional view of woman's role. They defined woman's goals and rewards, and they set her priorities. Largely cutting across the lines set by class and regional differences, they provided a comprehensive framework within which most women ordered their lives. In a woman's youth, ideally, she prepared for the day when she would become a wife and mother. In her adult life, the homemaker role came first, and activities not relating to home and children were by definition secondary.

Society did offer a range of alternative role options to women. To become part of the *mizu shobai*, the demimonde of geisha, entertainers, and prostitutes who provided leisure activities for virtually an all-male clientele, or to eschew normal family arrangements for a solitary life as a nun, scholar, writer, or the like—these were also possibilities. They were open throughout history to certain of the very beautiful, the very talented, and the unconventional among women, or, in the case of many who made their way into the demimonde, to the poor and the fallen. But to elect or even consider these routes was hardly the normal course for the great majority of Japanese women, who sought the security of a permanent marriage arrangement.

The traditional view was in virtually no respect unique to Japan. The assumptions just described have operated in most societies evolving from patriarchal traditions. What was unusual to Japan, perhaps, was the persistance of the view, with only minor challenges, well into the twentieth century. After Japan emerged from centuries of feudalism and national isolation in the 1860s, most of these assumptions passed intact into the modern period and were reaffirmed by legal code and custom until the end of World War II.

Three features of the traditional view had particular impact on the lives of women before that war and to some extent influence attitudes today. The first was the degree to which status differences between men and women were thought natural and legitimate. Whereas in Europe romantic and chivalrous traditions had developed in the feudal era to soften the very real lines of status difference between men and women, in Japan, with different feudal traditions, the lines were very stark indeed. In the prewar period women showed deference to men of their own as well as of higher classes by the use of polite language and honorific forms of address, by bowing more deeply than they, by walking behind their husbands in public, and in numerous other ways. In the extended family arrangement common before the war, ideally a new bride coming into the house was expected to acknowledge her status inferiority in a number of ritualized ways: getting up first in the morning, going to bed last at night, taking her bath only after all other family members had bathed, eating after other family members, and taking the least choice servings of food.

Another feature of the traditional view, supported not only in custom but in legal codes in the modern period, was the husband's authority over the wife. In the prewar family system, the head of the household assumed full legal responsibility for all family members. Upon marriage, a woman could act in any legal matters only with the approval of her husband's family. In provisions relating to divorce, marriage, property rights, and other questions coming under family law, the Civil Code consistently favored the husband.[5] Adultery constituted legal grounds for divorce only if committed by the wife. Where there was a dispute over the custody of a child, the wishes of the husband were controlling. It was regarded as proper, if painful for the wife, for a husband to divorce her, keeping the children in his own family to bear its name. By the same token, if a man fathered children by women other than his wife he was legally entitled to adopt them into the family. If her husband died, a wife came under the authority of her eldest son as soon as he became of age. Most women in prewar Japan spent their entire lifetime before and after marriage as legal dependents of male family heads.

A final feature of the traditional view that has endured well into the twentieth century is the notion that husband and wife belong in separate spheres of activity. As many writers note, industrialization has supported sex-role specialization by taking husbands out of the family productive unit (the farm or shop) and into the office or factory.[6] But the prevalence of attitudes supporting sex role segregation today is also traced to the strength of this aspect of the traditional view in prewar society, especially among the upper classes. Upper-class married women in prewar Japan played few roles in affairs outside the home circle and neighborhood. In contrast to Europe and the United States, where upper-class leisure patterns brought husbands and wives together in many social contexts, Japan provided few such opportunities. Wives hardly ever ventured into the demimonde where many well-to-do men spent their leisure hours. Sex role divisions were less rigid among the working classes, where work roles were often shared and where husbands had limited means for leisure activities, but the traditional view of woman's role among upper-class people has had more support than their numbers suggest. For as prosperity has spread, it has been natural that those ascending the social ladder aspire to the style of life of those above them. Sex role division stressed in the upper-class version of the traditional view of woman's role has thus survived in the twentieth century and spread to other levels of society, accelerated by the impact of industrialization.

But the traditional view of woman's role, reinforced by certain changes in the modern period, has been challenged by other views, especially in the postwar period. Japan's surrender in 1945 set off a series of changes that have affected women at almost every level of Japanese life. The Constitution of 1947 explicitly forbade discrimination on the basis of sex. Through reform of the Civil Code, the United States occupying forces attacked the basis of women's status inferiority in the family by guaranteeing women free choice of a spouse, equal recourse to divorce, equal property rights, and so on. Meanwhile, democratization and legal reform in their impact on women's status have been supported by other postwar forces. Urbanization has sped the demise of the extended family system. Within the urban nuclear family, even where status differences are acknowledged they are far less ritualized than before. Prosperity, another force for change in postwar Japan, has made higher education available to daughters as well as sons. Improvements in home facilities resulting from a higher standard of living have lightened the burden of housework, freeing women for other pursuits.

These recent forces for change impinge on the traditional view of woman's role described earlier. Multiple currents, often pulling in opposite directions, conjoin to shape definitions of woman's role in present-day society. For the individual woman, meshing legal norms with social reality may be a major challenge. The result is the three views of woman's role in postwar Japan that will now be described in turn.

Neotraditionalists

In a coffee shop in Osaka, I sat with Honda Akiko, a young woman activist of nineteen who is eagerly awaiting the day she becomes twenty and can be an official member of the Komeito Party.[7] At the time of the interview, she was participating in party activities unofficially by helping her older sisters, already Komeito members, count out campaign pamphlets at home.

Akiko is the youngest of four girls, the daughter of an iron parts maker who has worked hard all his life, and a mother who has spent most of her married life doing double duty as a housewife and part-time factory worker. Together they have struggled to make a living for the six of them, and if they have a single ambition for a family of four daughters, it is to see them marry into a life of greater ease than they have known.

The year before I interviewed her, Akiko had graduated from senior high school and immediately taken a job in a large company. There she performs the duties that thousands of young Japanese women today undertake for a few years before marriage. She is what today is called an "O.L." in Japan, an "office lady" hired to do routine office work, to pour tea for company members several times a day, and to create a pleasant working environment for the men who do the serious work of the office. To suggest to Akiko that she apply for the kind of job done by the men would be like suggesting that she try for the position of prime minister. In the business world, men and women are almost always hired for different kinds of work, and there are few ways in present-day society in which she could cross those lines. More important, in her own mind she really does not see herself as able to do men's work. As she explained to me, in words echoing centuries of Japanese history, "Men are superior to women in every field. Women have a narrower mind, a more limited view." Finally, not only would men's kind of work be beyond her abilities, as she sees things, but moreover it would interfere with the main life plan of Neotraditionalists like Akiko: to become a full-time housewife and mother to the exclusion of most other pursuits.

As we sat there, I had asked her a number of questions about the future, about her long-term plans and goals. Like many of the young activists I interviewed in Japan, she asked me about my own plans. I told her I aspired to be a college professor, but that I hoped to marry someday, too. With great tact, she asked me how old I was, and when I said I was twenty-eight she looked worried and concerned for me. Then she said in a soft but firm voice, resounding with the hopes of a great many young women all over Japan today,

> As for me, I have no special person in mind, but I have a dream of marriage. It is stronger now than when I was graduating from high school. My dream is to create a warm atmosphere in a home even if it turns out to be a humble home.
>
> To find someone, first I must polish myself. That is what I am doing now. I am improving myself so that I can find an ideal husband.

For Akiko's plans, her job now is perfectly suited to her needs. Her salary is low and she must live with her family, but she has funds to pay them for her upkeep so that she does not feel herself a burden on them. And beyond that, she has pocket money for clothes, makeup, magazines, and an occasional trip to a coffeehouse with former high-school friends and girlfriends from the office. At work, she has a chance to gain the kind of practical experience with life that most young women feel is today an important credential for marriage. She is "polishing herself," and in the back of her mind is the hope that in the company she might be able to meet an eligible young *salariman*, one of the middle-class salaried workers who are symbols of postwar prosperity.

Once she finds someone suitable, Akiko will quit her job. It is her earnest hope—shared by a great many young women today whose mothers in their early married years struggled to combine housework and child rearing in prewar Japan with a tiring industrial job or hard work in a home productive unit—that she will be able to give full time to the life task of making a home. But Akiko is realistic. If she does not meet a *salariman* and instead marries someone of her own class, she will probably have to work, for it is not yet possible for most young working-class couples in Japan to live on the husband's salary alone. When I asked her if she would work after marriage, I was obviously touching on a subject that occupied many of her thoughts.

> If there is no way around it, of course I will. I'm hoping, though, that I won't have to. I would rather stay at home and keep a perfect house. I'd prefer that life—waiting for my husband to come home.

Many young women like Akiko, once they wed, are finding married life somewhat different from the way they had envisioned it. With the inflation that has been endemic for much of the postwar period, young middle-class husbands have a hard time providing for two people, even when a wife is frugal. Furthermore, the dreams of a great many young women today grew out of the aspirations of mothers who started out young in a different Japan when housing was more spacious, housework more demanding, and family size much larger. Today, in the highly urban society Japan has become, many young housewives in big cities find themselves living in an apartment smaller than an average American living room. "Keeping a perfect house"—Akiko's dream—is a matter of a good two hours' work, and after that is done, until they have children, they may find themselves with a great deal of time on their hands.

The problem is often especially acute if the husband is a *salariman*, for often he must work overtime, and in the typical pattern of Japanese business life, may go drinking with co-workers after office hours several nights a week. The *salariman's* wife, eager to serve and please her husband according to traditional formulas, may find herself waiting alone many nights in front of the television set in a tiny apartment, not sure when he will come home. He, to meet his job responsibilities in Japan, may not be able to return in time for dinner, and because of long-established social custom, would look askance at the idea of telephoning her to forewarn her. While her children are young, the full-time urban housewife may feel that she has her hands full. But family size is small today, and soon the children are in school. The housewife then may find her hours empty indeed.

Today it is common to hear the men joke about the modern wife.

Shaking their heads, they say that unlike the industrious, hard-working mothers they remember, she spends much of her time sleeping late or sitting in front of the television. But this kind of joking may be one reflection of an increasingly serious problem in Japan—the growing dysfunctionality of woman's major social role as it has been defined traditionally. What many Japanese men describe as the life of leisure of the modern wife can, from another point of view, be seen as a life of boredom, personal inertia, and considerable loneliness. Women's magazines today reveal the other side of the picture in articles dealing with how to be more sexually attractive to bring a husband back from the office on time, how to prepare meals such as stews which can simmer for hours and be ready whenever he happens to return, articles on hobbies to fill the housewife's long hours at home, and others on how to put idle time to good use by helping children with homework. Some of these articles reflect considerable frustration—sexual, emotional, and otherwise—as well as many women's concern today for finding traditionally acceptable ways to adapt to a role whose terms have changed profoundly in recent years.

The views attributed to Akiko so far appear to put her in the category with prewar traditional women. In what sense, then, is Akiko Neotraditional? What distinguishes her attitudes from those of prewar women? Certainly one area of change was in her attitudes toward a political role. Most Neotraditional women do not aspire to become active members of a political party, but there is no question that attitudes toward women's political participation have changed. Today, defying trends in other countries, the overall voting rate is slightly higher for women than for men in Japan, and among young people in the 20-to-29 age group it is substantially higher.[8]

Another area of change is in attitudes toward education. In the prewar period, girls were educated in a separate girls' track with a program explicitly designed to prepare them to become "good wives and wise mothers." Today, however, there is little doubt that most people regard the serious study of basic subjects as necessary for youth of both sexes. Ministry of Education figures show that when choosing among several curriculum options in senior high school, only 11 percent of the girl students elected the home-economics concentration that almost surely would have been the natural preference of a great many prewar girls, had they been confronted with study options.[9] The level of women's educational aspirations has also been rising. Whereas relatively few girls went on beyond their six years of compulsory schooling in prewar Japan, it is now within the ordinary hopes and expectations of most young Japanese women like Akiko to go to senior high school. In fact, by a slight margin, the rate of advancement to senior high school is higher for girls than for boys and now stands at 82.7 percent.[10]

Even more significant are changing attitudes toward higher education. Akiko herself had not sought education beyond the high-school level. But her older sister, another Neotraditional woman, had managed to finish junior college by working part time. In the prewar years, the percentage of women advancing to higher education generally was around 1 percent.[11] By 1972, it stood at 28.4 percent.[12] Many of these women, like Akiko's sister, attend junior colleges where they make up 84 percent of the enrollment, rather than four-year colleges and universities where they represent only 19 percent of the total; but compared to the prewar situation, these developments are quite remarkable.[13] Following from their attitudes toward woman's role, many Neotraditionalists want a college degree as a new kind of marriage credential that many people now see as necessary for a young woman of the middle or upper middle class who wants to attract a suitable husband. Because Neotraditional women want to marry a man who is somewhat superior to them intellectually, they are careful not to become more educated than the kind of men they hope to marry. Junior college is a particularly safe choice because it makes them eligible to marry almost any college-educated male. On the other hand, Neotraditionalists of upper-middle-class backgrounds, feeling fairly assured that they can marry a graduate of one of the top universities of Japan, may attend a middle-ranking university or a four-year women's college.

Views of marriage have also changed, as evidenced by present-day attitudes toward mate selection. As many writers note, the arranged marriage system itself has changed remarkably in the postwar years, while overall the percentage of "love" marriages *(renai kekkon)* has outpaced that of arranged marriages *(miai kekkon)*. A recent report of the Economic Planning Agency showed that in large- and medium-sized cities, around 60 percent of all marriages were "love" matches.[14] Akiko's desire to find her own mate, then, is quite usual in postwar Japan. In a recent study, 82.7 percent of those under twenty years of age who were questioned said they would prefer to have a "love" marriage.[15] The actual figures as cited above lag behind these expressed desires, but nevertheless the change in attitudes is a major one.

Finally, Neotraditionalists' feelings toward work reflect major signs of change. In the prewar period, many young girls took jobs for wages because of severe family hardship. Many would have preferred to stay home to prepare for marriage by studying cooking, flower arranging, and the like. Today, however, most young women like Akiko accept it as a matter of course to take a job for a few years before they marry. Of women in the 20-to-24 age group, 70.5 percent are now in the labor force.[16] As indicated by figures cited earlier, most of the others are in college. Obviously, few girls stay home any more preparing for marriage, and for most—whether for pocket money, personal enrichment, to find a husband, or, recently, to save money for a trip abroad—taking a job has come to be accepted as a natural and necessary stage of growing up.

For Neotraditionalists, basic goals and views of their role and place as women in Japan have not changed. But compared to the women of the prewar world, there is no doubt that the movement is in the direction of more civic participation, fuller involvement with national life through work, an increasing quest for higher education, and in all activities a search for greater personal independence.

New Women

One woman who typified many of the New Women I interviewed was Takai Setsuko, a quietly dressed young woman of twenty-three who at the time of the interview was a Japanese equivalent of a Nader's Raider. As a specialist in the chemical composition of fabrics, she was a persuasive and committed advocate of consumer protection, working full time at the headquarters of the Housewives' Association *(Shufuren)* in Tokyo.

In Setsuko's early experience there is little that readily meets the eye to set her apart from the Neotraditional woman. She grew up far from a major urban center in a small village in southern Shikoku, and she told me forthrightly that when she had graduated from high school she had had no particular thoughts except to marry someday like other girls. Then, over the summer after graduation, she had talked to former high-school classmates back from their freshman year in various colleges in Tokyo. She had said to herself, "I've been thinking in my own limited world. I ought to go to college." Her father, a local official, was not enthusiastic, expressing fears that in their rural locale a college education would hurt her marriage chances. But he agreed finally to pay for her schooling. Thus in 1967, five years before I interviewed her, Setsuko had come to Tokyo to attend a women's college where she majored in home economics. So far she was on the Neotraditional course.

But at some point in her senior year in college, something appears to have changed Setsuko. She was then doing her graduation essay, a requirement for all seniors, and she became increasingly interested in the topic, which dealt with the safety of commercial fabrics used for clothes. She began interviewing manufacturers and consumer groups, including the Housewives' Association, and she was shocked to find that many widely used fabrics are inflammable and dangerous. Late in her senior year, she decided that she would have to do something with the knowledge she had acquired from her research, and she began to formulate plans. Her family back home, worried about a daughter alone in distant Tokyo, wanted her home after graduation. In letters, they were beginning to mention likely candidates for an arranged marriage. But Setsuko pressed to be allowed to follow her own course, and in the end her parents reconciled themselves. She accepted a job that she had been offered at the Housewives' Association and set out to find an apartment in Tokyo. Because she had heard that many Tokyo landlords might be reluctant to rent to a young single woman, she began looking for a place long before her job began. Most young women from distant parts of Japan who work in Tokyo live with relatives or girlfriends. Their reasons are partly financial, but many would also be afraid that if they lived alone they would endanger their reputation and thereby hurt their marriage chances. Setsuko, however, went ahead with her plan because, she said, she wanted a taste of the independent life. At the time of the interview she was living by herself in a tiny apartment, and spent most of her time in activities related to her job at the Housewives' Association.

When Setsuko is asked about the future, she immediately talks about her plans to improve her competence at the job she is doing. When I asked her about marriage, she obviously felt great discomfort. She wants to marry, but she wants to continue her job afterward, and she wonders if she can find a husband in Japan who will understand how she feels.

Whereas Neotraditionalists, even when they become deeply absorbed in a job or other activity, are apt to see it as only a passing phase of youth before they take on their main life role, many New Women like Setsuko do not want to give up their outside interests. They want to marry, and they accept the sex role tradition in marriage that allocates to them the role of homemaker and child tender. But they want to play other roles as well.

What New Women want in terms of the actual content of the marriage relationship varies with the individual. Some, while handling their job or other activity, would want to assume all the traditional obligations that go along with the homemaker role. They talk of taking on full child-care responsibility, paying for it themselves, and say they would expect no help from their husband with housework. Others (though they, too, do not question that the homemaker role is really their responsibility) express the view that their husband should occasional helping hand. In their criteria for a husband, some ·nly hold certain traditional views and say forthrightly that ·nt someone more intelligent than they. Others say they prefer someone closer to their own age (but generally, slightly older), and of similar educational attainment. All express the hope that in the marriage they ultimately enter there will be somewhat greater companionability and more opportunity for sharing thoughts and feelings than tend to be anticipated in the Neotraditionalist's model of marriage. Most New Women, however, are engaged in an experiment with their role, an experiment where neither their ideology nor the behavioral requirements for implementing it are clearly formulated in their own minds. Those who are unmarried have no clear model of what they actually want in the marriage relationship, and those who are married know only what they do not like. If Freud were to talk to the New Women of Japan today, he might well be led to repeat his famous query, "What do women want?" New Women do not yet know in precise terms. They are searching for answers.

Many New Women who are not yet married have difficulty finding men who share their new view of woman's role and place in Japan today. Their problem in finding a husband is complicated by the fact that the arranged marriage system, which even the most independent-minded Neotraditionalists consider a reasonably acceptable fallback, is largely unsuited to their needs. Even with all the recent changes in the system, it still functions to bring two people together in a traditional marriage relationship where the wife is expected to follow a course set by the husband. As one New Woman, a freshman economics major at Tokyo University, explained:

> There are two kinds of arranged marriages in Japan. One is the old feudalistic kind where parents and relatives put a lot of pressure on the parties concerned. The other is the modern kind, which is basically an introduction method. I don't like either kind. I don't want to have to agree with a man's opinions about everything.

Even when they find a marriage prospect on their own, New Women may run into problems. Many men who want to assert their independence by having a "love" match still have traditional expectations concerning woman's role. The number of New Women is growing rapidly today, however, and increasingly they are able to find men sympathetic to their views at work, in school, or, in the case of many New Women I interviewed, in their political group.

Women already married who come to the New Woman's view within a traditional marriage relationship have other kinds of problems. The experience of Tanaka Keiko provides an example. At age

32 she is a member of a Tokyo women's group composed of upper-middle-class Tokyo suburban housewives, all of whom want part-time or full-time jobs. At age 25, Keiko, a graduate of a women's college, had an arranged marriage to a young engineer whom she dated only eight times before the wedding ceremony. Following the accepted pattern—which she herself thought quite natural at the time—she quit her job at an electric company near her home in the Kansai when she married, and moved to Tokyo to make a new life with her husband. Now, seven years and two children later, she wants a part-time job as soon as the children are both in school. Her reasons are those heard with increasing frequency in Japanese upper-middle-class suburbia: Housework is monotonous, she has too much free time, and she is lonely in a community where she still knows very few people after seven years.

Keiko's husband is frankly astonished at her attitude. From his standpoint, he has gone above and beyond the traditional responsibilities to a wife by providing her with a more than adequate home, a car that she is able to use during the day, and ample spending money. Since he provides so well, it makes no sense to him that his wife would want to work. He also has the view, widely shared in Japanese society, that children require a mother's full-time physical presence and fairly constant attention, not only in the early years but well into the school years and even late adolescence as well, and that giving herself over to these tasks should be a woman's highest satisfaction and main life purpose. Thus he can only see her plan, which calls for placing the children in a day-care center or in the care of outside help for a few hours several afternoons a week, as serious neglect of her responsibilities and a failure of moral purpose as well. To heighten the tension, his own mother vehemently agrees with him and sides with him in disputes. The Tanakas' traditional marriage is undergoing considerable strain as the discussion continues. Some New Women who came to their view after marriage have achieved more success in gaining their husband's cooperation, particularly where the activity they want to take on is a job that would supply needed extra income to the family. But where family income is adequate, husbands generally are much harder to convince. The work available to even highly educated women without special skills generally pays very little—in many cases, barely enough to pay for day care or for a housekeeper to mind the children.[17]

A wide variety of environmental influences directs women toward a New Woman's view today. The experience of higher education is often a major factor. It is true that more than half of the women in higher education attend junior colleges and women's colleges, many

following the typical Neotraditionalist path. But the number
ng four-year coeducational universities is increasing rapidly.
0, women made up only 2 percent of the university enrollment,
but by 1972 the figure had risen to 19 percent, with a spectacular rate
of increase in number far outpacing that for male students.[18] Even at
prestigious Tokyo University, the percentage of women almost tripled between 1960 and 1970. By the latter year, 10 percent of its
students were women.[19] Not all women attending universities are
New Women. But there is much evidence of an important correlation
between educational level and views of woman's role. A study by
Blood conducted in a middle-class suburb shows that 69 percent of
the college-educated wives in the sample worked, whereas only 24
percent of the high-school graduates were working.[20]

In my own study, I found far more New Women who had come to
their ideology of woman's role as a result of educational experiences
than had done so as a result of working. Cases like that of Takai
Setsuko, who had found an interesting job with a consumer group,
were rare. Japanese employers show great reluctance to hire women
for challenging jobs at good pay. Women's average wage in 1971 was
still less than half that received by male workers.[21] Women hold less
than 4 percent of the jobs in the category of managers and officials,
and the figure in 1970 was slightly less than the one ten years before.[22]
As one New Woman, a Tokyo University graduate, remarked bitterly
after she was turned down for low-paying editorial jobs at two big
publishing houses, "Japan is an escalator society, and women just
never get on the escalator."

For a number of women interviewed for the study, the situation in
the job market had been a major contributing factor in leading them
to political and civic groups. Eager to develop new interests outside
marriage, they had first sought interesting work; failing to find it, they
had turned to political activities.

Radical Egalitarians

After a long series of introductions, I was at last able to meet Suzuki
Fumiko, an 18-year-old member of the Red Army (*Rengō sekigun*).[23]
Fumiko had a manner that conveyed a sense of confidence and strong
determination. Sitting before me in the coffee shop, her eyes seldom
left my face as we talked. When she laughed, it was with great zest and
feeling. Unlike many women I talked to in Japan, who accepted the
terms I had set for the interview and left me the initiative, Fumiko
took a much more active role in the exchange. She would answer no
questions until she had asked me about my ideology, my family

background, my own relations with men, my plans, how I would use my research findings, and what I had found out so far about Japanese women. Only then, and after she had made clear what she would and would not discuss, was she willing to proceed.

Fumiko's feelings about woman's role came out rather early in the interview when I asked her how she felt about men and marriage. Thinking a moment, she made a strong statement of the Radical Egalitarian view and then described the course she had chosen:

> The war destroyed the [traditional] family system in Japan, but the basic problems remain. Marriage in this society involves a relationship between possessor and possessed, not between two individuals who think of each other as equals.
>
> My own relationship with a man is not that kind of relationship. It is a face-to-face relationship where we look directly into each other's eyes. We live together in the course of developing our ideas and thoughts.

At the time of the interview, Fumiko was living with a man, also a Red Army member, in a tiny apartment they had found together. Both were agreed, she told me, that the duties of daily life in the apartment should be shared and that each should have large areas of personal freedom to do what they wished.

How the several Radical Egalitarians I met had come to their view is a highly complex matter that does not lend itself to easy generalization. It is dealt with at length elsewhere.[24] Briefly, however, many did appear to have at least one parent, most often a mother, who had given strong support, whether tacit or expressive, for the daughter's personal explorations. In Fumiko's case her mother, left a widow early in her forties by the sudden death of her *salariman* husband, had suffered severe financial hardship in trying to make her way alone as a woman in Japan. It was this experience, in part, that appeared to have made her supportive of a daughter's search for autonomy. Piecing together a marginal income from her deceased husband's pension and from making garments, she had given her tacit consent—while outwardly voicing disapproval—when her daughter became involved in radical political activities during junior-high-school days. While her mother sewed upstairs in their large, rambling house in Kamakura outside Tokyo, Fumiko had turned the downstairs into a commune for the Red Army. The year before I interviewed her, Fumiko had dropped out of senior high school and had begun to live with her present lover, again with her mother's full knowledge.

Though the Radical Egalitarians I talked to had come to their view by somewhat distinctive routes, and differed widely in personal qualities and in such factors as class and educational background, they had certain characteristics in common. One was a distinct personal style. Whereas virtually all Neotraditionalists and most New Women tended to express themselves somewhat indirectly, uniformly using the polite forms of speech and expression considered appropriate for women, Radical Egalitarians spoke with great frankness and directness. In many cases they used plain forms of speech and numerous expressions that are commonly regarded as "men's language" in Japan.

Another characteristic was that most had given considerable thought to where they stood on many issues, both political and personal. Whereas Neotraditionalists and especially New Women often discovered inconsistencies in their behavior and feeling over the course of the interview, Radical Egalitarians, even the younger ones like Fumiko, had gone through fairly extensive self-examination. They were quick, in most cases, to admit shortcomings and failures to live up to their ideals. But in a way that was quite striking, they had thought things through.

Unlike the New Women I interviewed, who differed with one another on what they wanted in a relationship with a man, Radical Egalitarians were fairly agreed. Uniformly they expressed a strong dislike of the widely accepted criteria for choosing a mate in Japan, such as family background, socioeconomic status, and educational attainment. Many were ideologically opposed to the institution of marriage for the kinds of reasons cited by Fumiko.

Almost all were struggling to achieve their personal aims in radical subcultures where they were surrounded by those who gave them strong personal validation. Although a number of them maintained close ties with their families, most lived apart from relatives, generally with members of their group or with a man who shared their view. Almost all the Radical Egalitarians interviewed for this particular study were engaged in political activities, in the context of which they were pressing for equality as women. Most were in two main types of groups. Half, like Fumiko, were in radical political organizations that are part of the New Left in Japan. These women were opposed not only to current notions of woman's role but also to the general pattern of social and family relations in Japan and other capitalist societies, to the work ethic as personified by the *salariman,* to the present government, to all the existing political parties in Japan, including the parties of the Left, and to an educational system in their country, which they see as overcompetitive and dehumanizing. Within their group, many were pressing for their right to participate on an equal basis in all group activities, ranging from assuming leadership roles to engaging in physical combat in pursuit of the group's objectives. Most said that there were major barriers to achieving equality in their political activities. Disputes between male and female activists had broken out in numerous groups over such seemingly simple but extremely significant matters as who should pour the tea at meetings.

The other half were members of radical women's liberation groups.[25] Many of these women had deserted the New Left because they felt that men in the movement failed to understand the seriousness of their struggle for equality and recognition. Joined by many young women not from the New Left, they have formed numerous women's groups and collectives. Those associated with *Tatakau onna* (fighting women) generally hold that before women can have equal relations with men they must first learn to express themselves among women and develop their self-confidence. This group operates several collectives where women live and study together, most supporting themselves by taking part-time jobs in coffee shops or wherever they can find work. While living in the collective, many have sexual relations with men outside it. Here they argue that Japanese women, long sexually repressed in a country with a strong tradition of a double standard, should overcome their timidity and sexual dependence on men by learning to have sex as many men do: with a variety of partners and on their own terms.[26] Radical Egalitarians in several women's groups not associated with *Tatakau onna* had different objectives. Individual members were living with a man, and met occasionally in groups that functioned much like consciousness-raising groups in the United States. These young women felt that women must struggle for equality and recognition not in a separatist movement but in a joint struggle waged with men who share their view of woman's role and who are willing to try for a new style of relationship between man and woman in present-day Japanese society.

The Future of Japanese Women

Amid the Neotraditionalists, New Women, and Radical Egalitarians were, of course, many young women trying to find themselves, moving back and forth between the various views at different stages of their life experience. In Japanese society, particularly among the older generations above the age range of my informants, many women are still struggling between the prewar traditional view of woman's role—which imposed extreme restrictions on women's right to participate in the affairs of society—and the Neotraditional view that is widely accepted in Japanese society today. Social values, including those bearing on woman's role and place, are in great flux today and it is only natural that a great many women find themselves vacillating between views, unsure of what they want, undecided as to whether they are willing to undergo the great personal and psychological risk that comes when human beings try to move in new directions.

In present-day Japan, the central tension is between the view of Neotraditionalists, who continue to have their strong one-role ideology that calls on them to subordinate all other major life activities to the role of wife and mother, and the view of the New Women, who want to be wives and mothers but who want to develop other personal interests as well. The Radical Egalitarians are far outside the mainstream of life in Japan. In society as it is today, their experiment is possible only within the subcultures they have created.

Over the next decade, there will be growing tension between the views of Neotraditionalists and New Women. By the middle of the 1980s, especially in the major urban centers, the view of the New Women will be vying for dominance in the culture.

The steps by which the New Women's view gradually will come to dominance are deeply rooted in the nature of postwar change, particularly in developments among the urban middle class.

In the wake of a devastating war, Japan's leadership guided the nation into a program of major rebuilding that required most Japanese to make a great many personal sacrifices. Husbands worked long hours, stayed overtime at the factory or office, often took little or no vacation, and came home exhausted on weekends, in many cases with only one day of rest to collect themselves for the week ahead. Because of the heavy work demands on men, husbands and wives saw remarkably little of each other. There was little money or time for joint activities. Husbands came home too tired to talk and develop serious communication with their wives. The home itself, for most urban Japanese, was a very modest place indeed. What with housing storages, living quarters were cramped and families living on extremely limited budgets had little money to improve the quality of their living environment. These conditions were certainly major factors supporting the traditional segregated leisure pattern of Japan. Men exhausted from their labors looked forward to the male leisure environment outside the home—the bars and cabarets where they could stop off on the way home from work for much-needed moments of relaxation. To take a wife out and relax together not only ran against the grain of custom but also required money for two people's leisure activities, money that simply was not available. All this is to say that the pattern of postwar life has supported the traditional sex role divisions of married life.

While these developments were taking place among adult Japanese, a great many young people who had grown up entirely in the world of postwar Japan felt a growing desire for new styles of social relationships in keeping with the democratic values supported within the school environment. For many young Japanese, the university world was a testing ground for trying to develop new styles of relationships with the opposite sex. Many, looking ahead to their future lives in the big cities of Japan, felt that the traditional marriage relationship, characterized by great social distance between husband and wife in the extended family, did not seem quite appropriate to the needs of two people making their way together in the urban setting. Young men's and women's hopes for new kinds of relationships with one another are mirrored in statistics cited earlier showing the strong desire of a high proportion of young people to choose their own mates.

But in a society struggling to regain its position in the world, these hopes, in a great many cases, were not realizable. Many young men left the university for a job and were soon caught up in a system that brought their period of personal exploration to a close. Many of them who at one point had wanted to find their own marriage partner turned to parents or others to find a mate for them. They had not enough time or opportunity, either at school or while working in a country where easy friendship relations between the sexes are still difficult to achieve, to meet someone on their own. Nor was there much time after marriage, for the work demands in Japan left them little time to spend with their wives or to build family lives. It was partly in anticipation of this aspect of the life ahead that many young Japanese, especially young men whose lives were soon to be spent almost wholly in the world of work, described feeling a certain emptiness in the 1950s and 1960s and dreaded leaving the university world to enter it.[27]

For growing numbers of young Japanese now becoming adults, however, some of these problems will gradually ease, and there will be subtle and gradual changes in the nature of relationships between men and women. The five-day week and increased prosperity will have major impact in support of the change. Men will have more time to spend at home. There will be more money in the family for taking family trips and for an occasional night out together. Vogel, in a report a few years back, noted signs of all these trends in urban middle class life.[28]

As a response to these developments, for the 1980s young Japanese women are going to be strongly attracted to the Neotraditionalist view. They will set about creating a pleasant home environment with family funds now more generously available for that purpose, and they will look forward to spending time with their husbands. For both the married and the unmarried, getting to know the opposite sex in a country where long-established traditions have kept men and women in separate spheres of activity will itself be a great adventure. In Tokyo offices there is already much joking and teasing of increasing numbers of younger men who are eager to get back home after work to be with their young wives. In English classes I taught in major companies in Tokyo while doing research in Japan, many young workers sheepishly admitted to their pleasure in occasionally preparing breakfast for their wives on a leisurely Sunday morning, or enthusiastically described a Saturday afternoon they spent in some activity with a son or daughter.

These incidents do not mean, of course, that there will be major changes in the basic sex role divisions in marriage. Most Japanese men and women, for a very long time to come, will continue to feel that homemaking and child-care responsibilities are primarily women's responsibility. For men, the segregated leisure pattern itself will continue to exist for some time; it is deeply a part of business and social life. Newer patterns of leisure activities where couples can take part will grow up alongside the traditional pattern, but will not replace it. What will change, however, is the emotional content of married life, the growth of mutuality and common understanding between people who are building their lives together in modern urban society.

Why, then, will the Neotraditionalist ideology gradually lose ground to the New Woman's view? My own feeling is that a major impetus for change will come from factors beyond the immediate control of today's Neotraditionalists. As noted earlier, a great many young women, eager to devote themselves to their husbands and children, even today are finding it difficult to employ their full energies in this way. The average Japanese couple, according to a study issued in 1972, now wants two children.[29] The average wife has the first child when she is 25.3 years old, and the second at 27.9.[30] By the time a woman reaches age 40, both children will be in high school and long past need of her full-time care. Hence, at age 40, because average life expectancy for women even now is over 75, she is likely to face at least 35 years in which the wife-mother role cannot conceivably take up all her time. For Japanese women, long brought up to believe that serving and caring for husband and children was their exclusive and all-consuming life purpose, this increasing obsolescence of their role as it has been conceived traditionally is going to require major adjustments. In recent years there has been much discussion in Japan of *ikigai* (the purpose of life). Growing numbers of Japanese women who have been involved in this discussion see the problem very much as described here: What is a mother to do with herself after her children are grown in a world where parents can no longer expect to live with their grown children? Where is she to find meaning in what will soon be the entire second half of her life?

A great many young Neotraditionalists face a major struggle in coming to terms with cold statistics that will force them to begin developing new interests outside the home. Some will be helped through their difficulties by the changing nature of the labor market. If current trends continue there will be an increasing bid on the part of the business and industry for the services of women workers over 40. Gradually the Neotraditionalist's work pattern is likely to change from what Ginzberg has called the "terminated" pattern, now the ideal, whereby young women quit the labor market to marry after a few years of work, never to return again, to "periodic" or "intermittent" patterns whereby growing numbers of Neotraditionalists will move out of the labor market when they marry and back into it again after their children are well in school.[31]

The spread of the New Women's ideology as it gains acceptance in Japan will cause many women to begin to give thought to their work prospects after their children are grown, and will lead others to consider the possibility of taking part in civic and political activities. Kiefer notes (in the Lewis Austin volume) the rising interest in civic participation among wives dwelling in Tokyo *danchi* (public housing projects) today. It seems likely that as husbands become somewhat freer from work responsibilities in the 1980s, there will be some tendency for young married people to join in civic affairs as couples, though this development will be fairly slow in coming, particularly outside urban areas. In the meantime, the most common pattern will be one where women develop new civic and other outside interests on their own while their husbands continue to invest much of their energy in their work. In Tokyo, Osaka, and other large cities, growing numbers of housewives are participating in some of the new civic movements in Japan, such as the citizens' movement and the consumer-protection movement.

Of the great dynamics operating behind the many changes that will occur in the lives of Neotraditionalists over the coming decade, one must be singled out for special note. This is the impact of higher education in changing women's notions of their role. In Japan today, an extraordinary thing is happening in higher education. Over the 1960s, within a decade, the number of women enrolling in junior colleges quadrupled and the enrollment of women in universities tripled.[32] Barring the unforeseen, it is very likely that these trends will continue in a prosperous society in which parents can educate daughters as well as sons. For a great many women now preparing to go on to higher education, their initial motivations will be traditional ones—to find a suitable mate or, at any rate, to collect important credentials for a good match. However, it is important to point out the latent function, the unintended consequences, of higher education now sought ostensibly as marriage preparation. Here is a remarkable case where a highly traditional attitude—a cultural stress on developing "credentials" for marriage, which grew out of a long tradition of arranged marriage in Japan—now is highly supportive of role change for women. Whatever the initial and conscious motivations for seeking higher education, there is little doubt that its long-range effects on the lives of growing numbers of Japanese women will be those already noted by many writers—to lead them toward new expectations as they become increasingly involved in what they study, and to make them less able to accept traditional marriage arrangements that restrict the outside interests of the wife.[33]

By the mid-1980s, if present trends continue, and if all these predictions are borne out, Japan will be well on its way toward becoming a nation of New Women, still managing the home and assuming responsibility for the children but gradually taking on a wide variety of other life activities—including part-time and full-time work at various stages of their lives before and after marriage, civic and political activities, and a great number of personal pursuits unrelated to homemaking.

If this is to be the future for the Neotraditionalists of today, what does the future hold for women who, in the mid-1970s, already held the New Woman's view? Many will experience considerable frustration trying to find life satisfaction in the years ahead. Some will look for fulfillment in hobbies and other activities. But many will be searching for part-time or full-time employment. It is here, as indicated earlier, that they will encounter major barriers. The present generation of business and political leadership has very little sympathy for the work goals of many New Women. The female labor market is almost exclusively geared to the needs of Neotraditionalist single women wanting to work for a few years as marriage preparation, or Neotraditionalist wives forced to work for family economic reasons. In 1970s Japan there are extraordinarily few job opportunities for young educated women. Unless the system changes radically in the future, the New Women of today and of the years immediately ahead are going to feel increasing disappointment with their life prospects as their employment needs are not met. The kind of clerical and factory work that industry will hold out to eager takers among Neotraditionalists will not be relevant to the needs, interests, and, in many cases, educational attainment of many of today's New Women.

Will the New Women of tomorrow turn in great numbers to the Radical Egalitarian view by the mid-1980s? No; role change of such magnitude for large numbers of women seems highly unlikely in such a short span of time in a society with such long traditions of male dominance in social and family life. By the 1980s, however, the Radical Egalitarian view will no longer seem quite so avant-garde, partly because it is already on its way to gaining currency in the United States and other Western societies that have major impact, through the media, on Japanese life and thought. Today many Radical Egalitarians combine their desire for equality as women with political aims and specific policy objectives that the majority of women in Japan cannot begin to accept. Many, it is true, have found their own answers. Many of today's Radical Egalitarians find satisfaction in living for and, in some cases, fighting for ideals they share with those around them. But their personal answers, developed in subcultures far from the mainstream of life, have very little relevance to the needs of most young Japanese women, who must struggle for their own answers in Japanese society as it is and will become.

Notes

1. This paper, originally prepared for the Advanced Seminar Series of the East Asia Council at Yale, has gone through several major revisions. Part of an earlier version was presented in April 1974 at the Annual Meeting of the Association for Asian Studies in Boston. I am grateful to Herbert Passin, David Plath, Lewis Austin, Marsha Hurst Hiller, Carol Berkin, and Stephen Butts for their valuable comments on the paper at various stages of preparation.

2. See Susan J. Pharr, "Sex and Politics: Women in Social and Political Movements in Japan," dissertation, Columbia University, December 1974.

3. For a discussion of sex role ideologies operating in other societies today, see Edmund Dahlstrom, *The Changing Roles of Women and Men* (Boston: Beacon Press, 1971) and Jessie Bernard, *Women and the Public Interest* (Chicago: Aldine-Atherton, 1971).

4. See Florence Kluckhohn's discussion of cultural ranking among value orientations in Florence R. Kluckhohn, "Some Reflections on the Nature of Cultural Integration and Change," in *Sociological Theory, Values and Sociocultural Change*, ed. Edward A. Tiryakian (New York: Harper and Row, 1963).

5. For a valuable summary of provisions in the Civil Code, see B. James George, Jr., "Law in Modern Japan," in *Twelve Doors to Japan*, ed. John Hall and Richard Beardsley (New York: McGraw-Hill, 1965).

6. See, for example, Ronald P. Dire, *City Life in Japan* (Berkeley: University of California Press, 1958), p. 116.

7. To protect their identity, the informants' names have been changed, along with minor biographical details. [The Japanese custom is to order the family name first, as here. Among residents of Western countries whose ancestry is Japanese, this custom gives way to the practice of placing the family name last. Thus this book presents an apparent inconsistency in name order: The preceding chapter cites the work of Shigeru Ishikawa, whose family name is Ishikawa; here the text mentions Honda Akiko, whose family name is Honda.—Ed.]

8. The voting rate for women has exceeded that for men in every national election since the Upper House election of July 1968. See table in Pharr, p. 19. For the 20-to-29 age group, one election study reported a voting rate of 74.7 percent for women and 66.5 percent for men, the widest gap recorded for any age group. See Ministry of Labor, Women and Minors' Bureau (WMB), *Me de miru fujin no ayumi (A Look at Women's Progress)*, 1971, p. 18.

9. Results of a study cited in Tomoda Yasumasu, "Educational and Occupational Aspirations of Female Senior High School Students," *Bulletin of the Hiroshima Agricultural College* 4, no. 3 (December 1972), 248.

10. The figure is for 1970, and compares with 81.6 percent for males. WMB, *Fujin no genjō (The Condition of Women)*, 1971, p. 6.

11. In 1920 the enrollment rate for women was .4 percent (for males, 3 percent); in 1930 it was 1.1. percent (for males, 6.4 percent); in 1940 it was 1.2 percent (for males, 8.1 percent). See Tomoda, p. 247.

12. WMB, *Fujin no genjō*, p. 6.

13. Ibid., p. 5.

14. Economic Planning Agency, *Kokumin seikatsu hakusho (Report on National Life)* (Tokyo, 1971), p. 30. Data are from a 1966 study.

15. Sankei Shimbun, *Iken to ishiki no hyakkajiten: Sankei Shimbun 1000-nin chosa kara (Encyclopedia of Thought and Opinion: From Sankei Newspaper's Survey of 1000 Persons)* (Tokyo, 1972), p. 85.

16. WMB, *Fujin no genjō*, p. 6.

17. Both public and private day-care facilities are available in Japan, but demand for placement far exceeds available space. As of April 1973 there were 16,140 centers accommodating 1,449,019 children. (Government of Japan, *Seminar in [sic] Public Administration Officers on Women's Problems 1973 Fiscal Year*, 1973, p. 65.) But for the working wife of all but low-income families, it is still difficult to make inexpensive day-care arrangements. Fees at public day-care centers are set on a scale based on ability to pay, with the fee determined by the income of the head of the household. Thus for married women whose husbands provide an adequate income the fee is likely to take a major portion of any income they can earn.

18. WMB, *Fujin no genjō*, p. 6.

19. Figures based on data provided in: Ministry of Education, *Zenkoku gakkō sōran (National School Report)* for 1961 (p. 2) and 1971 (p. 2).

20. Robert O. Blood, Jr., *Love Match and Arranged Marriage: A Tokyo-Detroit Comparison* (New York: Free Press, 1967), p. 149.

21. WMB, *Fujin rōdō no jitsujō (The Status of Women Workers)*, 1972, p. 38.

22. WMB, *Fujin no genjō*, p. 52.

23. For a study dealing with Japan's factionalized student movement, see Stuart Dowsey, ed., *Zengakuren: Japan's Revolutionary Students* (Berkeley: Ishi Press, 1970). Formed out of previous groups in 1969, the Red Army *(Rengō sekigun)* has engaged in a variety of terrorist activities inside and outside Japan. The informant referred to in the text was active in the Red Army before the merger.

24. See Pharr.

25. Japan has a number of organizations and groups committed to the goal of improving the status of women in society and in the family, and thus could be considered a part of a "women's liberation movement" in the broad sense in which that term is used in the United States. However, "women's lib" *(ūman ribu)* as used in Japan has a much narrower meaning. Specifically, it refers to a small number of groups which appeared in the early 1970s and which take sexual liberation as a primary objective. A

major political goal of these groups is to end the ban on birth-control pills in Japan and counter the government efforts to tighten restrictions on abortions. (See Nagano Yoshiko, "Women Fight for Control: Abortion Struggle in Japan," *AMPO*, 17 [Summer 1973]: 14–20.) The actual membership figures for these groups are fairly low, probably numbering in the several hundreds. But interest in their aims and activities is somewhat higher than this estimate would indicate. In May 1972, for example, a conference in Tokyo on "women's lib" drew about 3000 participants.

26. Interview with Tanaka Mitsu, age 28, leader of *Tatakau onna*, Tokyo, 1972. Her views on women's liberation are set out in her autobiography: Tanaka Mitsu, *Inochi no onna tachi e (That Women Might Live)* (Tokyo: Tahata Shoten, 1972).

27. Many writers dealing with the causes of student activism in Japan in the 1960s describe this feeling among Japanese youth. See Robert Jay Lifton, "Youth and History: Individual Change in Postwar Japan," in *The Challenge of Youth*, ed. Erik H. Erikson (New York: Doubleday, 1963).

28. Ezra F. Vogel, "Beyond Salary: Mamachi Revisited," *Japan Interpreter*, Summer 1970, pp. 105-113.

29. Results of a 1972 study conducted by the Ministry of Health and Welfare. Cited in *Japan Labor Bulletin*, 1 July 1973, p. 2.

30. Ibid.

31. For a discussion of women's work patterns, see Eli Ginzberg, *Lifestyles of Educated Women* (New York: Columbia University Press, 1966), p. 78.

32. Ministry of Education, *Educational Standards in Japan 1970* (Tokyo, 1971), p. 30.

33. See Blood, p. 149, and Herbert Passin, *Society and Education in Japan* (New York: Teachers College, Columbia University, 1965), p. 111.

3   Women in the People's Republic of China

Kay Ann Johnson*

Women and the Traditional Chinese Family

In order to understand and evaluate the recent process of women's liberation in China, it is important to begin with some understanding of the roots of female oppression in the traditional Chinese family. Although the traditional Chinese family, and the norms and customs which defined the status of women within the family, varied geographically and with social class, it is nonetheless possible to make some generalizations about the traditions of the Han family in China.

Probably the safest generalization which cuts across history, geography, and class in China is that the status of women within the family was universally low. The subordination of women to men was inherent in the patrilineal and patrilocal nature of the family and in the broader kinship system that allocated status and authority. Women in the attendant outlook lacked rights of property ownership and management, and carried no independent decision-making authority in important matters affecting the family and clan. The status and power of women did, however, vary with different phases of their lives and there were a few avenues for women to increase their family position somewhat. Most notably, women gained status through childbearing and with middle-age, when they gained greater supervisory and religious functions in the home.

The most difficult and degrading phase of life was that immediately after marriage. The arrangement of blind marriages by family heads, a custom that greatly enhanced the control of family elders over family life, was usually done without consulting their children. The young people therefore usually never met or saw each other until at or near the marriage ceremony. Under this arrangement, the groom's

*This chapter appears in a different form in Joan I. Roberts, *Beyond Intellectual Sexism: A New Woman, A New Reality*, New York: Longman, 1976.

family paid a "body price" to the bride's family, in effect buying the young woman as a chattel and reimbursing her natal family for the expense of raising her. The marriage was not so much a contract between the couple as it was a contract between the families, transferring the woman to the husband's family for the purpose of bearing male heirs for the patrilineal family and performing necessary domestic work.

Thus the young woman entered an ongoing family as a stranger and an outsider. Physically severed from affectionate relations with her own family, she did not find the buffer of immediate affectionate ties with her husband to ease her initial transition. In fact, one of the functions of the arranged marriage was to protect the filial bond between son and parents from being undermined by a strong conjugal bond that could threaten the family hierarchy. The young wife, lacking status and the protection of affectionate ties, came abruptly under the authority of her husband and her in-laws. In day-to-day affairs, she was supposed to be most directly under the authority and supervision of her mother-in-law, who organized and controlled the "women's work" within the household. Because the husband and his family had paid, often dearly, for the bride's services as a wife and daughter-in-law, they felt they had the right to regulate her labor and activities according to family needs.

Under this system, divorce was almost impossible for an unhappy wife. Even if her husband died, her in-laws, if they were still living, retained control over her. If she was allowed to leave the family and remarry, they would expect the new husband to pay them the body price they originally paid for her. Similarly, a divorce was not likely to be granted by the husband or family unless the woman could buy back her freedom. Since the woman was totally dependent on the family economically, it was most unlikely she could meet the price. In some areas of China, remarriage of widows was not uncommon, although it was usually looked down upon.[1] However, divorce for a woman was very rare, being sharply circumscribed by law and custom.

The brutalizing effect that this family system had on young women was a common theme of revolutionaries and progressive writers of the early twentieth century. These writers reflected on the physical and mental abuse suffered by young women and their not infrequent resort to suicide as the only escape from intolerable circumstances. One of Mao Tse-tung's earliest articles concerned the suicide of a young bride in his home village. He asserted that her death, and the deaths of many others like her, was the inevitable result of the iron net cast around her by the old Chinese family system and the society that supported it.[2] The well-known writer Lu Hsun described the system as a flesh-devouring monster because of the physical and mental destruction it wrought on its own youth, particularly on young women.[3]

One left-wing writer described the typical, almost routine, physical abuse suffered by the wife at the hands of husband and mother-in-law:

> For women the old rule still holds good that as a daughter-in-law you have to put up with beating and abuse, but once you become a mother-in-law yourself you can beat and curse your daughter-in-law. If you don't you're failing to put up a good show of being a mother-in-law. The old rule for men in handling their wives is "a wife you've married is like a horse you've bought—you can ride them or flog them as you like." Any man who does not beat his wife is only proving that he is afraid of her.[4]

A woman began to gain some status and respect in the family if and when she bore sons and if and when she developed a warm relationship with her husband that could partially shield her from arbitrary beatings and from her in-laws' authority. If a woman bore and raised a son to maturity and got a wife for him, hence a daughter-in-law for herself, she then gained the first real position of authority and control in her life. As a mother-in-law she gained household supervision over her son's new wife and her labor. As the passage quoted above suggests, the now older woman, having suffered abuse under the authority of her mother-in-law, assumes the same role over her young daughter-in-law. Even at this stage in life, with the greater status of age, she remained subordinate to her husband (and in theory to his brothers) and, to a lesser extent, to her adult male children.

The control of women's lives by family males and elders was reinforced by the physical seclusion of women within the home—a seclusion that restricted their contact with nonfamily members and insured economic dependence. A strict division of labor within the family was buttressed by traditional customs, norms, and superstitions that restricted proper women's work to manufacturing and processing materials for household consumption and other work that could be done near the home.[5] There were, however, important regional variations in the norms that restricted the physical movement and economic activities of women. In areas of Southern China, women often participated in subsidiary agricultural work, such as weeding and transplanting, and helped during the busy harvest times. This productive, income-related activity probably improved the position of women in the home. Yet even in these areas, women's activities were supposed to be closely supervised and controlled by family members, and women were generally barred by custom and superstition from many of the main productive activities. One survey taken in the 1930s showed that women comprised only 16.4 percent of the agricultural labor force, mostly performing secondary chores.[6]

Although it was important for all but the wealthiest women to learn a range of domestic skills, educational opportunities of all kinds were generally denied to girls. Given the economic importance of the family unit, family resources were more profitably invested in sons than daughters. Daughters would permanently leave their natal families at marriage and were of little economic use to their original family and parents. The denial of education to women was also a natural outgrowth of the accepted sexual division of labor. Since women were barred from most occupations, they could find little use for an education. Sons, on the other hand, could gain official positions or enter various crafts and professions through educational achievement. And, unlike daughters, sons were permanent members of the family and had lifelong obligations to work to support their parents.

Thus the general economic and social restrictions placed on women made them wholly dependent beings, reinforcing their subordination to men and to family authority. The practice of footbinding, which crippled and partially immobilized women for life, symbolized this overall crippling of women's spirit and lives. (It is significant that in the South, where women were allowed to participate more actively in economic activity, footbinding was much less prevalent than in the North. In the South the practice tended to be limited to leisured women of the upper classes.)

The hierarchy of status and norms governing the proper roles and behavior of women assumed, to a large extent, the "ideal," the multigenerational stem or joint family. In fact, such families were in the minority, especially among the poor.[7] Predictably, family size and complexity were directly correlated with wealth and status,[8] conformity to traditional and Confucian norms being more easily maintained by the wealthy landowning classes. Because of high mortality rates, famine, war, and disruptions of the rural economy in the nineteenth and twentieth centuries, many poor peasants were incapable of raising and maintaining the ideal large families. For many peasants poverty greatly weakened family life and often destroyed it, making conformity to accepted norms impossible. Sometimes the sons of the poor could not even raise a "bride price" or afford to feed an extra mouth and hence could not marry at all. Thus, despite widely accepted norms that confined women to the home, economic necessity often forced poorer women out of accepted family roles to obtain food.

But it should not be inferred that less conformity to social norms among the poor necessarily meant that poorer women were more liberated or suffered less under male supremacy. Some poor women who were compelled by poverty to engage in income-related work no doubt did gain greater independence and power in family affairs.[9] But poverty also frequently compounded for women the suffering and humiliation that resulted from their subordinate status. Even in economically compelling situations where the alternative might be starvation, ingrained taboos and lack of experience might make it extremely difficult for women to take the necessary steps to fend for themselves. When the poor aspired to maintain the proper socialized values, the inability to do so painfully affected poor women's self-esteem and community respect for them.

This point is well illustrated by the testimony of a poor young peasant woman in North China at the turn of the century. Her unreliable opium-smoking husband rarely brought home food for her and her baby daughter. Finally, facing starvation, she was tormented over what she should or could do:

> A woman could not go out of the court. If a woman went out to service the neighbors all laughed. They said "So and so's wife has gone out to service." I didn't know enough even to beg. So I sat at home and starved. I was so hungry one day that I took a brick, pounded it to bits, and ate it. It made me feel better.
>
> How could I know what to do? We women knew nothing but to comb our hair and bind our feet and wait at home for our men. When my mother had been hungry she had sat at home and waited for my father to bring her food, so when I was hungry I waited at home for my husband to bring me food.[10]

In order to survive, the most poverty-stricken families were sometimes forced to sell their infant children, especially daughters since daughters held less promise of being able to contribute to the economic future of the family. Husbands might have to sell wives as servants or concubines to those who could afford them. In the worst circumstances, infanticide was practiced, mostly against baby girls. The generally reported high ratios of males to females in the population throughout China (as high as 156 to 100 in one Shensi county in 1829) can probably be partly explained by the practice of female infanticide and by a higher mortality among young women in general by reason of low status and the resultant neglect.[11] This population imbalance strongly suggests the disproportionate toll that poverty took on women. Incidents such as female infanticide, the selling of wives and infant daughters as concubines or slaves, and the denial to women of equal access to scarce family food supplies frequently emerge in the social literature of the revolutionary period as illustrations of a brutal and sick feudal society—a society in which women especially were the victims, regardless of class.[12]

Reform of Marriage and the Family

The family system was seen by many as intimately tied to those social norms and economic structures that defined this sick society. The fact that the family system and its norms pervaded nearly all aspects of local Chinese society[13] made it a necessary target for any movement that hoped to bring about fundamental social change. So from the very beginning, the movement for revolutionary change in China had to relate to family reform and to the small but growing women's movement for sex equality.

The introduction of Western ideas of democracy and equality greatly influenced the early twentieth-century May Fourth generation of progressive youth. This youth movement enlisted growing numbers of educated urban women who demanded equal economic and political rights. Both left-wing Nationalists and Communists sought to enlist the support of women and supported the principle of sex equality. The Nationalist government's constitution and laws promised to improve women's political and economic rights. But during Nationalist rule the practical effect of these reforms, and the women's movement itself, remained confined to a small segment of urban intellectuals and had little or no effect on the vast rural areas. Significantly, an independent and meaningful women's movement never really developed in the rural areas owing to the particular kind of overwhelming female oppression and the social isolation of women from each other. The only political force in China that was willing and able to carry out family reforms was the Communist Party, which brought marriage reform and women's property rights to the remote liberated areas and after 1949 to the whole country. Two of the first major reforms undertaken by the new Communist government were land reform and the new marriage law. Both of these reforms affected the nature of the traditional family and the status of women.

The Marriage Law of 1950 was aimed at directly subverting the authoritarian age and sex hierarchy of the family by abolishing the system of arranged "buying and selling" marriage, prohibiting child betrothal, concubinage, polygamy, and interference in the remarriage of widows. The law also gave women the right to sue independently for divorce. The marriage contract was made one between two freely consenting adults, at a minimum age of 18 for women and 20 for men, and "no third party shall be allowed to interfere."[14]

The abolition of arranged marriage obviously weakens the control of parents over their children. Marriage by the free choice of the couple strengthens the conjugal relationship between husband and wife and potentially makes this relationship the core of a new family, equaling or superseding the relationship between parents and sons. This change, ideally, increases the status and position of the young bride, since she no longer enters an ongoing family as a stranger and outsider. From the outset, she can lay claim to her own volition in choosing her mate and entering his family. This new and more nearly equal position gives the young woman some leverage to gain control over her life and respect from family members. Coupling this improved status with the right of divorce further increases her leverage, for if she finds her treatment unbearable the woman can now legally choose to leave her husband and in-laws. An account of the early days of implementation of the new law in a northern village indicates that some women were able to take quick advantage of this new leverage to gain better treatment in their homes.[15]

But for women to take meaningful advantage of their new legal rights in marriage and divorce, they had to have some basis of economic independence outside the family. Land reforms, which distributed land equally to every individual man and woman, were necessary to give fuller meaning to family reform. Women likewise needed and were also given formal rights to shared household property. Chinese Marxists have always emphasized the need for women to gain economic independence in order to achieve true equality. Owning land and family property in their own names was seen as essential to begin the process of liberating women.

Land ownership gave real bite to the right of divorce, since it made such a choice economically feasible for women. However, the inexperience, the lack of necessary skills, and the persistent taboos against women participating in certain kinds of labor made it difficult for all but the most determined women to assert their complete independence from husband and family. Nevertheless, the property reforms had a more general psychological effect. Many women felt their bargaining power had been enhanced and thereby assumed greater confidence and self-esteem. One peasant woman expressed this sense of new status and self-respect:

> Our husbands regard us as some sort of dogs who keep the house. We even despise ourselves. But that is because for a thousand years it has been, "The men go to the *hsien* [county] and women go to the *yuan* [courtyard]." We were criticized if we even stepped out the door. After we get our share [of land] we will be masters of our own fate.[16]

Another woman said:

Always before when we quarrelled my husband said, "Get out of my house." Now I can give it right back to him. I can say, "Get out of my house yourself!"[17]

It was necessary to invest a great deal of organizational and political energy in popularizing and actually carrying out these new reforms in the villages. In addition to mobilizing the new government and party apparatus, women themselves had to be organized to help overcome resistance. For the most part, local women had no previous experience in organizing themselves; but setting up local women's associations was crucial to the initial success of family reform. These women's organizations were to help oversee the implementation of the new Marriage Law and the new property rights, to educate and raise the political consciousness of women, and to mobilize women to take part in land reform and village political life. Most importantly, the women's organizations provided an essential base of physical and psychological support outside the home that women could rely on for help in asserting their new rights.

Probably the most crucial and difficult task of these early organizations was to break down the psychology of deference, fear, and fatalism that kept women passive, mystified, and incredulous about any possibility of altering their fate through collective political action. To this end, women were encouraged to come to meetings, to "speak bitterness," and to report gross mistreatment so that the women's association could take collective action to reform or chastise the culprit. Predictably, the initial efforts to bring women out of the home to attend meetings often met resistance by men and in-laws who could intimidate women with threats and beatings to keep them at home. Women organizers investigated and attempted to bring pressure on family members who obstructed the right of women to go to meetings.

Occasionally a public show of force by the women's association against a few reluctant men was a necessary and effective means of breaking down such barriers to organizing women. The worst husbands and fathers-in-law might be forcibly brought to public meetings for mass criticism and even beatings by angry women taking their long-sought revenge. Such incidents often had an explosive, catalytic effect on the participants, showing women for the first time that they could stand up to men, that they need not passively accept their abuse and inferior status, that they could, under the system of the new people's government, "turn over" *(fanshen)*.[18] These women's organizations thus served to create pressure for changing the most personal relationships that oppressed women by politically mobilizing women for collective action and by politicizing family relationships. The way in which a man treated his wife was no longer a private matter but a public political issue.

Between 1950 and 1953, the nationwide effort to popularize the new Marriage Law also broadly mobilized the joint organizational and political energies of the trade unions, youth organizations, the mass media, and Communist Party branches at all levels. The courts were moved to action as large numbers of matrimonial and divorce cases were brought for litigation. The overwhelming majority of divorce suits in rural areas were brought by women,[19] indicating the practical effect of women standing up to take advantage of new freedoms.

Though there were many important legal, psychological, and practical effects from this early period of intense pressure to transform the family and status of women, the effect was far from an unqualified success by the time the campaign began to subside after 1953. There were many problems of implementation, and local resistance to such radical changes was evidently widespread.

The liberation of women was considered an important and necessary theoretical concomitant of general political and economic transformation of society, and in many areas the mobilization of women did add important support to the new political and economic order. However, in many ways the struggle for women's equality seemed to complicate, and even threaten the success of, reorganizing political power in the villages. The assertion of new rights for women threatened the economic and psychological prerogatives of all men, regardless of class. It thereby created between the sexes a political cleavage that cut across the class lines and categories that formed the basis for the consolidation of the peasants' new power. Men who had fought against the Japanese, the Nationalists, and the landlords to bring the Communist Party and peasant association to power were now being asked by their political allies to give up much of the ingrained, traditional, socially fixed basis of their manhood. Many men who had struggled for a radical transformation of political and property relations in the villages nonetheless accepted reactionary traditional views about the "proper" subordination of women to men. For some men, having to give up such views was particularly ironic. Many of the poorest peasants had been unable to afford marriage or to raise and keep their families intact. Their poverty had thus denied them dignity of being complete men. Land reform and the new society promised economic and social benefits that could reunite separated families and enable men, previously unable, to start families of their own. Now, as this vision was within reach, these men, allies of the revolution, were being pressured to make painful adjustments that undermined their concept of a man's rightful authority within his own family.[20]

The predominantly male central leadership was not unresponsive to such resistant sentiments. As early as 1948, a Central Committee directive indicated that the organization of women was to be carefully managed by the Party so that it would not endanger land reform.[21] In other words, the most militant manifestations of the women's struggle against male oppression were to be contained so as not to alienate peasant men and detract from the struggle against the landlords. At the same time, the directive indicated that in some areas the family reforms were being completely ignored by local cadres and that this defiance also should be remedied. However, it was probably much easier for the party to contain historically more disadvantaged women than to quickly gain cooperation from recalcitrant male comrades.

Furthermore, the tensions and conflicts engendered were not simply between oppressed women and their male overlords. There were also inherent tensions and conflicts among the women themselves, particularly between the young daughters and daughters-in-law and the older mothers and mothers-in-law. Part of this opposition was due to the greater difficulty that older women had in accepting new ideas so late in life.[22] This conservative-progressive split between old and young was reinforced by the fact that traditional norms inflicted the greatest stress on young women, and this stress eased somewhat with age. But the split was more than a natural generational gap over new ideas. The mothers-in-law, in particular, experienced many of the demands for change put forward by younger women as real threats to their interests and their basic needs—their emotional and economic security in old age. These demands also threatened the mother-in-law's single privilege of commanding the labor of her daughter-in-law so as to lighten her own work load as she grew older.

As an illustration of this conflict, one perceptive observer, William Hinton, recounts an incident he witnessed at a village meeting. One man was criticized at some length for siding more with his wife than his mother in family affairs. He was accused of not being a proper "filial son." This criticism hardly seemed in line with the spirit of the new marriage reforms that were aimed at strengthening the bonds between husband and wife and ending the worst oppression, which fell on young wives who had always occupied the lowest rung in the family hierarchy. Hinton explains this apparent contradiction:

> When I thought it over, I realized that it was the older women who had "mounted the horse," and with millenniums of tradition on their side, no

one dared contradict them. They saw in the new equality which gave a daughter-in-law the right to challenge her mother-in-law a threat to the only security they had ever known: filial obedience from their sons and absolute command over their son's wives. Bought, sold, beaten, and oppressed as they had always been, they traditionally had but one chance for power, one opportunity for revenge, one possibility for prestige, and that was as a mother to a grown son, as mistress to a daughter-in-law. Now, it would appear, even this was threatened. Young women no longer obeyed. Sons sided with their wives. Old women might well pass out of life as girl babies came into it, unwanted, neglected, and quickly forgotten when gone. Unable to comprehend the many-sided security which the land reform and the new property laws were bringing in their wake, many older women were fearful lest reforms destroy the one traditional prop, the one long-awaited support of their old age.

Old Lady Wang felt this keenly because her only son was soon to marry. She herself had handpicked the girl and had tried to choose a compliant one. But still she feared that new ideas might transform even this young bride. What would happen then?[23]

As Hinton implies, the key to resolving this conflict in favor of the young and future generations of Chinese women lay in making the older generation feel that new social and economic forms offered them a new and dependable source of security and dignity, that they need not fear an old age of poverty and neglect, and that they need not rely on particularistic control of younger and weaker family members. In the future people would be guaranteed economic and social security by the community and state. In other words, the rights of guaranteed social welfare must supplant reliance on the small family in order that the particularistic, selfish, and oppressive relationships of the family be transformed into broader community identities and more humane personal relationships. This transformation, as I shall discuss later, has not yet been brought about. The problems encountered are not only the force of old habits, but factors related to general economic underdevelopment and the persistently low level of community social services and welfare that such an under-developed economy can support, particularly in the countryside. Top-level political awareness and choices about economic and social development and organization also influence the degree and speed of family reform and women's emancipation. These political and economic policy choices sometimes conflict with and sometimes reinforce the needs of women's emancipation. After 1953 this complex of factors created temporarily insurmountable obstacles for the women's liberation movement for equal status in the home and the economy.

Probably the greatest single obstacle arose from the potential for serious disruptions, even backlash, as a result of the local resistance inherent in the types of conflicts already discussed. While there was great local variation in the success and intensity of the early campaign for women's rights and family reform,[24] in some areas the conflicts and tensions apparently brought fellow villagers to the brink of covert sexual warfare. Not only were men sometimes violently beaten by organized women, but there is also some indication that the rate of suicide, torture, and murder of women alarmingly increased during the 1950s. That these deaths were connected to the struggles to transform the family is indicated by one Communist writer who claimed that most of the deaths were of young progressive women who were active in the struggle for women's rights and against the old family institution.[25] It seems safe to infer that many of these women were victims of a backlash by men and elders against the unprecedented rebellion of women in those areas where they were not adequately protected by the new women's organizations and the local party branch. Such violent and uncontrolled confrontations, even if limited to a minority of villages, indicated the potential for disruption and discord created by the national campaign to enforce the Marriage Law. Many local cadres were probably relieved when the intensity of the movement was allowed to subside after 1953 so that they could turn their energies more fully to other economic and political priorities and restore stability.

Other problems encountered in the implementation of the reforms involved the nature and responsiveness of the apparatus expected to carry them out. Local courts were not always dependable in enforcing the new law, finding it difficult to break with traditional legal views that discriminated against women. Traditional views were also deeply rooted in the local, predominantly male party organizations and village administrations which sometimes showed reluctance in carrying out central directives that challenged their male supremacy and prerogatives. Repeated press criticism and directives issued by central authorities indicated concern over the persistent problems in getting local organs to respond effectively to their legal and political responsibilities.[26]

Where such problems existed, they created an atmosphere in which activist women could not be certain of local support. This situation no doubt dampened enthusiasm and made women wary of going too far. Given the thorough and widespread nature of centuries of female oppression—oppression that kept women isolated from each other and from meaningful community life, oppression that made them almost wholly dependent beings within the narrow circle of the family—it was impossible for women to take the necessary psychological, political, and organizational steps to liberate themselves without

external encouragement, dependable support, and ultimately, protection. Even when such support was supplied by the top leadership,
local party, and courts, the process was difficult and sometimes brutal
for men and women.

The concern at upper policymaking levels over minimizing the
potential for further domestic disruption and local strife at the outset
of the First Five Year Plan seemed to sanction an end to the intense
political and legal attack on the family and female subordination.
After land reform, urgent priorities focused on increasing production, nationalization, and collectivization of agriculture. Under such
circumstances, the costs of the struggle against the old family institution, in terms of increased tension and the local political energy that
was being distracted from more urgent and basic needs, seemed too
great. Furthermore, many rationalized at this time that proper
socioeconomic conditions did not yet exist for more complete reform.

Women in the Economy

In light of the problems of local resistance to ideological pressure, of
economic priorities of the central leadership, and of the apparent
conviction that change of the family institution is ultimately dependent on transformation of broader social-economic forces, the policy
of a political and ideological frontal attack on the family shifted to a
more exclusive emphasis on changing the economic position of
women by gradually bringing them into the productive labor force in
industry and agriculture.

Therefore, in the mid-1950s it was emphasized that "real equality
between men and women can only be realized in the process of the
socialist transformation of the entire society."[27] The argument in
detail: Through this process, women play an increasing role in the
collective economy. Particularly in the countryside, eliminating the
family as the primary unit of ownership, production, and labor
organization through collectivization, helps break down the strict
division of labor within the confines of the family. Labor can be
organized on a broader, more rational basis and women can then be
encouraged to work outside the home to earn wages from the collective or state. By earning wages and contributing labor to the economy,
women presumably gain higher status in the community and greater
independence and power within the family. Bringing women into the
economy as a means of gaining greater sexual equality is particularly
important in a society where the ruling ideology places the greatest
value on productive social labor and service to the collective, and
where old norms, as well as new ones, reinforce the low valuation of

domestic household labor as compared to income-producing labor.

Yet during the mid-1950s and the initial collectivization of agriculture, the level and pattern of both urban and rural development, coupled with the scarcity of welfare and social services, made it extremely difficult for women to move out of the home and into the economy. At least until 1958, there continued to be serious economic and organizational obstacles to going beyond ideological exhortation and legal reform for women's rights.

During the First Five Year Plan, which emphasized the development of capital-intensive heavy industry, the creation of new jobs was not equal to the large numbers of people seeking nonagricultural employment.[28] Under these circumstances it was impossible to bring large numbers of young women and previously unemployed housewives into the urban economy. Women suffered a further disadvantage in competing with unemployed men for those new jobs that were available, owing to norms regulating "women's place" that mitigated against hiring women in heavy industry. Women were more equitably represented in some light industry and handicraft production, but these sectors grew much more slowly than heavy industry under the First Five Year Plan. The percentage increase of women workers and employees during this period therefore was very small, rising from 11.7 percent in 1952 to 13.4 percent by the end of 1957.[29]

Factors contributing to differential and discriminatory employment patterns for women were many. They ranged from those internalized attitudes, creating difficulty for women to leave the home and labeling certain kinds of work as inappropriate for women, to blatant discrimination in hiring practices. Factory managers and administrators often refused to hire qualified women because, it was argued, women were inherently a less efficient investment than men. Under labor insurance guarantees, factories and offices had to pay women during maternity leave; nursery services needed to be set up. Even concern over women's presumably special problems during menstruation made them seem less efficient and reliable workers. In short, it was argued that hiring women increased operating costs and was uneconomical.[30] Young educated women might even be denied jobs if they had future plans for marriage or childbearing.[31] Since there was a surplus of unemployed male labor competing for scarce jobs, it was doubly difficult to eliminate such practices in hiring. Given priorities for increasing heavy industrial production and pressure on factory management to meet new quotas within a set budget, adequate pressure from the top was not forthcoming, despite complaints by top women leaders.

As unemployment grew in late 1957 and early 1958, it was even suggested in such authoritative organs as the Women's Association journal, *Women of China,* that some employed women should return to housework so that men could fill their jobs.[32] So, while women were told in the early 1950s that the road to their full emancipation required participation in productive labor, for most urban women the obstacles to participation were insurmountable. There was some attempt to reconcile this obvious conflict by rationalizing that women's domestic labor can indirectly be considered productive social labor in that it serves and encourages husbands and children who are socially productive. In other words, by being good socialist family women, women can contribute to socialist construction without appreciably changing their traditional roles. Such an argument, however, seems to beg the question of creating the prerequisites for raising the status of women. It ties their possibilities for social worth to the role they play in maintaining the still largely patriarchal family unit. Thus women remain socially and economically dependent on—and hence controlled by—men, in-laws, and childbearing functions.

Despite the serious consequences for women, some policymakers were apparently arguing that at this stage of early industrial development, full employment for men should be given priority over the political and social goal of liberating women. This argument is similar to one that has arisen in debates over the proper role of women in economic development in many other developing countries. Many economists have argued that at early stages of development, when unemployment and labor-utilization problems commonly arise, women should not be encouraged to change their traditional roles. According to this argument, because of rural-urban migration patterns and population increases, new and more nearly socially equal roles for women within the economy cannot be accommodated. While heavy and time-consuming traditional housework continues to be necessary or useful, it is counterproductive to add women to the labor force while men remain unemployed. Women seeking new jobs outside the family simply contribute to labor discontent and greater unemployment among men by creating an even larger pool of surplus labor. Therefore during early development, employing male breadwinners should be given top priority and policies furthering women's equality should await a later stage of economic development.[33] This line of reasoning has further ramifications detrimental to women: It encourages educational policies that give priority to males and perpetuates differential socialization of females to prepare them for traditional, subordinate roles. The inescapable conclusion of this argument is that women's emancipation—political, social, and economical—is a threat to early economic development.

Others, however, have pointed out that it is not necessarily correct to assume that early large-scale unemployment due to rural-urban migration is initially unavoidable. The rural labor problem is usually not one where a sizable percentage of the population suffers from total year-round unemployment and consequent destitution. Rather, it is more often a problem of functional seasonal unemployment or underemployment. Many men who seek better jobs in the cities can return to at least subsistence-level living in the villages. Further, economic policies that emphasize developing more labor-intensive agriculture and diversification could provide fuller year-round rural employment that would slow or prevent migration. Industrial economic development in the towns and cities could then benefit from mobilizing women into new jobs.[34] It can even be argued that bringing urban women into the industrial labor force is more economically efficient because it provides new labor for development without proportionally increasing the size of the urban population. Rapid urban population growth, compared to general population growth, places a much greater burden on public-investment budgets in terms of housing, light, water, sanitation, schools, hospitals, and the like.[35] Rural populations, on the other hand, can be more adequately self-reliant in dealing with some of these needs. Yet, because economic development is so often thought to be synonymous with industrial development, because of private and foreign investment patterns, and because of the frequent urban biases of political and economic elites, employment opportunities in agriculture have often been overlooked and public investment in agriculture neglected. In China, too, the early pattern of industrial development began to give rise to these problems.

Although the extreme economic arguments against women's liberation never officially gained ascendancy in China, the First Five Year Plan did not deal adequately with urban/rural labor utilization. It therefore led to economic policies that indirectly conflicted with avowed social-political goals of sex equality. Later, during the Great Leap Forward and again during the Cultural Revolution, Maoist politics and policies challenged these policies, arguing that progress in ideological social goals and progress in economic development can be made to reinforce each other, not conflict.

In the pre-1958 period, however, rural women, like urban women, encountered serious obstacles to doing productive work outside the home. In addition to the persistent norms and attitudes that made it difficult for women to leave the home, the nature of the agricultural economy and the lack of organized social services for women kept women confined to domestic work most of the time.

In many areas, the rural economy, like the urban economy, could not in its then current state absorb much new labor except during periodic busy seasons. Seasonal underemployment was widespread even for men.[36] Even after initial collectivization, the scope of the rural economy did not change appreciably to accommodate underemployment and seasonal fluctuation. Part of the reason was the lack of capital investment in agriculture under the First Five Year Plan.[37] In addition, the organization of labor and resources in the early cooperatives was not rationalized enough to take advantage of the pool of underutilized labor.[38]

Another factor inhibiting women's participation in the rural economy was the heavy burden of domestic work. In the countryside the burden of household and family responsibilities was, and continues to be, much greater than in the urban areas. The rural family traditionally has manufactured most of its own consumer goods. Throughout the mid-1950s and to a lesser extent in the 1960s, the manufacturing of household goods was not socially organized on a large scale and therefore continued to be done on an individual basis within each family. This redundant labor consumed almost the full time of one or more females per family. Making clothes, shoes, and bedding; processing and preserving foodstuffs; taking care of children, the elderly, or the sick; cleaning house and preparing meals— all without the benefit of time-saving conveniences—were the individual responsibility of the women within each household. Such heavy and unpaid work left most women with little time to join in the wage-earning collective work of the production teams. For the most part, the traditional division of labor that kept women tied to the home, maintaining their dependence and lower status in the family, was not greatly altered. Changes in the organization of work and village life were needed. Simply removing the family as the primary unit of ownership and production by socializing the means of production was not enough. And as long as there was no labor shortage in most areas, there was little economic pressure to collectively liberate women from housework and mobilize them into the economy.

The ambitious policies of the Great Leap Forward and the commune movement were meant to deal simultaneously with urban and rural unemployment and underemployment. This alleviation was to be done at a time when the rate of capital formation alone could not meet these needs. Therefore, these policies emphasized the rapid expansion of labor-intensive enterprises and projects, attempting to turn China's huge population and labor surplus into an immediate asset. Human capital became a major source of investment for rapid development.

These policies dealt in two ways with the obstacles hindering the liberation of women. First, new jobs were created by dealing with unemployment through reorganizing and mobilizing labor, and large numbers of women were organized to take part in work. Second, since many women were prevented from working by the burden of domestic work, community welfare and social services were organized to socialize some of the redundant household labor. In urban areas, small-scale labor-intensive factories were set up as satellite factories to large industrial enterprises and as "street industries" operating within residential areas. These factories relied on waste material from large industries, locally available capital, low-level indigenous technology, and the intensive labor of the previously unemployed, particularly women. By 1960, 85 percent of 4 million new workers in these enterprises were women.[39]

Although in 1958 the employment of women in industrial and office work more than doubled,[40] the proportion of women in nonagricultural labor increased only 1 percent. By the end of 1959, this proportion had increased another 3 percent, putting the total proportion of nonagricultural female labor at 18.8 percent.[41] One reason for this relatively small increase in nonagricultural labor is that women were prevented from taking equal advantage of the large number of new jobs opened in heavy industry, where norms concerning proper women's work inhibited female employment. The Great Leap policies, it seems, did not attack norms that operated against women's participation in certain types of work as much as it created new jobs in areas that women could more easily enter.

At the same time, the rural economy was diversified and intensified by the establishment of small commune-run industries: projects for water conservancy, afforestation, and construction, and increased sideline production in fisheries and animal husbandry. These created a demand for more labor and thus led to the mobilization of under-utilized labor, including large numbers of women. The bulk of the several hundred million people mobilized for water conservation and afforestation projects between 1958 and 1960 were women.[42]

In order to free women for these new jobs, many household women's tasks were collectivized. Nurseries and kindergartens were rapidly set up in the villages and urban centers. Urban canteens and commune-run dining halls were also set up to rid women of time-consuming chores in food processing and cooking. Other services—such as laundries, weaving and sewing cooperatives, shoe-making and shoe-repair shops—were organized in many areas to further reduce the need for individual women's work within the family. Not only did these socialized services greatly reduce the need for women to stay at home, but they also created a large number of income-earning jobs filled almost exclusively by women, who staffed the nurseries, dining halls, and shops. More than half of the 10 million workers in the commune dining halls were women and almost all of the 6 to 7 million workers in commune nurseries were women.[43]

Thus in many areas the mobilization of women did not break down norms concerning the type of work appropriate for women. Rather, it involved taking traditionally defined, unpaid, redundant female labor out of private homes and collectivizing it. The labor thereby becomes socially productive, and for performing it the women usually receive income. The change both raises the status of such work and contributes to the economic independence and authority of women within their own families.

The importance of economic independence as a central factor contributing to the emancipation of women has been, and continues to be, much emphasized by the Chinese:

> In the old society, women were generally regarded as men's dependents, no matter how hard they worked at home. The profession of housewife did not pay. Apart from political and social discrimination against women, the economic dependence of women was the source of men's superiority complex and their undisputed authority as head of the family. Under such circumstances, notwithstanding all talk to the contrary, inequality between men and women existed in fact so long as women had to depend on men for their support. . . .
>
> Liberation brought political and social discrimination against women to an end [sic]. But the problem of economic dependence of women took a long time to solve, with the result that women were usually at a disadvantage in public life. This unfortunate state of affairs changes rapidly when women stand on their own feet economically and become equal partners with men in supporting the family. In this way the status of women is raised. . . . Thus women acquire an increasing sense of their economic independence and the old practice of the male head of the family bossing around the home is on the way out.[44]

According to this view, socializing housework and giving women wage-earning jobs outside the home will inevitably revolutionize the old patriarchal family relations. The socioeconomic changes brought on by the Great Leap policies were, indeed, intimately related to the emancipation of women and the transformation of the family system. Such socioeconomic developments are portrayed as the key, at times the only, way to further sex equality. Only during the Cultural Revolution is it suggested that a return to direct ideological and political attack on male chauvinist and feudal patriarchal attitudes is necessary before further socioeconomic change can fully benefit women. This latter strategy, as will be discussed later, implies a more militant, politically activist approach to the problem. It points to the existence of special normative and ideological problems operating against sex equality that are not easily swept away by changes in the socioeconomic realm and that in fact stop women from fully taking part in those changes.

As mentioned earlier, the employment policies of the Great Leap period did not aim specifically at destroying a sexually defined division of labor beyond the point of socializing women's work. The main objective was to get women out of the home and into the economy where their labor could be used more rationally and productively. In fact, sex-typing in jobs was actually encouraged in some areas and was considered natural. At a women's conference held in Peking in November, 1958, Tsai Ch'ang, Chairman of the National Women's Federation of China called on women

> to take a yet more active part in cultural, educational, medical and public health work as well as in welfare and other social services. She said women should gradually replace men in all such work that was specifically suitable for women so as to attain a more reasonable distribution of social labor force.[45]

As a transitional step, this sexual division of labor can make it psychologically easier for women to enter the labor force and can help shield women from job competition with relatively advantaged and more experienced men. Furthermore, from the point of view of national decision makers, it may seem more rational, efficient, and less disruptive to channel women into jobs for which previous social tradition has deemed them best suited. Thus child care, elementary and secondary teaching, nurturant jobs in public health and medicine, community services, and many handicrafts are considered particularly suitable to the temperament and special responsibilities of women. Only a few have seriously questioned the permanent or long-range legitimacy of this pattern, which assumes innate female characteristics that are relevant to employment patterns. Nevertheless, legitimizing such sex-typing serves to rationalize and institutionalize discriminatory attitudes and authority structures that limit women's access to jobs in many areas of the economy. It also helps perpetuate a "natural" division of labor and authority within the family. In particular, such attitudes justify and reinforce the continuing low representation of women in more prestigious and higher-paying modern and heavy industrial sectors. For the most part, those areas where women work in large numbers are lower-status and lower-paying jobs.

Regardless of how one evaluates the patterns of female recruitment, the Great Leap period did significantly increase the participation of women in the economy and mobilized them into broader social roles outside the family. Unfortunately, the serious economic difficulties that followed this period, due to unusually bad weather and problems in policy implementation, caused a setback in the mobilization of women during the 1960s. Nurseries, mess halls, and other services were scaled down or abolished. The massive water conservancy and other special projects that had employed so many women were halted. Many of the street industries that had been run mainly by and for housewives were consolidated or closed. The result was that women were laid off in large numbers in the early 1960s. Although general unemployment also rose, not surprisingly women were affected disproportionately by the recession. Thus many women returned to the home and full-time household duties.

In the mid-1960s the official view of the prospects of women's equality was more pessimistic than in 1958. While serious inequities were recognized, it was implied that economic circumstances would allow little alteration in the situation:

> Concerning the status of women, marital status and family relationships, survival of old ideas and viewpoints still remain.
>
> On top of this, the extent of women's participation in social labor, viewed either from the number of persons employed or from the role they have played, still suffers a certain limitation *although it is the correct proportion in relation to the present stage of development of our national economy.* As a result of this limitation, there is still a difference, in fact though not in law for women in the enjoyment of equal rights with men both in society and in the home. This difference will gradually disappear following the further development of production. That is to say, to do away completely with the old survival in marriage and family relationships, it is necessary to create the more mature socio-economic and ideological conditions this requires.[46] [Emphasis added.]

The insistence that liberation could be furthered, at this point, only through increased economic development and "more mature socio-economic conditions" discouraged women from politically organizing to oppose the old survival in marriage and family relationships as they had been encouraged to do in the early 1950s. The official view expressed above could be used and apparently was used to shield authorities from criticism for not moving to remedy the low representation of women in industry and political organizations. Although general economic recovery during this period gradually did reopen jobs, little renewed concerted effort was made on the economic and political front for women until the Cultural Revolution when, in addition to general political mobilization of women, many of the Great Leap innovations were reemphasized on a smaller scale and in a more orderly manner. Until this time, the problems and contradictions facing women in the 1960s were similar to those of the pre-1958 period. Women were told that the only road to liberation was through participation in productive social labor, and yet the problems of heavy domestic work and scarcity of jobs made it very difficult for women to obtain paid work.

Coincident with the return of many women to home life and with the absence of political agitation for women's rights was a reemergence in popular literature of the legitimacy of certain traditional kinship relations, though in reformed guise. One analyst found that the fictional literature of the 1962–1966 period, in contrast to previous periods, stressed the value of filial obligations, of respect for older generations, and of partriarchal authority within the family.[47] Elders were depicted as having a legitimate, if sometimes misguided, interest in the marriage of their children, particularly in the acquisition of a daughter-in-law. These stories continued to portray the conflict between a liberated woman's obligations to her work in socialist society and her duties to her family and household. But the mother is now shown as more home-oriented and the father as more dominant compared to earlier literature.

Articles appearing in the youth and women's journals during this time confirm this interpretation of the fictional literature. In 1962, the *Chinese Youth Journal* carried several articles on the filial obligations of children to parents. One of these articles was written in response to a letter from a mother-in-law who was distressed by a daughter-in-law's attempt to interfere in the son's filial obligations to his parents— specifically his obligation to live with them and support them.[48] Although the surface issue was one of financial support, the underlying problem is the tension engendered by a rebellious daughter-in-law who seeks greater independence from traditional norms and thus threatens the control and security of her in-laws. The editor's response to this letter supported the mother-in-law's position, saying that a daughter-in-law is obligated to support parents-in-law and should not instigate her husband to ignore his responsibilities by leaving his mother's household to set up a separate one with his wife. While adult children in general are obligated by law to support elderly parents, it is asserted that there is a special obligation of sons and daughters-in-law to support the husband's elders. Significantly, the editor points to the moral force of tradition as the mainstay of this duty and asserts that in a socialist society this duty is even greater. What is most important to remember is that "it has always been a traditional practice in our country for a son and his wife to support his parents."

The individual rebellion and defiance of young wives, once encouraged as a means of politicizing and transforming the family, are now depicted as selfish, disruptive, and counter to broader socialist duties. (Compare this attitude also with the militant slogans of the Cultural Revolution—"Rebellion is justified," "Dare to struggle"—and the call to attack the "Four Olds"—old customs, old habits, old culture, and old ideas.) It was thus difficult for women to use the ideology of sex equality to directly attack the authority of traditional relations within the family.

The persistence and qualified sanctioning of traditional family patterns points to the continued importance of the family as an essential provider of welfare and social security. Significantly, filial obligations are emphasized during a period of economic recession when state and community welfare services, particularly in rural areas, continue to be inadequate: old-age and hardship security require major responsibility from family and kin whenever possible. Only 1 or 2 percent of the average commune's income is invested in general welfare funds, hence the level of commune support for a needy individual is usually quite low. Furthermore, commune welfare services take the form of public assistance rather than the fixed and guaranteed social-security system found in state industries and offices.[49] Commune welfare is usually administered on an individual basis after a local investigation to determine the cause and level of special hardship and to determine whether the problem can be handled by immediate relatives. Some of the same social stigma seems to be attached to this process of receiving aid as might be attached to receiving charity. The stigma makes it psychologically a less attractive form of support than that afforded by children. Under such circumstances, parents continue to seek old-age security through their relations with adult children. Thus traditional filial relations continue to have vital economic significance. If young women rebel against old customs that subordinate them to husbands and in-laws, the strength of those traditional obligations that guarantee support are threatened.

Particularly revealing is the editor's statement in the *Chinese Youth Journal:* "Sons and daughters-in-law care for parents and society is responsible for those with no sons and daughters-in-law."[50] The prestige and economic value of having many sons in traditional China has often been noted. The religious incentives for bearing many sons have largely been removed by the disintegration of clan organizations since 1949.[51] So have some of the economic incentives, such as the family patriarch's ability to invest the labor of many sons and thereby greatly increase family property and improve social class.[52] But as long as state or commune support is psychologically and materially insufficient, it seems that the traditional preference for sons over daughters is still reinforced. The Chinese leadership, including Mao Tse-tung, has frequently commented on the continued preference for male children among the peasantry.[53] Since daughters continue to be only temporary members of their natal families, moving away to join their husband's family at marriage, they still do not fulfill the social and economic security needs as well as sons do. Even though more and more women are likely to become economically capable of support, mother-daughter ties and obligations are likely because of tradition to remain weaker than father-son ties.

The persistence of these traditional patterns continues to influence the differential social development of sons and daughters since the family may continue to prefer to invest in a son's income-related skills and education. A daughter is more likely to be encouraged to leave school early to help at home, where she learns domestic skills.[54] The reluctance of villages, as well as families, to invest scarce resources in the educational and political development of girls also continues to be a problem. The frequent custom of girls marrying outside their natal village leads local leaders to feel they are likely to lose their investment if they cultivate the skills and leadership abilities of young girls instead of boys. As recently as 1971, an article in *People's Daily* complained about the existence of this view among party cadres on the question of giving special training to women:

> [Some] people said: "No matter how well we train them, they [young women] will be taken away one day." This is a result of viewing the matter from the standpoint of only one village or one brigade without considering the interest of the revolutionary cause as a whole. As long as we can train outstanding female Party members, they will help make the Party strong even when they are married away to another village. How can we say "it does not pay"?[55]

The article noted that the common expectation that young women will become housewives after marriage also contributes to discriminatory attitudes about training young women. Significantly, this article implies that this real practical problem, arising out of concrete socioeconomic conditions, can be appreciably alleviated through correct ideological and political work. However, such ideological and political work was hardly emphasized in the 1960s until the Cultural Revolution. Rather, the "need for more mature socioeconomic conditions" was emphasized as a prerequisite for furthering sex equality.

Relieving women of heavy household work and mobilizing them

into the economy will not necessarily nor quickly destroy accepted customs and stubborn social norms that significantly differentiate the life patterns of males and females by reason of marriage and patriliny. Nor does collectivizing broader areas of work and social services inevitably destroy public and private views that uphold sexual stereotyping. Such problems are deeply rooted in patterns of village and family life in which they are accepted as natural and politically neutral. In many ways the development of sexual equality directly threatens the political and economic power of men who have controlled village and family life. The problem, then, is not simply one of cultural adaptation to economic role changes, but it is also one that requires a fundamental redistribution of power at all levels of society. As such, it is a distinctly political issue.

Women in Politics

In both urban and rural China since 1949, women's political participation has been generally low. Those capable and determined individual women who were able to hurdle the initial obstacles to women's participation have been encouraged and promoted to high-level political positions in line with the leaders' commitment to sex equality. But women as a group have attained only a small percentage of middle- and upper-level leadership posts. The campaign to popularize the Marriage Law did significantly increase the proportion of women cadres from 8 percent in 1951 to 14.6 percent in 1955. However, at the higher levels of leadership their proportion declined from 6 percent to under 3 percent during this same period.[56] In 1956, only 10 percent of the membership of the Communist Party were women.[57] These figures probably did not change appreciably before the Cultural Revolution.

In general, women hold a relatively larger proportion of leadership posts at local levels but their share declines at progressively higher levels. At the top, only 13 of 170 Communist Party Central Committee members were women in the early 1970s. In 1965, it was reported that 25 percent of the production-team (lowest rural unit) cadres in Kwangtung province were women. But in the commune-level organizations, probably only 5 percent were women.[58] In urban areas these percentages are generally higher, especially at lower levels. Over 30 percent of all cadres in Peking in 1963 were women.[59] But since women are heavily represented in the leadership of local neighborhood organizations (sometimes as high as 50 to 80 percent), the percentages of women cadres above these local levels of leadership are sharply lower.

Many of the same obstacles that have hindered women's economic participation also block their political participation. Heavy housework and family responsibilities make it difficult to find the extra time required by political and organizational work. Even in routine mass political activities, such as all-village meetings, women often are unable to participate because they are expected to stay home to take care of children and the household while the men attend the meetings.[60]

As mentioned earlier, this accepted sexual division of labor within the family makes local Party branches hesitant to recruit and train young women.[61] Furthermore, parents, husbands, and in-laws often discourage young women from political work because it causes them to neglect family responsibilities and, contrary to old norms of proper behavior, it brings them into contact with men outside the family. The kind of behavior and social contact required of a political cadre may, some families feel, compromise a woman's reputation and cause a loss of face within the community.[62] One woman cadre in North China complained that most of the older women in her village think it "indecent and immoral and shocking that young people talk with each other," and "they scold their daughters and daughters-in-law and granddaughters for not observing decent behavior."[63] These attitudes are often a more serious obstacle to political activity than to participation in collective work outside the home. In rural work, women are usually organized to work in women's brigades or to do "women's work" together. But in political work, women may have to work with young men. Rural women activists complain that it is often difficult for young women to ignore the pressure and influence of the older women because they must live and work together.[64]

Women cadres who are undeterred by such pressures must sometimes endure rumors about their moral and sexual behavior.[65] Old superstitions that stigmatize women are also used to keep women out of important positions usually reserved for men:

> When the brigade Party branch committee was re-organized and I was elected secretary, these class enemies spread rumors and superstition about me. "With a woman at the head the trees won't grow," they said. And, "A woman in the leadership will bring bad luck." They reinforced their rumors by compiling a list of crimes I was supposed to have committed in order to disqualify me from the post.[66]

Such attitudes obviously discourage women from seeking political posts and make it even more difficult to overcome the sexist division of housework and family responsibilities. It takes an unusually self-confident and capable woman to overcome these handicaps and pressures in order to become permanently involved in politics.

For several reasons urban women have experienced greater ease in taking up political activity, at least at the lowest local level, than their rural counterparts. First, attitudes about acceptable female behavior and old superstitions are probably less prevalent in more modern urban settings. Young married women are less subject to conservative pressures from relatives and in-laws because, in the urban living setting, they are less likely to live or work together. Compared to rural women, young urban women have more peer-group and nonfamilial contact.[67] Second, urban women have greater access to social services and goods such as day care, laundries, canteens, preprocessed foods, and a wide range of consumer goods that women must still manufacture in many rural households. Urban husbands also seem somewhat more willing to help out around the house occasionally.[68]

Probably the most significant factor related to greater local political participation of urban women occurs because residential areas are organizationally and often geographically separate from major production units. In rural areas, the composition and functions of the commune, brigade, and team leadership groups reflect the greater integration of rural living with the work setting. In this situation women compete with the most active working men for political posts (except for positions in the women's association, of course). Therefore, women who participate in collective production only part-time or not at all rarely gain access to such positions. In urban areas, residential leadership groups take responsibility for the wide range of social problems and activities not directly related to the activities of state factories and offices. Women who are not employed full-time outside the home play an important, often predominant, role in these community organizations.

Residents' committees were set up in the early 1950s to provide organization for aspects of urban living that fall outside the scope of the major enterprises and to provide organization for the otherwise unorganized—the elderly, the disabled, retired workers, housewives, and other family dependents.

The tasks of these residents' committees originally included neighborhood public security, fire prevention, and street sanitation; organizing public education programs, such as political study groups and literacy classes; carrying out welfare work and investigation of special needs; organizing community services such as day care; arbitration of local disputes; and mobilization of residents to participate in periodic national political campaigns.[69] During the 1958–1960 Great Leap period, when small neighborhood factories and socialized household services were established, production-related activities within the neighborhoods increased. The organization and mobilization of labor for these activities increased the scope of residents' organizations. During the years of economic retrenchment in the early 1960s many of these production and service facilities were scaled down or closed. During this period the residential organizations seemed to lose political vitality as well. The Cultural Revolution revitalized these local organizations and again increased their scope. Residents' committees helped run neighborhood schools and the rapidly growing neighborhood health clinics. Increasing the number and size of neighborhood factories or housewife factories is again emphasized and residential nursery services have been enlarged.

Most of the neighborhood political work and many of the community-run services such as the health clinics and the smaller nursery stations are undertaken by unpaid volunteer workers, drawing heavily on unemployed women and retired workers. Such work carries political responsibility and prestige within the community and provides women with accessible avenues for entering community social and political life. But this kind of work does not fulfill the often mentioned requirement of economic independence for women within the family. The small neighborhood factories and many of the service-related work shops (for tailoring, laundering, repairing, and the like) do provide wages, although they are low compared to the wages of regular industrial and office workers. As these small-scale enterprises increase, more and more women will be able to gain a source of independent income and access to the leadership posts within these enterprises.

In contrast to local leadership in residential organizations, leadership groups in state-run factories and offices show underrepresentation of women similar to that in rural political organizations. Women's representation in political and administrative groups in factories is usually far below the proportion of women in the factories' total labor force. One visitor to China who investigated 35 industrial enterprises in the late 1960s estimated that 25 percent of the workers and employees in China's major industrial cities were women. The percentage for all urban areas is probably lower.[70] Yet he reported that women comprised only 8 to 15 percent of the middle- and top-level leadership. He found no women directors of industry. Women were better represented at the lower levels of factory leadership.[71] My own observations in the summer of 1971 confirm this pattern. Even in those types of light industrial factories where women often constitute the majority of workers, such as textiles, food processing, and some kinds of handicrafts, women usually comprise only a small percentage of the leadership in these units. In one Sian textile factory, 60 percent of the 3350 workers were women in 1971. Yet only 20 percent of the leadership in the newly reconstituted (after the Cultural Revolution) Party Committee and Revolutionary Committee were women. In an embroidery handicraft factory in Suchow, over 80 percent of the 1400 workers were women, while 35 to 40 percent of the Revolutionary Committee and Party Committee, respectively, were women. The heads of these committees and of the factory were men. In both of these factories the percentage of women leaders was said to reflect an increase from the levels before the Cultural Revolution.

Women who work in state-run industries enjoy advantages and access to services that other women often do not have. They usually have access to conveniently located full-time inexpensive infant- and child-care services. (Rural women working in the neighborhood factories and organizations may have access to local day care, but it is often a makeshift arrangement, or limited to certain hours of the day or available only during busy seasons.) State workers also have access to minimal-cost dining services and canteens for all meals and in some factories for their families if they wish to avoid preparing meals at home. They receive high wages compared to peasants and other nonagricultural workers, and they get guaranteed retirement benefits. Their relatively high income, which is usually in addition to a husband's income, affords them access to many household consumer goods and services that other women may have to spend much time making or doing themselves. In other words, these advantaged working women have the material means to solve many of those practical obstacles that hinder women's emancipation. In addition, they have gained a large measure of economic independence from, and equality with, their husbands. Yet, as the figures on factory leadership suggest, even those economically liberated women who have been mobilized into the mainstream of the nation's economic life continue to encounter systematic discrimination against their full and equal participation and representation in political life.

It needs to be recognized that even for those women who have largely resolved the present contradiction between domestic labor and collective labor, this achievement has not been enough to gain them true sexual equality. Subtle attitudes that characterize their temperaments and special duties as specific to their sex help to perpetuate the notion of women as followers and men as leaders. Thus women have been unable to gain their share of political representation where they have had to compete with men for these positions. The accepted functional division of labor within the economy also spills over into political organizations. Women who do gain political posts often do so specifically in the capacity of advising on and implementing policies concerning special women's welfare work such as helping with day care needs or maternity problems. In other words, they are recruited to serve as women leaders of women. While this area is obviously one where women are needed, when this recruitment pattern is viewed together with the overall low percentage of women participating in leadership groups, it further underscores the extent to which other more general leadership concerns are dominated by men. Furthermore, recent press criticism indicates that, in general, this political work concerning specifically women's problems has been treated by party cadres as less important and less prestigious than other types of leadership work. Women's political functions, like many of their economic ones, tend to be both separate and unequal.

In light of the centuries of total exclusion of women from political activity of all kinds, special widespread and long-term efforts to give women political education, leadership skills, and experience seems necessary to promote women's political equality. Traditionally, the exclusion of women from political and decision-making activity was even greater than their exclusion from economic activity. This pattern seems to continue in the factories and communes, with families and the community more readily accepting women in productive work than in decision-making roles. A recent article pointed out the existence of this pattern. It stated:

> Some people do not believe in the revolutionary consciousness of the broad masses of working women. They think that while women may participate in productive labor, politics is certainly not for them. This viewpoint is not a Marxist one.
>
> . . . As Lenin pointed out, "Our task is to turn politics into something in which every working woman can participate." Those ideas and practices that regard women as incapable of engaging in politics and exclude them from proletarian politics are all wrong.[72]

This article, written in 1971, implies that a successful policy toward the problem of sex equality must give greater emphasis to mobilizing women politically while attacking male supremacist attitudes. Yet from 1954 to the Cultural Revolution the predominant policy toward the problem emphasized, almost exclusively, the need for women to engage in the collective economy to gain full equality. It was more or less assumed that little else needed to be done, or, alternatively, could be done to destroy the ideological vestiges of feudal patriarchy, male chauvinism, and female subordination in the family and community. An accepted division of labor based on sexual stereotypes and restrictive norms defining "appropriate women's work" within the collective economy escaped serious scrutiny and criticism. The important thing was to get women out of the restricted circle of the family to transfer their labor into the collective economy.

At the same time this policy tended to neglect the political education and mobilization of women for many years. Women failed to gain
the political skills, understanding, and self-confidence necessary to
assert themselves effectively when they were in situations competing
with more advantaged men.

The Cultural Revolution and After

The Cultural Revolution represented, among other things, an attempt to promote revolutionary political and social goals, such as sex
equality, by directly revolutionizing the superstructure of society. The
voluntarist Maoist assumptions that led to the notion of cultural
revolution opened the way for mass mobilization to further revolutionary political goals and to attack entrenched bureaucratic and
political interests that obstructed such action. As noted before, in the
early and mid-1960s as the economy was just pulling out of a recession, it was suggested that little more could be done to further the
social and political goals of sex equality or to destroy old ideas and
habits concerning women without further development of
socioeconomic conditions. The Maoist assumptions of the Cultural
Revolution suggested that through the use of mass political action and
revolutionary ideology such revolutionary goals could be, indeed
must be, furthered at the current stage of socioeconomic development. The key to furthering revolutionary goals, and thus the transformation of society as a whole, lay in "putting politics in command,"
in transforming people's way of thinking and ideological consciousness.

The Cultural Revolution affected women through the general
political mobilization of the population, including working women
and housewives, for political action, political study, and mass criticism
of established structures of authority. Women were encouraged to
organize in order to criticize and question the power structure in their
places of work, their communities, and their families.

In some factories militant women accused the leadership in the
trade unions, Women's Associations, party branches, and management of revisionist and feudal thinking on the question of women.
Such revisionist thinking was said to manifest itself in the theory that
women are backward and useless, that women lack political consciousness, and that women should therefore be "combatants not
commanders." These attitudes led the leadership to neglect the
training of women cadres, impeded the political education and activity of women, and dampened their enthusiasm.

Women were also encouraged to form political study groups in their neighborhoods in order to discover and repudiate the "Four Olds" (old ideas, old culture, old customs, old habits) in their families and communities. Criticism by women of their families' undemocratic authority structure and of their treatment by parents, husbands, and in-laws was encouraged by articles in the press such as the following:

> Over thousands of years our family relations have been that son obeys what his father says and wife obeys what her husband says. Now we must rebel against this idea. ... We should make a complete change in this. ... It should no longer be a matter of who is supposed to speak and who is supposed to obey in a family but a matter of whose words are in line with Mao Tse-tung's Thought.[73]

In line with the Cultural Revolution's more radical approach toward women's roles, the journal of the Women's Association, *Women of China,* was attacked for past editorial policies and for trying to resist the policies of the Cultural Revolution.[74] The chief editor, Tung Pien, was accused of slighting women's potential political role and emphasizing women's "natural duties" to nurture children and care for a family, thereby encouraging women to become "intoxicated with the small heaven of motherhood." She was said to have echoed modern revisionist theories of mother love and feminine tenderness and reactionary and feudalistic concepts such as "respecting men but denigrating women and demanding obedience at the three levels (obedience to father, son, and husband)."[75] As noted earlier, some of the writing that appeared in journals and short stories between 1962 and 1966 did in fact subtly reinforce traditional notions of patriarchal authority, of patrilineal obligations, and hence of the subordination of women. Though the criticism leveled at Tung Pien was somewhat overdrawn, the women's journal had for many years emphasized the special responsibilities of women in reproduction, raising, and socializing youth, and in household economy.[76] In contrast to this, during the Cultural Revolution women were portrayed primarily as participants in revolutionary politics.

Thus the Cultural Revolution, more than previous periods, placed emphasis on the need to mobilize women to participation in politics as well as production. Not only were barriers to women's rights of participation attacked, but intense normative pressure was also generated to impress upon women that they had an obligation to devote themselves more fully to social and political responsibilities outside the home. Red Guards and the mass media widely propagated norms of behavior which stressed that the individual's role and responsibilities to the collective should take precedence over more narrow and individualistic family roles and responsibilities.

But the high level of political participation fostered during the Cultural Revolution could not be maintained for long. The general mass mobilization tapered off in the late 1960s. Though it had left its mark throughout Chinese society, it had not, of course, solved social and political problems, including the many problems that hindered sex equality. It did, however, leave in its wake several more permanent political and socioeconomic improvements in addition to the less tangible effects of ideological radicalization.

In line with the new ideological emphasis on women's political participation, the top leadership took measures to insure the institutionalization of a higher level of female participation in leadership groups. In the later stages of the Cultural Revolution, when new leadership groups were being set up and when party committees were being reconstituted, Mao Tse-tung directed that a reasonable percentage of women should be included in all new party leadership groups. When new committees submitted their membership to higher levels for approval they were supposed to be rejected if they did not contain women. The actual size of the quotas set up was to be appropriate to local circumstances. They were usually modest, flexible, and varied geographically and according to level of leadership. Nevertheless, they seem to have led to a definite overall increase in female representation.

In one rural Kwangtung commune that I visited in 1971 the improvement was quite modest. Three of 21 members of the commune Party Committee were women, and two of the 25 members of the Revolutionary Committee were women. Two of these women apparently gained their position as a result of the Cultural Revolution directive.[77] One commune near Shanghai, however, had a minimum guideline of 25 percent for top leadership groups. In fact, the commune's Revolutionary Committee was 30 percent women and the vice chairman was a woman. Many of the brigades and teams had even higher percentages.[78] The quota levels in this commune were comparable to those set for the urban districts of Shanghai. In another part of the country in the northeast, a brigade visited in 1962, and again in 1969, also showed improvement. In 1962 only one of 12 brigade management committee members were women. In 1969, three of the 11 members of the new Revolutionary Committee were women.[79]

There has also been a revitalization of organizations and policies that directly and indirectly benefit women. Communes and neighborhoods have been encouraged to expand social services such as crèches, cooperative sewing shops, and food processing facilities to aid women with household duties. There have been renewed efforts to deal with the needs of underemployed and unemployed house-wives. The economic policies coming out of the Cultural Revolution again stress decentralization of light industry and the creation of small, self-reliant agri-industries in rural areas. These enterprises promote a fuller utilization of the locally available surplus and seasonal labor, including women. In the cities, there has been a new emphasis on creating and expanding small-scale neighborhood factories that employ housewives. For example, in Nanking in 1972 there were 500 such neighborhood enterprises employing 20,000 people, 75 percent of whom were women. Women served as directors in 300 of the 500 factories. It was reported that the total output value of neighborhood industries in Nanking was 43 times that of 1965.[80] These figures obviously indicate a policy of rapid expansion.

The expansion of this type of industry is significant because these factories provide women who otherwise would not find full-time wage-earning employment with the opportunity to do useful work outside the home. The wages are usually sufficient to noticeably increase family income and they therefore create an incentive for women to rearrange family duties so they can work. Also, employment in some of these neighborhood factories is somewhat more flexible than in state factories so that women may be able, in special circumstances, to maneuver employment around heavy family demands. It should be noted, however, that this flexibility may simply encourage a situation where family women are expected to take up a job without decreasing their family burdens or changing the sexist division of labor within the home.

In spite of the fact that these neighborhood enterprises are in many ways an innovative and practical way to deal with women's employment in an undercapitalized economy, they are not, from the standpoint of sex equality, an adequate substitute for increasing the proportion of women recruited into the main industrial sectors. The housewife factories lack the status of other industries because they are engaged in production of subsidiary importance to the economy, frequently using discarded industrial equipment and wastes as their main source of capital. Because they are indigenous, self-reliant undertakings that receive no state investment, the level of technology, working conditions, wage scale, and welfare benefits are necessarily far below the standards of state-run enterprises. A few of these housewife factories have succeeded in developing into fairly mechanized modern enterprises with increased wages, improved working conditions, and better welfare services.[81] But for the most part the neighborhood industries seem to constitute a second-class employment sector in which women predominate. At the same time, there is little evidence that the proportion of women in state industry has increased significantly since the Great Leap or that it will in the near future. Men continue to enjoy priority in recruitment into most modern sectors of the economy. Although occasional stories appear in the press about determined women who defy public opinion and expectations and successfully take up men's tasks,[82] little effort has been made to significantly alter the basic patterns of recruitment.

After the height of the Cultural Revolution passed, concern for women's political participation and education also seemed to subside. Party branches again gave women's political work low priority. Interviews with several women leaders in 1971 revealed some current thinking on the issue of sex equality.[83] Many urban women cadres maintained that women and men were now basically equal as a result of the Cultural Revolution. Presumably because the Cultural Revolution had been so effective in exposing and isolating serious revisionist thinking on women's equality, there was no longer need for special women's groups or special party work concerning the recruitment and training of women. In the factories the Women's Association groups, like the trade unions, had been disbanded during the Cultural Revolution because of alleged political conservatism and their overemphasis on the special welfare privileges of state-employed workers. It was maintained now that working women did not need special representation for their welfare interests because they enjoyed full labor insurance guarantees. Nor did they need special channels of representation for their political interests since these interests were the same as those of fellow men workers. The Revolutionary Committees and Party Committees within each factory represented the political interests of the working class, including women. The continued low representation of women on these committees was therefore not an urgent problem, but one that would naturally correct itself with time. The militant criticism and mobilization of the Cultural Revolution had apparently given way to efforts to achieve political conciliation and stability by depoliticizing grievances and conflicts. The problem of sex equality no longer seemed to be a salient political issue.

Views on the nature of the problem of sex equality and how best to deal with it are not uniform. In late 1971, several articles appeared that again stressed the urgency of the problem and pointed out that too many party members do not take the issue seriously enough and resist efforts to promote sex equality. These articles asserted that remaining problems were not only serious ones, but that they involved issues central to the continuation of the revolution. One article argued that the central problem was the failure to recognize widespread male supremacist attitudes which still blocked the economic and political progress of women.[84]

Another article, which appeared in the party's theoretical journal *Red Flag*, recognized that such practical difficulties as insufficient socialized domestic services still exist. But it was stressed that these problems should not be used as an excuse to slow the progress of women's liberation, to subordinate women to housework, or to exclude them from political leadership.

> Perhaps some comrades say: "A home must be run by somebody. This is a practical problem." . . . As long as we have the correct idea of supporting women to participate in the three great revolutionary movements, we will be able to think out ways to solve these practical problems, patriarchal ideas, vigorously promoting the "four olds" of the exploiting class, spreading the "theory that women are backward" and the "theory that women are useless," and stirring up the evil of pre-arranged marriages in order to disrupt the women's liberation movement. Within the ranks of the people, there still are present mistaken ideas of various sorts which belittle women and impede the coming into play of women's revolutionary strength. For this reason, to make a success of women's work is a serious class struggle as well as a battle for changing customs. We must not lose sight of this. As for the destructive activities of the class enemies, we should resolutely strike at them. As regards the various "four olds" viewpoints that belittle women as promoted by the exploiting mass criticism, . . . Party committees at various levels should put women's work on the order of the day and grasp it seriously and properly as an important task of struggle-criticism-transformation.
>
> We must continue to carry out Chairman Mao's proletarian revolutionary line, "wage a resolute struggle against the concepts of belittling the women's movement," and completely get rid of the old idea of having high regard for men and belittling women.[85]

This emphasis probably represents a radical minority view within the party. The criticisms it and subsequent articles raise indicate that among party cadres there is resistance to implementing a special policy to train more women and to giving high priority to the issue of sex equality.

In contrast to this radical view, other women leaders have expressed the view that the use of frontal tactics to change the views of family members and men is disruptive and counterproductive. Lu Yu-lan, a prominent women's leader, implicitly argued for a somewhat different approach when she recently wrote:

> A current wrong idea is that women win their freedom by seizing control in the family and this wrong idea leads to a lot of fruitless quarrelling among husband, wife and in-laws . . . disrupted family harmony and failed to win public sympathy and achieve its aim. . . . Women began taking a broader

view, to understand that to achieve their own emancipation they must look at things in terms of the entire society, to see the family as a basic social unit, as changing with the transformation of society as a whole. It was realized that after women take their position in society, changes in family relations will follow, and men and women can be equal.[86]

Again the emphasis is being given to relying on broader socio-economic changes to modify family relations and women's status. During land reform and the campaign to enforce the Marriage Law, the political tactic of politicizing the personal grievances of women within the family was used to mobilize women and bring about political change. In this way, political struggle was brought into the private structure of family relationships in order to liberate women for political participation and productive work. The Cultural Revolution created a similar politicization of private attitudes and relations in order to raise political consciousness and release new energies for social and economic change. Some apparently felt that the ensuing tensions and fractionalizing in interpersonal relations caused too much disruption. When production was endangered, many leaders sought to restore stability through conciliation of various social groups and the de-politicization of interpersonal relations and griev-ances. Thus Lu Yu-lan asserts that struggle within the family is counterproductive and fails to win support for women. Instead, she suggests that women should put more exclusive emphasis on taking up work and increasing their contribution to socialist construction. As a result of this participation, the family authority structure and attitudes that discriminate against women will be transformed.

But this approach tends to mask the still widespread existence of discriminatory attitudes and ignores the independent role that such culturally defined attitudes and norms can play in obstructing the progress of sex equality. Simply urging women to take a fuller part in production does not necessarily deal with the continuing existence of contradictory values and expectations, imposed on women by family members and men, that make it difficult for women to achieve sex equality. Family members not only continue to expect women to respond to special obligations in ways that take up a great portion of their time, but they also impose norms regarding proper behavior and appropriate women's work that make it difficult for women to interact equally with men even after they take up productive work. The special emphasis on ideological reform among family members and men, as put forward by the radicals on the women's question, might help resolve these tensions in favor of greater and more nearly equal social participation by easing the pressure of traditional and proprietary family norms and obligations. From this perspective, some disruption of family harmony may be a necessary by-product of liberating women. The liberation requires a reordering of family roles and a lessening of family control over the economic, social, and political activities of women. The contrasting propositions—the insistence that men and women are now basically equal, that the Cultural Revolution swept away most of the remaining barriers, that equality will automatically accrue to women as they take up productive work—intentionally obscure the need to take special political action to further sex equality.

Recently, those concerned with the continuing inequality between the sexes seem to have received some top-level support for renewing a more politically activist approach. This effort apparently includes encouraging a more critical appraisal of current problems, and rebuilding and strengthening special women's organizations at all levels.[87] As mentioned earlier, in 1971 such organizations were still inoperative in urban factories and the dominant view seemed to be that they were no longer necessary. At the national level too, attempts are under way to reconstitute the Women's Federation.

Conclusion

To date, progress for women has been fairly dependent on a general leadership commitment to the ideology of sex equality, prodded on by the small number of high-level women leaders. But the leadership has also been able to quietly shelve women's demands when these have not coincided with other interests and priorities. The initial militance of oppressed women in many areas during the family-reform campaign indicated that many keenly perceived their inferior status and suffering. The issues raised by some women during the Cultural Revolution illustrated a continuing base of unfulfilled aspirations and perceived tensions. But women are a politically and culturally disadvantaged group with a unique history of social isolation. They have generally lacked the experience, awareness, and independent social resources necessary to turn their power into a consistent organized political force capable of compelling greater sensitivity to women's particular cultural and social handicaps. Without this organized power, women's groups have been unable to sustain their demands when these have met with resistance from stronger groups.

For the most part, various leadership groups have tended to view the liberation of women primarily as an economic problem and only secondly as a political and ideological problem. Thus policies have usually failed to deal directly with cultural barriers and traditional sexist attitudes. While women leaders might be more sensitive to these problems, they are a tiny minority among the top circles. Further-more, many of these top women have in a sense been co-opted by virtue of their past experiences and their individual success. For this small percentage of talented, educated, politically active women, most of whom have personal knowledge of the wretched female past, the new system has worked well. They are a symbolic testimonial that women are liberated. Such radical symbolic changes may actually help to mask the fact that for most women real changes have been far less substantial.[88]

However, the Cultural Revolution may have accelerated the cre-ation of a generation of young women leaders of a new type. These women, without personal knowledge of the wretched female oppres-sion of the past, may be more conscious of the serious discrimination persisting into the present. Like young Red Guards who, taking their elder's socialist ideal seriously, became critically aware of the elitist nature of established institutions before their elders in authority, young educated women may be more likely to take the propagated ideals of sex equality to demand more complete equality in politics, family life, and work. They are less likely to be co-opted in the ways their elders were. In proportion to their larger numbers, a smaller percentage will be drawn away into middle- and top-level leadership groups, despite the absolute increase in female representation. If these assumptions are correct, one might expect local organization and representation of women's demands to be relatively stronger and more self-consciously assertive.

Notes

1. For example, see Jan Myrdal, *Report from a Chinese Village* (New York: Signet, 1965), pp. 235–241.
2. Stuart Schram, *The Political Thought of Mao Tse-tung,* rev. ed. (New York: Praeger, 1969), pp. 334–337.
3. For examples of writing that portrays the brutal circumstances of women under the traditional family system see Pa Chin, *The Family* (Peking: Foreign Languages Press, 1958). Also see Jou Shih, "Slave's Mother"; Chao Shu-li, "Meng Xiang-ying Stands Up"; Lu Husun, "New Year's Sacrifice"; translated in W. J. F. Jenner, ed., *Modern Chinese Short Stories* (London: Oxford University Press, 1970). One of the most poignant autobiographical stories recorded is "Gold Flower's Story," as told to author Jack Belden in *China Shakes the World* (New York: Montly Review Press, 1970), pp. 275–307.
4. Chao Shu–li, translated in Jenner, p. 121.
5. C. K. Yang, *The Chinese Family in Communist Revolution* (Cambridge, Mass.: MIT Press, 1959), p. 139.
6. John L. Buck, *Land Utilization in China* (Chicago: Statistics, 1937), pp. 301–303, cited in C. K. Yang.
7. Irene Taeuber, "The Families of Chinese Farmers," in Maurice Freedman, ed.,

Family and Kinship in Chinese Society (Stanford: Stanford Univeristy Press, 1970), pp. 81–85.

8. Ibid., p. 3.

9. Mao Tse-tung makes this point in his "Report of an Investigation into the Peasant Movement in Hunan," 1927, in *Selected Works of Mao Tse-tung* (Peking: Foreign Languages Press, 1965), I, 44–47. In the original report, he also makes the point that poor peasant women enjoyed greater sexual freedom, although this was later deleted from the text. See Schram, p. 258.

10. Ida Pruitt, *A Daughter of Han: The Autobiography of a Chinese Working Woman* (Stanford: Stanford University Press, 1967), p. 55.

11. Hou Chi-ming, "Man-Power, Employment and Unemployment," in Alexander Eckstein et al., eds., *Economic Trends in Communist China* (Chicago: Aldine, 1968), pp. 336–338. Underenumeration of females in population registration is also thought to contribute to the high sex ratios reported.

12. For an illustration of the special burdens imposed by poverty on women, see Jou Shih, "Slave's Mother," in Jenner.

13. C. K. Yang, p. 138.

14. Text of "The Marriage Law of the People's Republic of China, 1950," appears in C. K. Yang, pp. 221–226.

15. William Hinton, *Fanshen* (New York: Random House, 1968), p. 159.

16. Ibid., p. 397.

17. Ibid.

18. For one account of these meetings and the psychological effect on women and their relationships with men, see Belden, pp. 288–307.

19. C. K. Yang, pp. 69–71.

20. For example, see Hinton, p. 159.

21. See Isabel Crook and David Crook, *The First Years of Yangyi Commune* (London: Routledge & Kegan Paul, 1966), p. 241.

22. For example, see Myrdal, *Chinese Village,* p. 252.

23. Hinton, pp. 353–354.

24. The village visited by Jan Myrdal, for example, appeared to have done little women's organizational work until 1955–1956. See Myrdal, *Chinese Village,* pp. 252, 255.

25. Ch'en Yu-t'ung, "Liquidation of the Old Legal View as a Condition for Thorough Implementation of the Marriage Law," *Hsin Chung-kuo Fu-nu (New Chinese Women),* no. 9, September 1952, pp. 7–8, cited in C. K. Yang, pp. 81, 109. Also see Yang, pp. 107–110.

26. C. K. Yang, pp. 36–39, 78–82.

27. Mao Tse-tung, *Socialist Upsurge in the Countryside,* vol. 1, editor's note, Peking, 1956, quoted in *Peking Review,* no. 11, 1964, p. 19.

28. John Philip Emerson, "Employment in Mainland China: Problems and Prospects," in *An Economic Profile of Mainland China* (New York: Praeger, 1968), p. 433.

29. Ibid., p. 433.

30. C. K. Yang, p. 151.

31. Ibid.

32. An Tzu-wen, "A Correct Approach to the Problem of Retirement of Women Cadres," *Chung-kuo Fu-nu (Women of China),* no. 2, 1 February 1958, pp. 14–18, cited by Emerson, "Employment," p. 434.

33. Ester Boserup, *Women's Role in Economic Development* (London: George Allen & Unwin, 1970), pp. 194–196.

34. Ibid., pp. 196–200.

35. Ibid., pp. 206–207.

36. Hou, pp. 378–379.

37. Ibid., p. 377.

38. See Franz Schurmann, *Organization and Ideology in Communist China,* rev. ed. (Berkeley: University of California Press, 1968), pp. 469–474. Also see *Peking Review,* no. 10, 8 March 1969, p. 7.

39. Emerson, "Employment," p. 435. Also see John P. Emerson, *Sex, Age and Level of*

Skill of Non-agricultural Labor Force of Mainland China (Washington, D.C.: Foreign Demographic Analysis Division, Bureau of Census, 1965).

40. C. K. Yang, p. 152.

41. Emerson, "Employment," p. 433.

42. Ibid., p. 434. Also see Hou, p. 380.

43. Emerson, "Employment."

44. Yang Kan-ling, "Family Life—the New Way," *Peking Review,* 18 November 1958, pp. 9–10.

45. *Peking Review,* 9 December 1958, p. 13.

46. Yang Liu, "Reform of Marriage and Family Systems in China," *Peking Review,* 13 March 1964, p. 19.

47. Chin Ai-li, "Family Relations in Modern Chinese Fiction," in Freedman, pp. 87–120.

48. "Is a Daughter-in-Law Obliged to Support Her Father-in-Law and Mother-in-Law?," *Chung-kuo Ch'ing-nien Pao (Chinese Youth Journal),* 12 May 1962, translated in *Selections from China Mainland Magazines,* no. 2756, 15 May 1962, p. 15. Although the questions of financial support for the husband's parents and living together with them are two separate issues, it is significant that the editor does not point out the distinction. It is thus indirectly implied that the daughter-in-law's obligations include living in her in-law's household if this is possible. Living together also has the practical effect of strengthening and insuring the financial obligations of son and daughter-in-law.

49. For a discussion of "public assistance" and "social security" for workers, see Joyce Kallgren, "Social Welfare and China's Industrial Workers," in A. Doak Barnett, ed., *Chinese Communist Politics in Action* (Seattle: University of Washington Press, 1969), pp. 540–573.

50. "Is a Daughter-in-law Obliged."

51. Janet Salaff, "Institutionalized Motivation for Fertility Limitation in China," *Population Studies* 26, no. 2 (July 1972): 243.

52. Ibid., p. 239.

53. Edgar Snow, *The Long Revolution* (New York: Random House, 1971), p. 44.

54. Myrdal, *Chinese Village,* pp. 245–246.

55. "Pay Attention to the Development of Female Party Members," *Jen-min Jih-pao (People's Daily),* 13 September 1971, translated in *Current Background,* November 1971, pp. 9–10.

56. Salaff, p. 256.

57. Ibid., p. 252.

58. Ibid., p. 257.

59. Ibid.

60. Jan Myrdal and Gun Kessle, *China: The Revolution Continued* (New York: Vintage Books, 1970), p. 134. Also: Committee of Concerned Asian Scholars, *China! Inside the People's Republic* (New York: Bantam Books, 1972), p. 162.

61. "Pay Attention to the Development of Female Cadre Members."

62. Janet Salaff, "The Role of the Family in Health Care" in Joseph R. Quinn, ed., *Medicine and Public Health in the People's Republic of China* (Washington, D.C.: U.S. Department of Health, Education and Welfare, 1972), p. 40.

63. Myrdal, *Chinese Village,* p. 252.

64. Interview with woman cadre, July 1971.

65. Salaff, "Institutionalized Motivation," p. 252.

66. Lu Yu-Lan, "A Liberated Woman Speaks," in *New Women in New China* (Peking: Foreign Languages Press, 1972), p. 12.

67. Salaff, "Institutionalized Motivation," p. 252.

68. Interviews, July 1971. Urban men usually acknowledge that they *ought* to share some household responsibilities. But most men and women readily admitted that the major responsibilities were still primarily looked after by women.

69. For a more detailed description of the early residents' groups, see Schurmann, pp. 274–280.

70. Salaff, "Institutionalized Motivation," pp. 255–256.

71. Barry Richman, *Industrial Society in Communist China* (New York: Random House, 1969), pp. 304–305, 396.

72. "Bring the Role of Women into Full Play in Revolution and Construction," *Hung-ch'i (Red Flag)*, no. 10, 1 September 1971, translated in *Selections from China Mainland Magazines*, October 1971, pp. 73–78.

73. Translated and cited by Salaff in Janet Salaff and Judith Merkle, "Women in Revolution: The Lessons of the Soviet Union and China," *Socialist Revolution* 1, no. 4 (July–August 1970).

74. *The Great Cultural Revolution in China*, p. 181.

75. Translated and cited by Salaff in Salaff and Merkle.

76. Ibid.

77. Interview, July 1971.

78. Interview, July 1971.

79. Myrdal and Kessle, p. 134.

80. *Peking Review*, 23 March 1973, p. 23.

81. *New Women In New China* (Peking: Foreign Languages Press, 1972), pp. 55–61.

82. Yin Yi-ping, "Half the Population," in *The Seeds and Other Stories* (Peking: Foreign Languages Press, 1972), pp. 27–36.

83. The following account is derived from interviews and discussions with a number of middle- and upper-level women cadres in Shanghai and Sian, July 1971.

84. "Bring the Role of Women into Full Play in Revolution and Construction."

85. Ibid., p. 78.

86. Lu Yu-lan, pp. 7–8.

87. See, for example, "Working Women Are a Great Revolutionary Force," *Jen-min Jih-pao (People's Daily)*, 8 March 1973, translated in *Peking Review*, 16 March 1973.

88. *Editor's note:* It is not entirely clear how Chiang Ch'ing, Mao's widow, fits into this picture. Criticism of her recent attempt to seize power does not seem to be based on the fact that she is a woman or even that she is Mao's widow, although she is accused of forging a statement in which Mao supposedly designated her as his successor. She and three other co-conspirators (all male) have been arrested and purged.

II   Southeast Asia

Southeast Asia is a land of great diversity with many nations and many religious influences. Buddhism, Islam, Catholicism and Hinduism have mixed with older animistic traditions. Further, the effects of Western imperialism have varied widely. Thailand remained unconquered while the British ruled Burma and Malaysia, the French ruled Vietnam, the Dutch ruled Indonesia, and the Spanish and Americans ruled the Philippines. Despite this visible diversity, the status of women is relatively high in Southeast Asia, particularly when compared with that of the women in East and South Asia.

The question is: What factors are held in common by the nations of Southeast Asia that contribute to the high status of their women? Two interrelated variables—the bilateral kinship system (the original though not at present extant family system of almost all Southeast Asian peoples) and the existence of an ample land supply that makes bilateralism possible—would appear to account for the relatively high status of Southeast Asian women.

Bilateralism, in which an individual traces his descent from both parents rather than through the single ancestral line recognized in patriarchal and matriarchal societies, has important behavioral consequences that greatly affect the status of women. Among these consequences are that women are never removed from the support of their kinsmen and that partial self-selection of mates exists for both males and females. The patriarchal dowry is replaced by a "bride price" which confirms the worth of women. Inheritance is partible and inherited property is usually divided equally among all children regardless of sex. All of these practices combine to give women psychological importance and decision-making authority over real wealth—including cash, land, and other valuable property. In Southeast Asia this outlook usually meant that women controlled the families' funds. As a result of this control women made many of the families' investment decisions, including the establishment of businesses in which women performed all the marketing functions, purchased the land, directed agricultural production, and determined which children would receive education and for how long. The latter power in a modernizing setting insured that women would receive the educational advantages that allowed them access to the new roles in rapidly urbanizing nations.

Finally, there is an important socialized self-image that attaches itself to bilateralism. Women gain a strong sense of self-esteem, in part because as children little girls are given a great deal of responsibility whereas little boys are not. Thus women in Southeast Asia feel that they are responsible for the survival of the nuclear family as opposed to the extended family. Since in Southeast Asia, both in the past and in the present, the nuclear family is the critical social unit around which most economic, political, and social behavior revolves, women have retained important decision-making roles.

There are, of course, differences in the relative status of women in Southeast Asia. These range from the high status of women in the Philippines, Thailand, and Burma to the somewhat lower status of women in Indonesia and Malaysia. In Indonesia, the customary law associated with high female status has been leavened by Hindu and Islamic influence and in Malaysia the strong influence of Islam has considerably lowered the status of women. Despite these differences, however, nowhere in Southeast Asia is the status of women, either real or ideal, as low as or lower than that of their sisters in either South or East Asia.

Part II of this volume deals with women in Southeast Asia. First, Justin Green examines attitudinal and value orientations of a Philippine female elite in an attempt to ascertain whether women as leaders can or will make those value choices that tend to lead their societies into sustained economic, political, and social modernization. He finds Filipina leaders to be of intermediate type, neither modernizing nor traditional. Rather, they are a self-preserving combination of both.

Next, Heather Strange examines the socioeconomic roles of rural Malay women in a coastal village of the state of Trengganu in Malaysia. Over a period of ten years she sees a great diversity of roles and significant changes influenced largely by the economic status of individual women.

Stephen Douglas, in examining Indonesian women's organizations, points out that when women are considered as a special interest group among many others, either because of their own behavior or because of directions the political process has taken, a consequence may be negative effects on long-term efforts at the macro level to raise the status and political importance of women.

Next Ann Ruth Willner suggests that at the micro level Javanese women are attaining more nearly equal status with Javanese men than Western women are with Western men and, further, that they are doing so without intersexual conflict. Willner believes that the greater recognition of equality and the absence of conflict are the result of Javanese culture and traditions. The lack of restrictions on "style" removes negative societal restraints which in Western society often prevent women from pursuing goals that are invested with masculine connotations. Such cultural factors produce a society peculiarly predisposed toward the attainment of "maximum equality with minimum conflict."

4 Female Elite Goals and National Development: Some Data from the Philippines

Justin J. Green

Many attempts have been made in recent years to classify the characteristics of modernity and the criteria for identifying development. It is not necessary to catalogue these efforts here, for the sterility of this enterprise has become self-evident to social scientists interested in the phenomena of social change. To many scholars it seems that such classification and identification suffer from either ethnocentric or teleological error, or both. Ethnocentric error may occur because some social scientists either covertly or overtly build into their studies assumptions about the ends of the development process that turn out to be their culturally biased notions of the good society. Teleological error may occur because the assumption is made that we can understand process through the actions observed rather than through the motivations of the actors. In order to escape these traps, some researchers have developed decision-making models that possess the virtue of locating the responsibility for societies' critical decisions in their leadership elites.[1] In these models, it is the leaders' goals that become societies' goals. The leaders choose the means to achieve these ends, and from these choices the future shape of their societies emerges.

This model does not exclude the many from any influence in the decision-making process. Nor does it preclude competition among several groups of elites for control of decision making in any given area. Influence and competition are, after all, what politics is about. To those who make the critical decisions, the efforts of the many and the competition for power are but two of the variables that, among others, influence their behavioral choices.

The point here is that since development is a self-directed process, its dynamics can be analyzed only by forecasting some set of goals for the process. To avoid teleological error in such forecasting the short- and long-term goals of society should be those emanating from societies' decision makers. In such an endeavor, the study of elites and of the decisions they make is critical. Moreover, these studies possess maximum value when they are able to aid us in understanding the process of elite goal formation, as well as the specific goals formulated.

The problem with such an approach is to operationalize it: to discover the goals of various elites and the means these elites are likely to use in the pursuit of these goals. Myrdal, for example, in seeking to understand the effect of traditional attitudes and beliefs on development, warns us of certain pitfalls.

> But an examination that confines itself to what is verbalized and explicit can convey only an inkling of the social significance of traditional attitudes and beliefs, some of which are very important inhibitions and obstacles to development. What is needed is intensive and empirical investigation of these attitudes and beliefs in different strata of the population and their influence on behavior. At present, solid knowledge about this highly relevant matter is scanty.[2]

Despite his warning to others, Myrdal develops a taxonomy of nonempirical modernization ideals that he ascribes to elites. These tend to be exactly those goals and values verbalized by elites in the public arena. It is our hypothesis that the underlying attitudes of elites will not support the modernizing goals and values they publicly articulate, and we plan to test this hypothesis in a Philippine setting by examining a group of Philippine women leaders.

Women in the Philippines

Philippine social life is the result of the intersection of several major forces, including the following:

1. The indigenous Malay culture with its emphasis on the equalitarian extended family and its wide network of horizontal multi-stranded dyadic relationships. These exchange networks constrained the acquisition of power and economic resources and tended to widely disburse decision-making roles.

2. Almost four hundred years of Spanish hegemony converted the equalitarian family system into multilayered patron-client networks that contributed to and were supported by a social class system consisting of a small group of very rich landholders and a large mass of poor peasants. The Spanish occupation, however, failed to shatter the bilateral extended family, which continued to provide support for all its members and underwrote the myth (and occasionally the reality) of mobility.[3]

3. A half century of American presence overlaid these networks with American-style democratic institutions including, among others, the tripartite division of political power, a bureaucracy staffed by a civil-service system, and an American-style educational system replete with English language, the Protestant work ethic, snow scenes at Christmas, and the liberal democratic credo. All this Americanization, however, had only a minimal effect on the existing distribution of political and economic power either in the institutional or family life of the society.[4]

The Filipino who emerged from these multifaceted experiences has a set of values and behaviors that enable him to mesh rather smoothly with this dualistic world of an indigenous social system and American institutions. Although linguistic and other cultural barriers continue to exist in the Philippines, family and value systems tend in the main, toward homogeneity. Although social structural ties tend to mitigate class disparities, wide gaps in life style persist between classes.

The persistence of the Filipino family, its important role in Philippine life, and its extended horizontal nature have been documented by many scholars.[5] The question is: What are the consequences for female status of this form of social organization?

Historically it would appear that the horizontal social structures that underlie the bilateral kinship group led to behavioral practices— "bride price," partial self-selection of mates, the female as manager of the family funds, and others—that made for high female status. During the Spanish period, however, the Filipina's (particularly the upper-class Filipina's) freedom was restricted, and her status suffered from the imposition of Spanish law. Among rural folk, however, it is doubtful that Spanish customs and mannerisms shaped the peasant woman's behavior patterns. The daily demands of existence, the multiplicity of roles she was called on to play, and the tendency in rural areas to tenaciously preserve pre-Spanish customs precluded the rural Filipina from accepting the "Maria Clara" image that had been adopted by her upper-class sister.

With the advent of American rule came a slow restoration of the legal status of women that had been voided by the Spanish Civil Code, which deprived women of such rights as those of engaging in commerce or owning property. Under the American regime, in addition to legal rights, the Filipina was given equal opportunities in education, business, professions, politics, and civil service. Few areas of endeavor were closed to her.

In the Philippines today few roles, if any, are denied women. Females hold important positions in the government bureaucracy as well as in the secretarial pools. Most teachers at all levels of education, including higher education, are women. In primary and secondary teaching positions women outnumber men three to two. At the college level women hold approximately half of all teaching positions. In public markets most vendors are women. The executive offices of family-owned corporations are occupied by women, and the financial pages of the Manila newspapers appear to mention as many females' names and pictures as those of males. In hospitals, pharmacies, industrial laboratories, or in any occupation requiring an advanced degree, women are very well represented. In the Philippine Congress during the period before martial law, women were outnumbered by men, but the numerical superiority of males was decreasing. The legal profession, once dominated by males, has increasingly become a female domain. Current bar-examination figures indicate that the majority of those who pass the bar exam are now women, and each year they have come closer to "topping the bar."

In the rural areas, except for plowing and other heavy field preparation, women work alongside men. Rural buses and jeepneys are crowded with women taking produce to market for sale or returning home with their purchases.

In summation, neither in the past nor in the present has the Filipina been yoked with inferiority. Hence it seems particularly appropriate to study the interrelationship of development and Philippine women leaders.

The Sample

In the course of a study that examined a group of Philippine female leaders, data were obtained that allow us to test the extent, if any, to which Myrdal's modernization ideals are held by a Southeast Asian female leadership sample. A group of 145 female leaders was located, using a three-stage reputational method. The method was partially validated by the degree to which the list of the sample members overlapped available positional and honorific lists of women leaders.

The method is biased in that it tends to locate those leaders who are either full-time residents of Manila or are rather frequent visitors to the capital. Some important provincial leaders appear to have been left out. The sample also is biased toward Christian leaders and thus may tend to eliminate the views of Muslim women. Finally, it must be remembered that this sample consists, in the main, of upper-class women, women of political, economic, and social power who play an important leadership role in the Philippines. There may be little or no resemblance between the attitudes and behaviors present in this sample and those present in the larger female population. Of the original group, 122 were interviewed by trained, experienced Filipino interviewers, using two questionnaires. The instruments were designed to disclose an in-depth portrait of the leaders' social backgrounds and those attitudes and behavior patterns that would allow the Philippine sample to be compared with elites in other nations.

An analysis of the social background data disclosed several important and, to some extent, contradictory trends. Among these were: (1) the elite were of high socioeconomic origin; (2) there are indications of decreasing mobility into elite ranks; (3) though their social characteristics were generally similar to those that might be expected in a traditional elite, some criteria, including level of education, travel abroad, and occupationally specific training, would suggest classifying them as a modernizing elite.[6] This divergent set of characteristics led to the conclusion that the Filipina fits into neither the traditional nor a modernizing elite category. Rather, as measured by social background characteristics, she is an intermediate, well adapted to the operation of what Nash has called a multiple society.[7]

The available attitudinal data do not enable us to establish a set of real goals that Filipina leaders formulate for their nation. The best we can do here is to compare the information about goal formation that was obtained with those modernization ideals Myrdal suggests are held, or at least expressed, by South and Southeast Asian elites.[8] Because Myrdal was primarily concerned with Indian elites, some of his modernization ideals are not applicable in a Philippine setting; and because the research on Filipina leaders did not possess instruments permitting the examination of others, what follows analyzes only those modernization ideals for which data are available and which are relevant to the Philippines.

The Ideal of Rationality

In discussing elite goals in South Asia, Myrdal suggests: "It is regularly assumed in public debates that policies should be founded on rational considerations. It is also taken for granted and often stressed that such a course represents a break with tradition. Superstitions, beliefs and illogical reasoning should be eradicated."[9]

One question we asked our respondents was, "Do you strongly agree, mildly agree, mildly disagree or strongly disagree that science has its place but there are many things that must always be beyond human understanding?" Such a question, we felt, might shed some light on the issue of Filipina rationality. While many people might subscribe to the central theme of this question, that some things are always beyond man's reason, the uncompromising words "many things" and "always be" should pressure the rational respondents to respond with disagreement or "mildly agree" rather than "strongly agree." Myrdal's expectation of rationality as a modernizing ideal is not met by these respondents: 67 percent of the female leaders strongly agreed with the statement, while another 21 percent mildly agreed. Only 12 percent of the sample disagreed, which could be considered the most rational response. Given this sample's high level of educational attainment (87 percent had college degrees), we had expected a larger percentage to fall at the rational end of the scale. We cannot suggest from this one response that Filipina policy makers are not rational decision makers, but there would appear to be a tendency among these leaders to accept an unhappy state of affairs rather than make rational attempts to solve the problem.

Ideals in Development and Planning for Development
According to Myrdal, elites believe that "development means improvement of the host of undesirable conditions in the social system that have perpetuated a state of underdevelopment."[10] Three areas—high population growth rates, graft and corruption, and a slow pace of social change—would seem to be candidates for consideration as undesirable conditions. We will examine our sample's attitudes toward these areas.

Population Control
Economists and demographers, admittedly with some dissent, have suggested that there is a positive relationship between a rapidly increasing population and a sluggish rate of economic growth. Given the existence of such a relationship, the figures in Table I indicate that the Filipina leaders neither practice nor serve as models of population limitation. The mean is approximately 3½ children per married

Table 1. Children Born to Married Filipina Leaders

Number of Children	*Percent of Leaders Having These Numbers of Children*
None	8
1	13
2	16
3	14
4	18
5	9
More than 5	22

leader. If this average were the critical figure in influencing others, then the example set by leaders, though not desirable if population limitation is a modernization ideal, might be tolerable. The general population, however, does not see means; what is more readily visible is the modal family size. Unfortunately, the question used to determine the number of children per leader in the research was not coded in such a manner that the modal number of children of the sample was obtainable. However, the large proportion of women (22 percent) having more than 5 children and the fact that this group includes many women with families of 9 or more suggests that the example set by the leadership group vis-à-vis any ideal of population limitation is not a good one. What is more troublesome is a positive correlation, though it is statistically not significant, between younger leaders and larger families.

Graft and Corruption

One need not have been an acute observer of the Philippines in the 1960s to be convinced that graft, nepotism, and corruption, as defined by Western culture, existed in Philippine society. The front pages of all the daily newspapers attested to their presence. It is probable, though not provable, that these practices slowed the nation's economic growth. However, because the culture sanctions the type of behavior that underlies these problems, female leaders, when confronted with questions that touched on these issues, responded with attitudinal and behavioral choices that would tend to perpetuate the problems despite the costs in economic growth. Answers to the questions below suggest that traditional political behavior based on personal contact and family connections, both of which are associated with graft and nepotism in a modern setting, is still perceived as the acceptable way to achieve one's goals.

Two questions were asked: the first called for an open-ended response; the second question forced the respondent to make specific choices.

1. Suppose a law were being considered by the Philippine House or Senate that you considered to be unjust or harmful. What do you think you could do?

2. Suppose several men were trying to influence a government decision. Here is a list of things they might do. Realistically, which do you think would be most effective here in the Philippines: (A) Work through personal and family connections; (B) Write to Government officials; (C) Form a group; (D) Work through a party; (E) Protest demonstrations?

Although these leaders were educated to support group-oriented approaches, the responses to both questions indicate strong support for the personalistic approach to political problem solving. In the open-ended question, 64 percent of the sample indicated that personal rather than group approaches would be their choice; 18 percent indicated that they would employ both the personal and the group approach; and the remaining 18 percent chose group-oriented approaches. One leader who advocated the personal tactic remarked, "I would talk to these leaders and tell them not to pass it. I am a friend of the most important leaders." Another leader, advocating both individual and group tactics, stated, "I would approach the senators personally and get a group together on an impersonal basis."

The responses to the second question indicated that 49 percent of the female leaders would work through personal and family connections or write to government officials, 29 percent would form a group, and 21 percent would work through their political parties. Given the personalistic factions that hold together Philippine political parties, the latter category could be seen as either a personal or a group approach to the political process. Further, the whole structure of Philippine politics discourages universalistic behavior. Given this cultural context, the expectation that these leaders or Filipinos of any sex or social class would make group-oriented choices is probably unrealistic.

Innovation

To measure the level of innovativeness of this female leadership sample, four scales were used. However, only one will be examined here. The questions used in obtaining values for this scale were for the most part open-ended. These questions dealt with each leader's subjective view of her most important occupational and nonoccupational achievements and were designed to separate innovative from normal patterns of behavior. The responses were coded to place the leaders on a scale of innovativeness. Though the coding was subjective, it was based on four criteria; what the subject did, her motivation, the amount of resistance met, and the manner in which such resistance was handled. The leaders' responses with reference to these criteria were compared with what seemed to be culturally more acceptable behavior patterns.[11]

Table 2 indicates the distribution of respondents on the scale of innovativeness that resulted from this coding. The results (supported by other measures not considered here indicate that levels of innovativeness among our sample are not high. From this we might hypothesize that leadership behavior which accepts and preserves the status quo is more likely among this group than activity producing

Table 2. Innovativeness of Filipina Leaders

Score on Scale of Innovativeness	Percent of Sample
0 (Noninnovative)	20
1	37
2	12
3	10
4	8
5	3
6 (Innovative)	0

innovative change. If, as Myrdal suggests, improvement of undesirable conditions is a modernization ideal and since improvement generally calls for innovative behavior, then this ideal may be unrealizable inasmuch as Filipina leaders give little indication of moving toward the innovative kind of behavior that would make this modernization ideal achievable.

Ideals Concerning Social Stratification

In discussing stratification, Myrdal comments:

> In all the countries of South Asia the ideal that social and economic stratification should be changed in order to promote equality in status, opportunities, wealth, income and levels of living is commonly accepted in public discussion of the goals for planning and for policies generally.[12]

In other words, Myrdal suggests that equalitarianism is not only an attitude that affects other behaviors but is itself a goal of Asian elites. We can test Myrdal's proposition by examining the equalitarian attitudes of our sample.

Equalitarianism was measured by a version of the Index of Equalitarianism used by Bell in studying Jamaican leaders.[13] Table 3 compares the equalitarian percentages of all Philippine women leaders with those of Bell's Jamaican leaders and with those of college students in 1959 at the University of California, Los Angeles.

The responses to questions 1, 4, and 5 indicate that the level of equalitarianism of the Philippine female leaders is considerably lower than that of the U.C.L.A. college students. On questions 1 and 5 the Filipinas' level is also lower than that of Jamaican leaders. On question 2, levels remain similar but are somewhat lower for both Filipinas and Jamaicans than for the American college students. Only on question 3 are there considerably higher levels of equalitarianism among both the Jamaican and Filipina samples. The similarity of levels on question 3, 63 percent (Jamaican leaders) and 66 percent (Filipinas) compared with 22 percent for the U.C.L.A. students, suggests that for Jamaicans and Filipinas this question had a meaning different from what it had for American college students.

Table 3. Percent of Equalitarian Responses of Three Leadership Samples Responding to Five Questions

Question 1: The income of most people is a fair measure of their contribution to human welfare.

		Filipina Leaders	Jamaican Leaders	U.C.L.A. Students
Equalitarian	Strong Disagreement	31	62	67
	Some Disagreement	33	20	24
Nonequalitarian	Undecided	4	8	7
	Some Agreement	19	7	1
	Strong Agreement	13	3	1
N		122	229	91

Question 2: We should not be too concerned if there are many in low positions in the Philippines since most of them do not want the responsibility of higher positions.

		Filipina Leaders	Jamaican Leaders	U.C.L.A. Students
Equalitarian	Strong Disagreement	43	45	37
	Some Disagreement	29	24	34
	Undecided	3	4	11
Nonequalitarian	Some Agreement	22	15	12
	Strong Agreement	3	12	6
N		122	227	91

Question 3: Difference in status among various occupations in the Philippines should be reduced.

		Filipina Leaders	Jamaican Leaders	U.C.L.A. Students
Equalitarian	Strong Agreement	43	39	4
	Some Agreement	23	24	18
Nonequalitarian	Undecided	7	13	13
	Some Disagreement	18	10	30
	Strong Disagreement	9	14	35
N		120	230	91

Table 3 (Cont'd.)

Question 4: Differences in rank among people are acceptable since they are chiefly the result of the way individuals have made use of the opportunity open to them.

		Filipina Leaders	*Jamaican Leaders*	*U.C.L.A. Students*
Equalitarian	Strong Disagreement	11	10	14
	Some Disagreement	15	11	29
	Undecided	5	4	9
	Some Agreement	37	30	34
Nonequalitarian	Strong Agreement	32	45	14
N		120	228	91

Question 5: People of the same social or economic position ought to pretty much mingle with their own kind.

		Filipina Leaders	*Jamaican Leaders*	*U.C.L.A. Students*
Equalitarian	Strong Disagreement	11	33	21
	Some Disagreement	6	17	20
Nonequalitarian	Undecided	—	8	14
	Some Agreement	25	21	29
	Strong Agreement	58	21	16
N		122	225	90

If we accept this explanation of the variance on question 3, it is apparent that Jamaican leaders and Filipina leaders are less equalitarian than American college students and that the Filipinas are the least equalitarian. Even this level can be further qualified. Two of the background variables correlated with high levels of equalitarianism in Bell's study were sex and education. Females and highly educated respondents were significantly more equalitarian than others in Bell's results. The data of this sample support Bell's findings that educational level is positively correlated with equalitarianism. If Bell's data on sex difference are transferable to other populations, then our exclusively female, highly educated sample should be higher in equalitarianism than Bell's sexually heterogeneous, less educated sample. It is not. It seems probable that if we compared Jamaican and Filipina leaders, holding sex and education constant, then the relative equalitarianism of the Filipinas would be even lower than is indicated by Table 3.

Although it should be noted that the strongly stratified nature of Philippine society makes it unlikely that equalitarian ideals would be dominant, nevertheless the fact that this sample has been heavily exposed to American ideals and the fact that Jamaica is as much socially stratified as the Philippines make the following conclusion inescapable: The Filipina's level of equalitarianism, as compared to available data from other societies, is quite low. We would suggest that equalitarianism as a modernization ideal is likely to be rhetoric designed to create a favorable image outside of the Philippines. There is little attitudinal or behavioral support among the members of this sample for creating the equalitarian society.

Ideals Concerning Institutions and Attitudes

Myrdal notes that South Asian elites, as part of their modernization goals, seek to improve existing institutions and popular attitudes toward efficiency, diligence, orderliness, punctuality, frugality, honesty, rationality in decision making, preparedness for change, alertness to opportunity, energetic enterprise, integrity and self-reliance, cooperativeness, and willingness to take the long view.[14] Improvement means, in this case, to become more efficient, more orderly, more alert, more honest, and so on.

We will examine next those attitudes for which there were satisfactory data in the Philippine study.

Efficiency

To examine efficiency as a desired attitude on the part of the Philippine elites, we asked, "What should people be like?" A very large majority chose the response, "Does his job well." This would suggest some fairly strong support for the hypothesis that efficiency is an important modernization goal.

Diligence

Our evidence indicates that Filipina leaders approve of diligence. Of the entire sample, 93 percent either strongly agreed (75 percent) or mildly agreed (18 percent) with the statement, "If people would talk less and work more, everybody would be better off."

Frugality

Referring again to our question "What should people be like?" none of the respondents selected "thrifty and saving" as the quality they admired most. Further participant observation would indicate that conspicuous consumption is the behavioral norm among Filipina elites. Our data indicate that frugality is not seen as an important or desirable characteristic.

Preparedness for Change

It was reported above that on one measure of innovativeness Filipina leaders are not prepared to act in order to bring about change. Another facet of the Filipinas' attitudes toward change is their views of the role of others in promoting and accepting change. Some indication of the Filipinas' views is obtained when we note that 83 percent of the sample agreed (50 percent strongly) that "young people sometimes get rebellious ideas, but as they grow up, they ought to get over them and settle down." This response might suggest that these leaders expect the young to follow in their footsteps rather than rock the boat.

Conclusion

Myrdal, as noted, ascribes to elites the desire for change. Others have gone a step further and prescribed this attitude as a requisite for elite rank. Coser, for example, says that elites

> must attempt to undermine and neutralize traditional modes of behavior. They must desire to create citizens free from particularistic loyalties to village, communal groupings, family, tribal chief or traditional aristocracy. They must attempt to legitimize secular power, even giving it a "social character," so as to free the polity from control by traditional powerholders and representatives of the religious order.[15]

The data on Filipina elites examined above suggest that any typology of elite purpose should avoid the teleological, be it Myrdal's ascription or Coser's prescription. The goals that will be useful in understanding the process of social change taking place in the developing nations are those that emanate from people who are influential in making policy. Discovering these goals is a matter for empirical investigation rather than ascription or prescription. Social scientists need not be bound by the elite's means and ends in ascertaining the outcome of change in the developing nations, for elite goals may be unrealizable and the means for obtaining them poorly chosen. However, the researcher must understand the subjective goals of the policy makers in order to explain and predict both the process of internal social change and the adaptability of these nations to the world environment within which they now function.

We would agree with Myrdal that his modernizing ideals might usefully be replaced by empirically verified elite goals. The data we have examined, though limited, indicate that in a few instances (those of value changes toward efficiency and diligence), Filipinas do support the modernization ideals ascribed to elites by Myrdal. However, in the majority of instances—rationality, stratification, equalitarianism, preparedness for change—we find among our respondents little attitudinal or behavioral support for Myrdal's modernization ideals.

Further, the patterns of the respondents' attitudes and goals that we are able to identify (little tendency toward alleviation of social stratification, little interest in or preparedness for change, greater interest in preservation of existing institutions than in changing them, little tendency for innovation but strong support for efficiency and diligence in others, little trust, satisfaction with the present political system and the feeling that one can efficiently manipulate the present system) support the statement made earlier that Filipina leaders are an intermediate type, neither modernizing nor traditional, who have adapted themselves to the conditions of the modern world.

The characteristics of this intermediate leader enable her to adapt to the modern world outside the Philippines and at the same time to perpetuate her own status in the multiple society. This society, as Nash defines it, is

> a segmented social order welding a territory and its population together by a single set of political and economic bonds. There is a class or segment which commands resources of national scope, carries in it the idea of nation, maintains relations with other nations, and is in some sort of touch with scientific, economic and political developments of the international community. It is this group, spread out through the national territory, in whom political control is vested and among whom political power is contested.[16]

Nash further states:

> The multiple society is different from our own in that the social and cultural variations are not class variations on a basically common culture in a single social structure, but rather the society exhibits poor articulation between segments, disparities in the principles of social structure from segment to segment, and allows only the national elite elements to be organized for purposeful political action.[17]

Attitudes present in this sample that envision no end to stratification, little change, preservation of present institutions, and the like, are not those of new women or modernizers about to overturn the established order and bring to their nation and its peoples modernity in its Western form. Rather, it is probable that many Filipina leaders seek modernity for only their own sector of the nation and at the same time act to preserve the gap between themselves and the more traditional sectors of Philippine society.

Notes

1. Karl Deutsch in his introduction to the new edition of *The Nerves of Government* (New York: Free Press, 1966) surveys some of the more important efforts in this direction, pp. vii–xxviii.

2. Gunnar Myrdal, *Asian Drama* (New York: Twentieth Century Fund, 1968), 1: 94.

3. F. Lande Jocano, "Filipino Social Structure and Value Systems," in F. L. Jocano, ed., *Filipino Cultural Heritage: A Lecture Series, No. 2* (Manila: Philippine Women's University, 1966).

4. David Wurfel, "The Philippines," in G. M. Kahin, ed., *Governments and Politics of Southeast Asia* (Ithaca: Cornell University Press, 1959).

5. See Jocano; Chester Hunt et al., *Sociology in the Philippine Setting* (Manila: Alemars, 1954).

6. The criteria for locating elites as either traditional or modernizing is taken from Suzanne Keller, *Beyond the Ruling Class* (New York: Random House, 1963).

7. Manning Nash, *The Golden Road to Modernity* (New York: Wiley, 1965), p. 16.

8. Myrdal, 1: 59.

9. Ibid., 1: 57.

10. Ibid., 1: 58.

11. An example of the kind of decision made on innovativeness is as follows: A subject who listed her achievement as bringing the idea of governmental sponsorship of social services to the Philippines was considered innovative, whereas the respondent whose achievement was to develop a small business into a larger one was not.

12. Myrdal, 1:59.

13. Wendell Bell, *Jamaican Leaders: Political Attitudes in a New Nation* (Berkeley: University of California Press, 1964), pp. 90–91.

14. Myrdal, 1: 60–63.

15. Lewis A. Coser, ed., *Political Sociology* (New York: Harper Torchbooks, 1967).

16. Nash, pp. 320–321.

17. Ibid.

5 Some Changing Socioeconomic Roles of Village Women in Malaysia

Heather Strange

In what follows we shall examine the socioeconomic roles of rural Malay women in Rusila, a coastal village of the state of Trengganu, during 1965–66 and 1975.[1] The focus is on those living in the village. Little is said about those who were born and raised here but now live and perhaps hold jobs in other parts of the country, although these formerly resident young women do have some influence on their friends and families in the village in terms of value change and attitudinal change.

There is great variety among the women in the village. Some are illiterate; two are educated beyond the secondary level. Most are married, but there are some divorcees and widows. A majority were born in the village, but some come from states as distant as Malacca on the other side of the peninsula. A few elderly women live alone or with a young grandchild for company, usually near the home of a son or daughter. Some younger women care for families of eight or nine. There are women who have made the pilgrimage to Mecca in Saudi Arabia or who have been to Singapore; others have never been as far as fifty miles from the village. A few women do no remunerative work while their neighbors engage in a variety of moneymaking activities.

Despite this diversity, the village women share a common belief system, customs *(adat)*, many values, and attitudes. They also share similar problems and rely on informal cooperative networks of women for assistance. All of them agree that being a wife and a mother are a woman's primary life goals. And they continue to see the "housewife only" as the most prestigious socioeconomic status for a woman although teacher and nurse now vie with it.

The village is the hub of their lives, the place where they spend most of their time. With increasing frequency, changes taking place in the larger society are affecting the village and the women in it: new economic opportunities, inflation, shifts related to agriculture, more education, and the introduction of television are a few. Such changes in the socioeconomic realm, as well as aspects of stability, are considered here.

Ethnographic Background

Every villager is Malay as defined in the Constitution of the Federation: a person who professes the Muslim religion, habitually speaks the Malay language, and conforms to Malay customs. In 1965–66 I was the only foreign resident in the area. By 1975 a five-member Canadian family and two American male Peace Corps volunteers were living in this village, and there were other temporary foreign residents nearby. None of these outsiders is included in the following numerical/statistical statement.

In 1965, there were 614 villagers in Rusila living in 134 households. By April 1975, 771 villagers resided in 165 households, with a range of from 1 to 9 persons per household. A majority of the households (68 percent, an increase of 7 percent since 1966) comprise nuclear families. Extended, polygynous, single-person, and subnuclear families account for the other 32 percent. The kinship system is cognatic, equal emphasis being accorded to mother's and father's kin.

The selection of a spouse for a young person of either sex continues to be a parental prerogative although changes are occurring in consequence of increasing education and new occupational opportunities for young people in urban areas.[2] Residence selection by newlyweds tends to be guided by economic opportunities. Recently, neolocal residence in or near urban areas has become an acceptable and increasingly chosen alternative.

A majority of the adults were born in the village; many others have points of origin within a ten-mile radius. People who were born here but now live elsewhere continue to have strong ties to the village. For an important ritual event such as a marriage or a funeral they arrive from many states of the Federation. And it is still usual for young women to return to their parents' homes for the birth of a first child.

Today, a government-trained midwife resides in Rusila. She is a capable woman who, knowing the limitations of her abilities, is not reluctant to request hospitalization in Kuala Trengganu, some eight miles away, for an expectant mother experiencing problems with a birth.

Many villagers are now willing to go to the hospital for treatment of minor as well as major ailments. The fears expressed in 1965 have abated. In part, people have been pushed into accepting alternative health care because there are no longer any local medical-magical practitioners *(bomoh)*. Postprimary education for increasing numbers of youngsters also contributes to attitudinal change.

A primary school was built in the village in 1952. Since that time almost all of the children from Rusila and two contiguous villages have attended it, sharply raising the literacy rate for the area. By 1975 almost all persons between the ages of 8 and 35 were literate. Children who complete the primary-school program can attend one of several secondary schools located between four and ten miles from the village. About half of them do so. The few who succeed at the secondary level may continue their studies in another part of the country with government financial assistance. Some of these young villagers have become teachers or medical-dental practitioners, or have taken other salaried jobs with the government or in the private sector.

The educated and the illiterate share a devotion to Islam. Adults, except menstruating women, observe the five prayer periods per day. Males above the age of twelve attend the Friday midday services at the mosque in the village. People vary in generosity, but all value the giving of food or money to the less fortunate. Everyone appears to observe Ramadan, the month of fasting, meticulously. And many adults express the hope that they will be able to make the pilgrimage to Mecca (the haj). The importance of the haj to the villagers is reflected in the respect shown to those who have performed this religious duty and by the growing numbers of individuals and married couples who have gone to Mecca not once but twice.

One Islamic practice, however, is coming under attack: polygyny. In 1965 many women privately expressed the view that they preferred divorce to a polygynous marriage. By 1975, young educated women openly expressed disgust with polygyny and the resulting economic burden for women who must share husbands with co-wives.

Besides the mosque, a prayer house, and the primary school, other public buildings in Rusila are a small community center and the *Medan Anyaman* (Weaving Center). The greater number of buildings in the community are privately owned homes. All houses are constructed of wood and elevated several feet from the ground, but there the resemblance ends. Some are small, rudely constructed, unpainted homes with thatched roofs and wooden shutters; some are spacious, painted dwellings with tiled roofs and glass windows; and there is a variety of intermediate types.

Differences existed in 1965, but the range was greater in 1975.

There is little change in the homes of the people at the low-income end of the spectrum, but among the more affluent there is elaboration in terms of more costly materials and construction by professional carpenters. Some of the latter homes have flower gardens around them and fences to discourage hungry herbivores. The only fences to be seen in 1965 surrounded rice seedling nurseries and fields. At that time no one grew flowers around a home.

The Household and the Village Economy

Each household in Rusila is a unit of production and consumption, but what is produced and consumed varies greatly from one to another. Two examples, each household composed of a married couple in their early thirties with four dependent children below the age of sixteen, illustrate some of the differences. Neither end of the local economic spectrum, the very poor household or the one supported by the salaries of two teachers, is represented.

Both couples have stable relationships. Their marriages were arranged by their parents and their weddings were celebrated with all of the appropriate festivities and rituals. Neither couple has ever been divorced nor have the husbands shown any overt interest in taking other wives.

Household A: Selmih and Rahman[3]

All income is from what is locally termed "village work" *(kerja kampung).* This family owns no rice land, but both husband and wife assist Selmih's parents in working their land. They are repaid with sufficient rice to last their family for two or three months. Selmih and Rahman jointly own and work on a plot of hillside land planted with tobacco, a cash crop recently introduced into the village. In addition, Rahman is a member of a fishing crew that works with a local owner-operator of a motorized boat, and Selmih prepares a rice snack that she hawks in the village each morning. Her eldest daughter, eleven, and Rahman, when he is at home, help by packaging portions. Selmih has above average skills as a weaver and makes pandanus mats for household use and for sale from a kinswoman's small shop.

The family's diet is usually well-balanced and consists basically of rice and fish with some vegetables and fruits. Fish is provided almost daily, except during the monsoon, by Rahman. Income allows for the purchase of other foodstuffs, including eggs about once per week. Meat, a luxury, is eaten only on special occasions. The two youngest children are allowed such daily snacks as ice cream obtained from passing vendors or fried bananas from a local shop. Rahman, like most village men, enjoys coffee and a snack with friends at a local shop most days.

Selmih and Rahman's home is small and simply constructed with few furnishings. It is located on land owned by Selmih's father. Although it is near the power lines that run through the village, the home does not have electricity. Selmih does all of her cooking over wood fires on a *dapu*, a boxlike structure packed with earth and raised on four legs to waist height. The family owns a treasured battery-powered radio.

All members of the family are more than adequately clothed. Selmih does some sewing for herself and her two daughters, using her mother's sewing machine. The school-age children have uniforms and sneakers; the younger ones wear rubber sandals and a variety of clothing. Although he prefers the comfort of the sarong (as most village men do), Rahman has western-style trousers and sport shirts for use as needed. He also owns an inexpensive wrist watch. Selmih wears Malay styles, casual or formal as the occasion merits. She has small, inexpensive, gold earrings—as do both of her daughters—and a heavy gold chain necklace that she bought with Rahman's approval after a particularly good fishing season several years ago. The fact that the chain has never been pawned says a great deal about this family's economic stability because gold jewelry is a wearable form of emergency funds. Rahman has a bicycle, which the eldest son also rides.

Household B: Mariam and Abdullah

Income is from Abdullah's wages as a blue-collar government employee in the town. He shares with siblings the ownership of two pieces of productive land. One piece is a beachfront property planted with coconut palms; the other, inland, is planted with rubber. During 1975 the price of rubber was so low that no one was tapping these trees. Mariam weaves mats, but only for household use and gifts.

All foodstuffs except coconuts are purchased. Compared with Household A, members of this family have a greater variety of protein foods in their diet. They eat chicken at least once each week, other meats occasionally, and eggs several times a week. But as in all local households, fish and rice are still the basic diet. The three children attending school outside of the village, one in an English-medium primary school, get snack money to take with them. The youngest child, of preschool age, is allowed to buy snacks from vendors. Abdullah takes a thermos of coffee to work and buys lunch from a wagon or shop in town.

Mariam and Abdullah's home is located on land given to him by his father at the birth of his and Mariam's first child. Their second child was a toddler before they could afford to begin building their home, which has been expanded as finances have allowed. It is now a spacious, solidly constructed house with glass windows, a stepped concrete porch, and a bathing room with the great luxury of piped water. In 1975 Abdullah was considering having a flush toilet installed indoors. If he does so it will be the first in the village. Household furnishings include a suite of "Danish modern" furniture in the living room, a television set and a radio, and in the kitchen, a refrigerator, a large dining table, and chairs. Mariam uses a kerosene stove for most of her cooking, but still has the *dapu* for baking cakes and roasting fish over wood embers.

The family's clothing is above average in quality and amount. Mariam sews some of her own things and makes clothes for her daughters. But many items for them as well as for Abdullah and the boys are purchased ready-made in the town or are ordered from tailors or seamstresses. Mariam and her daughters have gold jewelry. Even the littlest girl has earrings, a locket, and a bangle-bracelet. None of it has ever been pawned.

Abdullah uses a Honda motorcycle, and his sons share the use of a bicycle.

Comparisons

Household A is based on a more or less typical economic pattern of a traditional type. Both husband and wife engage in remunerative activities, some of which are cooperative although there is usually a division of labor along sexual lines. With regard to the growing of tobacco, for example, Rahman does the bulk of land preparation while Selmih plants the crop and tends it with some assistance from him. They work together to harvest it. If they are atypical it is in the very high degree of cooperation between them. When a broker comes to the village to buy tobacco, Rahman is the one who transports it to the weighing area and deals with the broker because Selmih is shy in dealing with people, especially men, from outside of the village—a not unusual situation for young traditionally oriented women. But in some families, particularly where the married couple is older, it may be the woman who deals with the broker.

Another typical aspect of this household is its dependence on several sources of income. Selmih's food sales and Rahman's fishing are the most important, but the other sources mentioned above help to keep the family out of debt during poor fishing periods and have allowed Selmih to keep her gold necklace out of the pawn shops of Marang or Kuala Trengganu.

Household B represents an economic pattern that is becoming more common as increasing numbers of young people in the village gain more education and qualify for wage-paying or salaried jobs. However, the wives of some wage earners are themselves employed for wages or do other income-producing work in the village. Mariam is atypical, one of ten village women who claim to be a "housewife only," a prestigious status discussed below.

Her husband is referred to as modern *(moden)* by neighboring women because he chooses to shop for meat or staples while he is in the town and he sometimes helps at home, for example, fixing his own breakfast. Mariam is considered lucky.

Housekeeping and Child Care

A woman's first responsibilities are to her husband and children, just as her primary goals in life are to be a wife and mother. Basically, a wife should "follow" *(ikut)* her husband, that is, do what he tells her to do. If he wants a meal at one o'clock in the morning, she should get up and fix it. Few men make such demands on a regular basis. Women give lip service to the idea of a wife "following," but in fact many of them are the leaders in their households, usually with some subtlety.

Women in all households are the financial managers; some are adept jugglers and wizards. The managerial role is integral to that of housekeeper.[4] Older widows and divorcees may have to be self-supporting, but most women have husbands who provide basic household income. A man is expected to support his family, and most men try to do so. Nevertheless, women must usually supplement their budgets with some of their own earnings while at the same time trying to save something.

Men generally keep what they will need for "coffee money" and transportation and give the rest of their earnings to their wives. Men acknowledge that women are superior to them in their ability to use money judiciously. Women gain the compliment, plus the burden of manipulating finances that may be inadequate for their family's needs.

Most men assume that their wives have secret savings hidden somewhere in the home, as is indeed a common practice. Such a cash cache is used by a woman to meet unexpected expenses. Perhaps a child needs a dollar for a special school fee or the license for owning a radio must be paid. Sometimes husbands borrow from their wives although it is equally likely that a wife will deny that there is any extra money or claim that her funds are exhausted. Years ago it was not unusual for a woman to keep even a large sum of money in the house. In 1965 a dying woman revealed the hiding place of several hundred dollars. Now, the woman who can accumulate such a sum is more likely to have an account at the Post Office, keeping only small amounts at home. However, as late as 1971, neither males nor females in a nearby village had opened Post Office savings accounts.[5]

Borrowing and lending between individuals who are kin or close friends is common and extends from money to household equipment to tools and bicycles. Neighboring women, who may also be kin, can usually rely on one another for such things as well as for assistance in occasional child care, in food preparation for ritual or other special occasions, and in emergencies of all types. However, the need for borrowing, lending, and offering or requesting assistance is not necessarily a daily occurrence. The experienced housewife is usually able to plan for her family's needs unless something unexpected occurs.

For a housewife who has small children, a more or less typical work day, except during the monsoon when strong winds and heavy rains may curtail activities, goes something like this:

She rises at around 5 or 5:30 A.M., bathes at the nearest well, and brings water to the house. She performs her morning prayers, rouses her family, and then prepares the first meal of the day or purchases something from an early hawker. Older children bathe and dress themselves and may also have the responsibility for some younger ones. After her husband and older children have eaten, she has her meal, probably after they have left for work and school, and feeds little ones who may have slept late.

She washes the dishes, puts all of the bedding outside to air, sweeps the floors, perhaps sprinkling water on them to lay any dust, and then collects the clothing and other things to be laundered. If she has a very young infant she will draw water and bring it to the house, washing her laundry in the kitchen. If her youngest children can walk, she will take them with her to the well and do the laundry there, probably in the company of other women performing the same chore. This can be a pleasant time of chatting and exchanging gossip despite the arduous chores of drawing water and hand-scrubbing clothes. When the laundry has been hung to dry she turns her attention to getting food for the midday meal.

Such staples as rice and spices are probably at hand but other foodstuffs will have to be obtained. She may buy eggs from a neighbor; perhaps there is fried fish left over from the evening before. Whatever the case, she will get and prepare the food so that it is ready when her children return from school. If her husband arrives much later she may cook for him separately.

When she has washed the dishes from the midday meal she will probably bring in the laundry, do any mending, and put the things away. Only rarely will she iron clothes because the iron must be heated over a fire. She also brings in the aired bedding and prepares the beds and other sleeping places. Older children, especially daughters, are expected to help with afternoon chores or to care for their younger siblings.

The main meal is served in the evening around seven or eight o'clock when everyone is usually at home. Hence the main job of securing foodstuffs takes place during the afternoon. Fish peddlers and other vendors pass through the village and are watched for, but a trip to the market at Marang may be necessary to buy some foodstuffs. Or perhaps a friend is going to Kuala Trengganu and will bring back the needed supplies.

All cooking is done on top of a one- or two-burner kerosene stove or a *dapu*. If the *dapu* is used, another chore for the housewife or for her older children is gathering fuel. The family generally eats its evening meal together unless there are guests. In that case, the men eat first and the women and children eat later. Cleaning up afterward is probably accomplished by about 9 or 9:30 P.M.

During the course of the day, more water will have been drawn from the well for cooking and washing dishes, for bathing young children before the evening meal, and for filling the water containers kept outside each door so that those entering may first wash their feet. If the family has an outdoor toilet, it will have been scrubbed. An infant is breast-fed and cuddled and other little ones are tended. Prayer periods are observed. If visitors stop by, they will be offered snacks and coffee if the family can afford it.

Occasional chores, those not done on a daily basis, include such activities as raking the yard and burning trash, scrubbing floors, cleaning prayer mats, removing the ashes from the *dapu*, shopping for staples in the town markets, scrubbing and whitening the children's school shoes, and a variety of other tasks.

Obviously there is variation from household to household, depending on the number of persons to be looked after and their ages. A woman whose children are all in school has much more free time during the day than a woman with an infant and children of preschool age. And the woman with older children gets assistance of various types from them, lessening the amount of work she must do.

A woman engaged in shopkeeping or agricultural work will have a much more crowded schedule or she may expect more assistance from her older children. The average woman will find some time during the day to weave and visit with neighbors, perhaps combining the two activities.

All things being equal, the woman with the most free time is the "housewife only" *(ahli rumah saja)*. Of the 158 able-bodied women in the village in 1975, ten (6 percent) claimed this status (see Table 1). A "housewife only" is not to be equated with the sometimes expressed western notion, "I'm only a housewife." To be a "housewife *only*" in a Malay village carries prestige; the statement is made with pride. A woman who can say this indicates that she does not have to engage in remunerative work; her husband provides adequately for her and their children. Her sole duty is to look after the family and their home. She is considered lucky.

Table 1. Occupational Status of Able-Bodied Adult Females

	1966		1975	
Occupation	*Number*	*Percent*	*Number*	*Percent*
Kerja Kampung (village work)*	125	92	143	91
[*Pandanus weaver*]*	[97]	[70]	[112]	[70]
Wage worker	2	1	5	3
Ahli rumah	10	7	10	6
Total	137	100	158	100

*Kerja Kampung includes pandanus weaving.

For the majority of local women, including several of the *ahli rumah saja,* household activities have undergone little modification since 1966. Labor-saving services and devices exist in the village, but most of them are beyond the means of the average family.

Electricity was introduced into the main area of the village in 1963. By 1966, it was found in 25 percent of the homes, but was used only for lighting and power for a few radios. By 1975, 41 percent of the houses had electricity and use had been extended to 15 television sets and 8 refrigerators. But electricity, because of the high cost of stringing wire to the inland hamlets, was still confined to those areas of the village near the power lines by the highway.

Water piped into the home is another service, first utilized locally in the early 1970s, and now enjoyed by six families. As in the case of the power lines, water pipes are near the highway, hence the homes that have this luxury are all near the highway. Only women whose husbands are wage earners have piped water in their homes. Of 5 adult female wage earners, only the teacher (whose husband is also a teacher) has this convenience. She also employs a housekeeper to do the family's laundry and other water-consuming chores.

The only appliances found in the village are kerosene stoves and refrigerators. The stoves have become common (there are now 78), in part because they are relatively inexpensive and in part because free fuel for *dapu* fires is said to be less readily available. The cost of a months' supply of prepared firewood is almost the same as that for kerosene during the same period, but kerosene has the advantage of being available at local shops, is less bother to use, and takes up little storage space. Nevertheless, all women do at least some of their cooking over wood fires and a majority continues to use them exclusively.

Refrigerators are a "dream appliance" to most village women, a luxury they do not expect to own. Any housewife recognizes the practicality of a refrigerator and is well aware of its high price. Time payments are possible but difficult to arrange for those without regular income. If funds are available for a major purchase, how will they be allocated? A refrigerator? Piped water? Or a television set?

The television sets found in the village are all of the large console type. The cost of a set is approximately the same as the cost of a refrigerator or of having water piped into a house near the pipeline and building a small bathing room. Most of the women who were interviewed expressed a preference for piped water or a refrigerator if only they had the money; most of their husbands and children opted for television. However, some of the children who were interviewed on a very hot afternoon thought of ice cream and cold drinks and hence of refrigerators.

All homes that have piped water and/or refrigerators also have television sets. Six additional homes have only television sets. These numbers seem to indicate that women have little to say in decision making. However, a realistic appraisal must also recognize a woman's elemental concern with the welfare of her family and their needs. Pleading children are difficult to ignore. And while a refrigerator or piped water will benefit a family, television will be appreciated by relatives, neighbors, and other friends and thus may raise the status of the owners in the community. A refrigerator or piped water might just arouse envy.

In 1966 there were no television sets, refrigerators, or piped water, and only two outdoor toilets were to be found in the village. Most people used the beach or the bush for their needs, allowing nature to dispose of waste. By 1975 a majority of homes had a nearby outhouse containing a gravity-flow toilet. These toilets make less demand on the clean-up capacity of the South China Sea but create another chore for the housewife. Toilets must be scrubbed and insects discouraged from taking up residence in the outhouses. And when the ground is waterlogged, gravity-flow toilets do not flow very well so the house-wife may be required to perform a plumber's work.

Another chore created for the housewife results from the intro-duction of "Danish modern" furniture into the village. In 1966 little furniture was used in most homes; a double bed and a standing clothes cupboard were most common. A few households had rattan tables and chairs, very practical in a tropical climate, but they were on the verandahs. Now, those who can afford it favor suites of "Danish modern"—a couch, two matching chairs, end tables, and a coffee table. Such furnishings are a status symbol and become a necessity if a family has a wage earner (everyone knows wage earners can afford furniture) or a child attending a postsecondary school (the child should not be ashamed to bring school friends home to visit). The furniture chores for the housewife include dislodging insects nesting between cushions and frame, dusting, and airing the cushions fre-quently. If she neglects the latter task, they mildew and acquire a very unpleasant odor.

The progression has been from sleeping mats to mattresses to additional stuffed furniture—more "woman's work" with each ac-quisition. Do women complain? No, they do not. They are proud to have modern furniture, to be able to entertain "town people" without apologizing. Social interactions with town people are becoming in-creasingly common as more villagers seek employment or education outside the village. And such furnishings are used by some families only when there are guests, a pattern similar to that found in some American households where family rooms get a great deal of use while "front rooms" are saved for visitors. Furniture upkeep is a relatively small investment for the return in feelings of pride.

Land Ownership

Women have always saved money when they could and have bought property or helped their husbands accumulate it. In the latter in-stance, during the past two decades, more women have insisted on their names appearing on the deeds, along with the husband's. Joint ownership of land by husband and wife is one indicator of a stable marriage of some duration. If a woman considers her marriage unstable, she will try to buy land in her own right rather than purchase it jointly with her husband. One woman borrowed money to buy a small piece of rice land from another villager rather than share ownership with her husband, although between them they had the money for the purchase. She later explained that he had already spoken two *talak,* the Muslim divorce formula; a third would mean an absolute divorce. If that happened, she did not want to have the land divided because the plot was small. Also, she knew of cases where land had not been divided equally even though the owners had invested equally. And once divorced from a man, it would be awkward for her to meet him or his next wife in the field.

Under Islamic law both females and males have inheritance rights with regard to the real property of a parent, a male being entitled to twice the amount his sister gets. Thus if a male decedent is survived by one son and one daughter, the son gets two-thirds of the property and the daughter one-third. This system eventually results in some odd arrangements, such as an instance where twenty people share the ownership, though not equally, of four coconut palms. It is possible for Muslims to make wills "with regard to one-third of their property only,"[6] but it is still unusual for villagers to make wills. They rely on customary practices about distribution and expect that accommodations will be made between siblings when dividing an inheritance. Joint exploitation of land is becoming more common because of government regulations that disallow partition of productive land below specified sizes. Or it may be decided that one person will work a piece of land while others receive a share of the produce. Individual need and location of the holding usually influence how and by whom such property is utilized.

"A widow will receive one-quarter of her deceased husband's estate if there was no issue, and one-eighth if there was."[7] The law is based on the assumption that a widow with children will receive needed aid from them. And because strong ties normally exist between a mother and her children, she does receive their aid more often than not. The woman with no children is in a more precarious position because one-quarter of an average village male's property may be very small indeed. Again, accommodations are usual. A man who would mistreat his brother's widow in a property division would have to live with a lot of negative gossip. Still, it can happen. And the fact that it can happen emphasizes the need for a woman's insisting that her name be on a property deed when she has worked and saved for the purchase of property along with her husband.

Agriculture and the Division of Labor
Rice is grown for family use; little, if any, is ever sold. Of all Rusila families, 74 percent grow some rice or receive it for work done on land owned by others; 26 percent must purchase all of the rice they

use. Only 15 percent of local families can grow or earn enough to meet their needs for a full year.

The sexual division of labor in rice production continues to adhere to traditional patterns although some means of production have shifted. Men repair the field embankments and prepare the land, but less often, with the hoes and buffalo-drawn plows common in past decades. Tractor-drawn disk-plows were being used in this village by eleven (17 percent) of all rice-field owners in the mid-sixties, and they have literally gained ground ever since.

But women's work here has not changed very much—yet. Transplanting rice seedlings and harvesting the ripe crop are still done by women, by hand. And it is women who perform all of the chores associated with processing harvested rice unless the rice is taken to a mill.

Between the time of land preparation and harvesting of the crop, some attention may be given to fertilizing fields with commercial fertilizers or with ashes and fish waste. This chore can be done by men or women. The crop here is not usually weeded although increasing government concern for bigger yields may focus more attention on this aspect of rice growing. Rice is a crop that responds to "tender loving care," that is, to more careful weeding, better use of fertilizers, and the like.[8]

One thing is clear: With present methods of work, women on the east coast put at least as much time into rice production as men do. This contrasts with estimates for the entire Malay peninsula (which presumably include those areas where men are engaged in reaping), that show female hours worked as only 45 percent (one annual crop) or 68 percent (multicropping) of male hours worked.[9] Here, there are variations by family and variations in terms of the use of hired labor for plowing, but the sexual division of labor has remained stable since 1965.

Cash crops include rubber, copra, vegetables and fruits, and recently, tobacco. During 1965–66, rubber was by far the most important. Both men and women participated in all stages of rubber production although most tappers and processors were male. The price of rubber on the international market had dropped so low by 1975 that few owners were tapping their trees.

Copra, in both 1965–66 and 1975, was a product that many families made on an occasional basis. Copra is dried coconut. It is made by a simple but laborious process. Usually men pick the nuts unless they have a trained monkey to do so or hire someone who has. After the nuts are collected, the division of labor usually breaks down like this:

males and females, teenagers as well as adults, may participate in the husking process or a man may be hired to do it; women or men open the nuts; men and boys usually stack them on the drying platform; everyone who is able collects firewood and tends the drying fire; women remove the meats from the shells; women and men set out imperfectly dried nutmeats for sun-drying; and both may collect and bag the dried coconut. Making copra is most often a family effort. Everyone who can work at a particular task is expected to help.

Raising vegetables was the occupation of several rice-growing families following the rice harvests during the 1960s, and others had hillside plots that were cultivated throughout the year. They provided variety and quality for the villagers, and women sold their surplus in the markets of Marang and Kuala Trengganu. Men prepared the land. Women planted the crops and weeded them on a regular basis. And when vegetables were ready for harvesting, it was usually women who picked them unless the crop was exceptionally large as in the case of yams. Other people grew fruits such as watermelons. By 1975 much of the land that had formerly produced greens, onions, garlic, chilies, beans, tomatoes, and tiny potatoes had been turned to tobacco production.

Tobacco is a big business, a business the government is encouraging in this village and many others in Malaysia. And the business is evidently great enough that men here were building drying sheds in 1975. The basic problem for growers thus far is that the leaf being produced is not of high quality and therefore income is less than it could be.

Fishing and Fish Processing

Fishing is a male monopoly just as any processing that is done is a female monopoly. In 1966, 31 of 134 adult able-bodied males considered fishing their primary occupation; other men participated as members of fishing crews occasionally or did some individual fishing from small boats or with nets from the shore. By 1975, fishermen numbered 40 of 150 able-bodied males in the village. Fishing continued to rank as the second most common occupation for males after agriculture, if all forms of agriculture were combined.

Most women do some fish processing. I do not refer to the daily preparation of fish for meals but to the preparation of a large number of fish or other seafood for purposes of preservation. Before the monsoon most women try to prepare dried, salted fish and prawn paste for the time when fishermen will be confined to the land because of heavy seas, the time when there will be no fresh fish or when what is available will be very expensive. And when catches are good at other times they do the same as an economizing measure.

For some men, fishing is an occupation on a more or less year-round basis. For a very large proportion of women, fish processing is part of the housewife's role.

Shopkeepers, Hawkers, and Salespeople

Shopkeepers and hawkers may be of either sex although there are cultural limitations on the types of goods sold. Shops that feature coffee and cooked snacks are the realm of women. I suggest three reasons for the predominance of women in local shopkeeping. First, because most shops are attached to homes or located near them, a woman can combine shopkeeping with looking after her household. Second, the belief that women are better at handling household finances than men is congruent with small-scale shopkeeping. And third, the view is expressed by both men and women that females are better able to be firm in dealings with one another while a man would be generous to women, or might be subject to their wiles. The latter idea supposedly would make it difficult for the male shopkeeper to be tough about prices for female customers while a male customer might not try to get a lower price from a female shopkeeper.

Male hawkers sell fresh fish and commercially prepared foods such as bread and ice cream. Some are local, but many who pass through the village are not.

Female hawkers are local (from this or a contiguous village), probably because they go on foot while male hawkers ride bicycles. They sell home-prepared foods. One woman basically supports herself and her aged mother by her sale of snacks. Selmih, referred to earlier, is not the only woman who adds to her family's income with such work.

There are also women who take goods, usually fabrics, on consignment from dealers in town and show them in their own homes or bring them to the residence of an interested person. The seller makes a small percentage on each sale; the buyer pays more than the town price but saves the time and expense of a trip to the town.

A new addition to the ranks of saleswomen operating in the village is the representative of an internationally known brand of goods, such as food-storage containers. During 1975 the few representatives were all town women who were married to men working for salaries. They arrive in the village by car, driven by their husbands, on the sabbath (Friday) when many people are at home. Relying on hospitality codes to assure them an invitation into local homes, they bring big cartons full of their wares, wares that are expensive and impractical for use by the average village housewife. They push and pressure a local woman to give a party for her neighbors during which the vendor can try to sell the particular brand, no money down, weeks and weeks to pay.

In 1975 Malay good manners combined with hardheaded common sense were dealing with this phenomenon. While the vendors were in the village on their initial visit, they were treated with the utmost courtesy and given vague promises that a party would be planned after neighbors had been consulted. Once the women and their samples were on their way back to Kuala Trengganu, the whole matter was discussed in practical terms, gossiped about, and dismissed. What will happen if the number of these representatives grows and they continue their bombardment of the village housewives or if their goods become defined as prestige goods—impractical or not— remains to be seen.

Entrepreneurs

Entrepreneurial activity on a small scale is common to village life. For example, a woman visiting another area will likely bring back goods or foodstuffs that are not found locally and offer them for sale at a small profit. In the recent past, women have operated such diverse businesses from their homes as making mattresses and the manufacture and sale of cement blocks. Shopkeepers, some hawkers, and local salespeople of all types are entrepreneurs, engaged in economic activities that are needed in the village.

Entrepreneurs in new economic areas are few because of the potential risks involved, especially if a sizable sum of money must be invested for an uncertain return. Villagers are not as conservative as they have been depicted by their urban contemporaries; they will utilize new means of production such as mechanized plows and experiment with new crops such as tobacco when there is some assurance of success with them. The margin for error, the few dollars which stand between being debt-free and pawning gold jewelry or going into debt, is extremely narrow for many families. Hence few can dare to face the insecurity of involvement with an economic unknown; few can save or borrow funds for investment in a new enterprise.

Some can and do. For example, Mohammed and Kulsum are a married couple in their late thirties. During 1965, Mohammed told me his occupation was lorry driver although he had not worked as one for several years. He had engaged in a variety of jobs; Kulsum earned money from weaving, sewing, sale of eggs and chickens, and other work. Their economic situation was precarious and it continued to be so for several years. Meanwhile the economic pace in the state accelerated. There was more demand for vehicles to transport goods of all types both within the state and between states.

Mohammed and Kulsum discussed the possibilities of going into the trucking business and got advice from Kulsum's educated younger brother and other relatives. The problem: money. Mohammed had recently inherited a share in a fishing boat and nets. He and his siblings decided to sell the equipment and divide the money, but his share was insufficient for a down payment on the desired truck. He could not borrow the money, perhaps because he has a reputation for being none too clever with managing it, as he readily admits. It was left to Kulsum, whose reputation is the opposite, to try to borrow the money. Taking her youngest child with her and relying on her mother to care for the rest of her family, she spent a month in Kuala Lumpur where she convinced a Chinese businessman to make the loan. Some years earlier she had served as his agent for the sale of cement well casings in the village, so he knew her to be reliable and, despite being illiterate, a careful account keeper with the help of her eldest son. He finally agreed to make the loan, on good terms, with only her name as surety. By 1975 the debt had already been repaid and during that year the last payment on the truck was made. Mohammed was kept busy with a fairly steady flow of requests to haul goods; Kulsum managed the finances. The family's income was not regular, but their economic position had improved to the point where Kulsum no longer engaged in remunerative work except pandanus weaving.

The important point in this example is Kulsum's ability to borrow several thousand dollars when Mohammed was unable to do so. In another family the situation could be reversed. A person's reputation for money management is more important than sex in effecting a loan, especially if one is not regularly employed for wages or salary.

Wage-Paying and Salaried Jobs

Most of the people from this village who are wage earners hold positions as government workers: teachers, crafts specialists, laborers, mechanics, office personnel, people involved in some aspect of health care, and policemen. The majority of these jobs are held by males. Village Malays tend to prefer employment by the government over jobs in the private sector because they provide greater security and more reliable fringe benefits.

In 1966, only two women residents, both employed at the Weaving Center, were earning wages, one as a clerk and the other as an instructor (see Table 1 above). By 1975 there were five adult female workers earning wages or salaries: a clerk-manager at the Weaving Center, a government-trained midwife, a secondary-school teacher, a craft instructor who teaches at a government training facility in Kuala Trengganu, and the clerk who works in the Kuala Trengganu police headquarters. There are additional salaried women from this village who live and work in other parts of the country, and there are a few young unmarried females, still living with their parents, who work as clerk, salesgirl, or "Mother's helper." While the number of local women earning regular income increased from 1 percent to 3 percent during the decade, the gain is hardly impressive. As of 1975, only the midwife and teacher earn more than M$200.00 per month. Throughout Peninsular Malaysia, only about 6 percent of all females working outside of the home earn above M$200 per month as compared with about 40 percent of all working males.[10]

The statistics must be examined in both rural/urban and older-illiterate/younger-literate contexts. The future looks economically hopeful for younger women who can gain the education necessary to qualify for a position that assures a reliable income. While female literacy is still "lagging behind the males" for all age groups in Malaysia,[11] impressive gains have been made during the past two decades. Locally, there has been more than a 9 percent increase in the number of females attending secondary and postsecondary educational institutions between 1966 and 1975.[12] Those who succeed educationally will become teachers and nurses or aspire to professions in which women are underemployed or not yet represented. But what of the older, illiterate woman or the young woman who does not continue her schooling beyond the primary level? A few of the younger ones have left the village for work in factories or as "mother's helpers" to women from their village who live in east-coast towns. But the majority, younger and older alike, are engaged in *kerja kampung* (village work) of one or more types. For them, handicraft production continues to be an important source of income.

Pandanus Weaving

Weaving has been referred to several times already. It is an activity from which a majority of women in this and nearby villages gain some income each month. It is a practical spare-time specialty that requires no cash outlay for materials beyond a few cents for dyes and no special equipment except what the weaver herself can make. It is a craft that can be practical year-round, indoors or outside. And it is highly congruent with the housewife and mother roles. It does require patience to master the necessary skills and hard work to gather and prepare the pandanus. It also requires time, but the hours necessary to complete a large mat can be allocated in segments from five minutes to several hours.

Both in 1966 and 1975, 70 percent of all women who did some work for remuneration stated weaving as their primary source, perhaps their only source, of personal income (see Table 1 above). The amount any woman can earn varies with her skill and the time she can devote to her craft.

The most expensive items that are commonly sold are prayer mats. A fine mat that measures up to 26 by 48 inches with as many as ten strands to the inch takes between 10 and 20 days of spare-time work to finish. In 1975, the modal price for a prayer mat was M$13.00, an increase of M$3.00 over the 1966 mode.[13] While in the process of weaving a prayer mat, a woman might also use some time to make smaller items such as fans or table mats. The point is that as of 1975 even a highly skilled weaver with a lot of free time cannot earn more than M$50 per month. However, even less money than that may be important if, as is true in a large majority of cases, the basic household income is below M$200.

In 1966, the Weaving Center was an important place for the weavers. It was not just a sales outlet but also had space where women could work and could store unfinished mats and baskets; there also, novices could receive both formal and informal instruction and help. The building had been opened by the government in 1957 and it was the government that encouraged teen-age girls to learn the craft by paying them fifty cents per day, later a dollar per day, to work there. Unfortunately, by 1975 the old building with its many functions had been replaced by a modern structure devoted almost entirely to sales. One woman and a teen-ager were still employed there, but the teaching of weaving had ceased.

Meanwhile a few other sales outlets have developed—small shops in Rusila and contiguous villages. And some women continue to deal with middlemen from Kuala Trengganu, men who supply stores as far away as Singapore. One Malaysian government agency also purchases, through the Weaving Center, woven goods to be sold from their tourist shops in Kuala Lumpur and Penang.

Demand for woven goods has grown since 1966, and outlets for them have increased. Women still work companionably with a friend or two on the verandahs of their homes; little girls learn the craft through observation and imitation of their mothers, as they did before. But the days are gone when 25 or more women might be found at the Center weaving, gossiping, and helping one another with handicraft technicalities or other problems.

Cooperation between Women

Cooperative relationships between women are important for the smooth functioning of daily life, especially when unexpected situations arise, and they are basic to the preparations for major ceremonial events.

Food is elemental and life-sustaining. Women prepare it several times each day for their families and use treat foods as a means for showing affection to their children. They offer something to visitors—a green coconut, fried yams, coffee and biscuits, or a meal. Newcomers to the village are welcomed with gifts of food. Food is used to celebrate a job promotion or the building of a new home, to thank those who helped to prepare the fields for planting, to dig a well, or to move a small home from one site to another. Food is important in the annual cycle of religious events, especially the Hari Raya observances following Ramadan.

Food is associated with all rites of passage: the seventh-month-of-pregnancy, ceremonies for infants, the circumcision of a son, the marriage of a child (especially a daughter), and the death of a family member. For these observances, not daily fare but special food is prepared.

Meat is essential to a meal accompanying a major celebration. The import of the event, the number of guests invited, and the social status of the hosts determine whether chicken, goat, beef, or buffalo is provided. For a wedding, beef or buffalo and sometimes both are offered.

Whatever is served, at any of these events, women will have worked to prepare it. Even in the case of marriage feasts, where men actually cook the meat, it is women who prepare all of the spices and determine how tasty the finished dish will be.

When a woman is faced with preparing a major ceremonial meal, she calls upon her kinswomen and neighbors for help. They give foodstuffs, time, and effort according to the degree of kinship—mothers and daughters are usually especially helpful to one another—and social indebtedness to the person requesting assistance or out of a desire to build a reciprocal relationship. Everyone keeps mental accounts of what has been given and accepted, who owes and is owed. This is not to suggest that women make crass calculations; rather, there is a rule of generalized reciprocity operant; give and

take should roughly balance through time. A woman who is habitually
stingy may find herself without help when she needs it, and the one
who has been generous is treated generously.

A woman who has given her time and efforts, has donated
foodstuffs, has baked cakes, and has prepared spices for curries
during a period of a few years without needing help in return can
build a backlog that may meet most of the needs for even a large feast.
An example was reported to me in 1975 by one woman with a
reputation for generosity and hard work. Approximately one
thousand people had attended her daughter's marriage feast a few
years before. The prefeast gifts of food (eggs, sugar, rice, flour,
coconuts, and other edibles) that she received were enough for all of
the feast needs except meat, but gifts of money from the guests were
almost equal to the cost of the cow and the water buffalo that had
been slaughtered for the occasion. While talking about that feast in
1975, the hostess was still feeling the prestige of a woman who could
plan and prepare such an event at small expense to her household,
the satisfaction of having been able to activate so many social obligations, and the pleasure of knowing that several years after the event
her daughter's wedding feast was still being used as a measure against
which similar feasts were being evaluated. This is an unusual case;
most families would have to meet a greater amount of the expenses
incurred.

What I wish to emphasize here is the reciprocity between women,
reciprocity that includes time, effort, and money or food gifts.[14]

No woman could hope to make all of the preparations for a major
ceremonial or social event by herself. Some preparations may require
the assistance of only one or two persons; others demand the cooperation of many women.

For example, during 1975, Rohimah's eldest son married a young
woman from a distant town. He and his wife did not want the
traditional, formal "viewing of the bride" (*tengok menantu*) at his parents' home, but they did agree to attend an informal gathering there.

Rohimah had not previously had to manage the planning and
preparations for such an event. She called upon her neighboring
sister-in-law and an older cousin who had the necessary experience.
They decided upon cakes and beverages, as the appropriate refreshments (refreshments traditionally offered at the *tengok menantu*),
calculated the number of guests, and figured the necessary ingredients: amounts of flour, eggs, sugar, and other things for two
hundred cupcake-size cakes and thirty large ones; beverages—
whether hot or cold, either requiring lots of sugar; numbers of brass
baking molds, serving dishes, and other kitchen equipment. All of this

was done by mental calculation because none of the three women is literate.

Further discussion involved which utensils might be borrowed from whom, which women could be called upon for foodstuffs, and who would come to mix the batter and bake the cakes. Two of her friends agreed to gather the cooking utensils; Rohimah visited all of the women whom she asked for ingredients or assistance. Some repaid debts to her; with others she became indebted.

Altogether, eighteen females, not all of them living in Rusila, ranging in age from 12 to 65, were involved in the preparations. Three loaned cake molds or plates and tumblers only; others were active in all phases. Just baking the cakes over outdoor fires involved nine women for varying periods of time during the entire day before the party. Several youngsters of both sexes were kept busy gathering fuel. Most active, including all levels of participation, were Rohimah's sister-in-law (planning, borrowing from other women, loaning her own utensils, preparing and supervising the preparation of cake batter, baking and supervising that process). In decreasing order of involvement were the sister-in-law's mother, Rohimah's eldest daughter, a first cousin, a neighbor who is not a kinswoman, two nieces, a neighbor who is also a third cousin *(tiga pupu)*, another sister-in-law, and two friends who live nearby. Other friends from this and a contiguous village and an older sister who lives four miles away completed the work force. Rohimah's mother offered encouragement and was interested in the proceedings at various stages, but being enfeebled by a recent illness she was not expected to take an active part in the work.

This example is more or less typical of the cooperative patterns extant in food preparations for any event where fifty or more people are expected to be guests. Women with expertise who are kinswomen and/or close friends are asked for advice unless the hostess is already experienced. And they, or other knowledgeable women, help supervise novices. Any woman who owns needed utensils, such as cake molds, will lend them. Those who owe the hostess food debts will try to make repayment. Kinswomen, including in-laws, will probably be the most active participants in the preparations, particularly if they live nearby and can tend to their own households' needs periodically throughout a baking or cooking day.

Events to which fewer people are invited require less preparation and the participation of fewer women. A family celebrating a son's job promotion might invite only close kin and neighbors to dine on goat curry. In that case the hostess, with the help of one or two others, could make all the preparations.

Reciprocity between women is important not only for special food preparations but for easing the day-to-day demands of child care, obtaining food for daily meals, aiding the ailing, or work such as rice processing. The expertise of some women is valued by others for planning and preparing celebratory meals and also for dealing with anything requiring special skills, such as weaving problems.

A woman's degree of involvement in cooperative networks with others depends on a number of factors such as her marital status, the number of her children, her involvement in remunerative work of various types, her religiosity, and her personality. But the structure of village life is such that no woman is isolated and left to confront problems—major or minor—alone.

Conclusion

Modernization trends were already affecting the village in 1965. The national and state civil-service bureaucracies, the systems of suffrage and representation, and political parties[15] all had some impact. Female and male villagers over the age of 21 could vote in elections. Some regularly dealt with a variety of civil servants in myriad government bureaus. Mechanization, specialization in cash crops, purchase of nonagricultural products in the market, and differentiation in the social structure due to increased occupational diversification were under way or well established.[16] Formal education, literacy, and increased use of printed media had been growing since the establishment of the primary school in 1952.[17]

By 1975 some of these trends had become stronger and a greater number of women were being affected by them. The two most obvious are formal education and literacy. These had had the most far-reaching repercussions on women's lives. However, most of the women who have been successful at or beyond the secondary level of schooling have moved to urban areas.

One basic value continues to be shared by Rusila-born women of all ages regardless of education or current place of residence: the primacy of marriage and children in a woman's life. Despite modernizing trends, a majority of these women are engaged in traditional occupations. They combine their central wife/mother roles with being rice producers, hawkers, shopkeepers, or weavers—all of which are extensions of the central roles: producing rice, cooked food, and household products or selling them to others. Work patterns in these and other occupations of long standing continued almost unchanged between 1966 and 1975.

The major shifts in agricultural involvement locally are in cash crops. Rubber production during 1975 was almost at a standstill, but tobacco growing had been introduced. As a result, vegetable production had decreased, a fact that might have long-term effects on local diets. Copra continued to be produced in 1975 as it had been in 1965, as occasional work by a number of families when the price was high.

Rice remains the agricultural product that involves the most people. Changes that are taking place nationally—multicropping rather than single cropping, increased use of mechanized means of land preparation, and harvesting by means other than the hand-knife—are, or will be, affecting local methods. Since rice harvesting in some parts of the country has become men's work, the same shift may occur locally. And while some women still process their rice using mortars and pestles and winnowing trays, many have their rice milled at a mill run by a man.

Transplanting rice is backbreaking work and reaping is tedious and can be very unpleasant because of the leeches in the wet fields. Thus some women might welcome being replaced by men with scythes or machines. But for the women whose labors earn rice for their families such a change could be disastrous. An alternative would be to involve women in the new mechanization. Typically, however, it is men who learn to use mechanical equipment while women continue to use traditional means of agricultural production.

"The productivity gap tends to widen because men monopolize the use of the new equipment and the modern agricultural methods."[18] Where mechanization becomes dominant women may be pushed entirely out of an economic field they once dominated.

Weaving continues to be important to local women as an activity from which they can earn monthly, if small, amounts of income. The demise of the Weaving Center as a multipurpose facility eliminated a gathering place for the weavers and stopped some experimentation with the craft that working together had encouraged. But its function as a sales outlet has continued in the new, modern building. Other outlets have opened, small shops here and in neighboring villages. No woman has a problem with selling a competently made mat or basket. However, when the peak of individual productivity is reached, increased income is impossible unless goods can command higher prices.

The modal price for a prayer mat increased from M$10.00 to M$12.00 during the past decade. But inflation has escalated the prices of necessities by a greater percentage. For example, during 1965–66, the highest price reached by rice of the top quality used for daily meals *(beras)* was M$2.40 per *gantang* (eight pounds, milled) in May 1966. In June, it dropped back to M$1.80, where it had been for most of the year. Several years later, in February 1975, rice of the same quality cost M$3.80 per *gantang,* an increase of 100 percent over the average cost during 1965–66. During the same decade sugar, an essential ingredient in all beverages, rose from 35 cents to 65 cents per *kati* (one and one-third pounds).

Quite obviously, income from weaving has not kept pace with the rising cost of living. Increasing foreign tourism on the east coast, already being encouraged by the government in 1975, could help to rectify the imbalance, assuming that tourist demand for woven goods is great enough. Then the new Weaving Center should prove its worth if primacy of place is given to local crafts rather than to silver work from Kelantan, aboriginal wood carvings, and Bornean bead-work.

Malaysians from other parts of the country were and are the primary tourists in this area. In 1965, during August, a peak month for Malaysians to be traveling, the old Weaving Center grossed M$2890.90, mostly from sales to nationals. Over M$1000 worth of woven goods were sold during other summer months, balanced by very low sales (M$239.90 in January 1966) during the monsoon period.[19]

The beautiful beaches of the east coast, some of the finest in the world, are definitely a tourist attraction—for Malaysians and for-eigners alike. And as facilities expand and attractions are elaborated, the number of foreigners can be expected to increase—for better or worse. For the weavers, given the propensity of tourists to purchase easily portable and "typical" handicraft items, the trend should be in the "better" category.

As previously noted, households vary as units of production and consumption, but in most of them both male and female adults make an economic contribution and each may engage in several types of work. This pattern is long established. For most work there is a sexual division of labor although cooperation between husband and wife in various activities is also found. Women are the financial managers in all households—the degree of juggling and a woman's own monetary contribution essentially depending on a husband's earnings. Secret savings are still common and give women some manipulative power in their households—giving or withholding loans to husbands, using money for their own ends. It is notable that in 1975 more women had Post Office savings accounts than in 1965–66. Women do save money to buy land or household furnishings and other things, and several have been able to make the haj to Mecca, with or without a husband, as a result of their own financial acuity.

The home is traditionally the woman's province; she expects assistance from her older children, especially daughters, but not from her husband, except in unusual circumstances. She is the one who makes decisions about household matters. A disadvantage of the few "modern" husbands who help at home and do much of the necessary shopping in the town is that women might have fewer contacts outside the village and be subject to more male influence within the home. The "housewife only" *(ahli rumah saja)* admittedly has prestige because her husband is a breadwinner *par excellence,* but in gaining prestige she has lost some of her controls in household decision making. On the other hand, she is the housewife who is most likely to be enjoying new services (piped water) and time-saving appliances (refrigerators).

The average housewife is still doing the same chores in almost the same way that her mother did them. It is doubtful that the average family presently living in Rusila will enjoy either piped water or a refrigerator in the next decade. But the probability is great that such services and appliances will become more common in the village. If more wage and salary workers settle here, either young educated villagers or people from the towns, they will expect to have services and appliances. There was already a housing shortage in Kuala Trengganu in 1975, and there were few areas for new construction. Hence people working there were beginning to look for homes in nearby villages. I assume that this trend will continue and soon encompass villages even further away than the one under consideration here. Some of the resulting changes are predictable; others at present seem unclear.

Predictably, as middle-income families move into the village, more well-constructed homes will be built. The differences between families who are well off and those who are barely subsisting will become more pronounced.

It is also likely that service personnel will be in demand by middle-class families. In 1975, gardeners were employed at the school and the Weaving Center; a man who worked as a mechanic for the government earned extra money doing the same work near his home on weekends. The female school teacher and the Canadian family employed village women as housekeepers, an occupation that is viewed positively by local women.

Most older women and some younger ones with no other economic hopes would be delighted to have jobs as housekeepers. A small but regular income is assured, one can usually expect to be treated like a member of the family if working for Malays, and there are numerous perquisites: having one's meals, taking extra food home, being given household items and clothing that are no longer wanted. Castoffs are not in the same category as new things one has chosen, but they are gladly accepted. During 1975, the housekeeper for the Canadian family received a large quantity of used children's clothing as well as some kitchen utensils and other household goods. Other women envied her good fortune.

A village is a community, a place where everyone knows everyone else, and where everyone depends on a supportive social network. Even if an influx of nonvillage families occurs, it seems doubtful that living patterns will change for the average villager.

Patterns of cooperation have been strong between women for as long as anyone can remember. The strongest ties continue to be those between mothers and daughters, a pattern that has led some mothers to oppose advanced education for a daughter for fear of losing her to an urban job. But the many ties, of blood and friendship, between women within the village and beyond, remain rooted in traditional values. They might be disrupted traditionally by disagreement and recently by the demands of education and jobs in another part of the country but they continue nevertheless to be strong.

New economic opportunities may become available to village women and shifts of authority or power within their households, based on economic contributions, may affect their abilities to influence their families, but women's cooperative networks that have economic, social, religious, and political components can be expected to continue. They may even be elaborated as a protective device in the face of an influx of outsiders or instead provide the fundamental device for involving new families in village life.

Notes

1. Research was conducted over fourteen months during 1965–66 and was sponsored by Fulbright Fellowship FH–4–89. Five months were spent in the field during 1975, made possible by the Faculty Academic Study Program at Rutgers, the State University of New Jersey. In Malaysia, the help I received from Abdullah Malim Baginda during the first research period and from Fred Dunn during the second was invaluable. But nothing could have been accomplished without the generosity, assistance, and kindness from the people of the village about which I write. Finally, my thanks to Kenneth R. Anderson, Jane Dorn, Cynthia Enloe, Jacqueline Nanry, and Christine Wilson for reading the first draft of this chapter and offering me many splendid revision suggestions. Since this report was organized in 1975, my references to "now," "today," "recently," and the like, are as of 1975.
2. Heather Strange, "Continuity and Change: Patterns of Mate Selection and Marriage Ritual in a Malay Village," *Journal of Marriage and the Family* 38, no. 3 (August 1976): 561–571.
3. Names used in this chapter are all common Malay names, but the people who comprise my main examples do not bear them.
4. The same pattern is reported by MiMi Khaing in a paper, "Women in Burmese

Economic Life," presented at the Association for Asian Studies in Toronto in March
1976; by Robert Youngblood for the Philippines in "Female Dominance and Adoles-
cent Filipino Attitude Orientation," *Journal of Asian and African Studies* 12, 1977; by
Judith Djamour for Malays in Singapore in *Malay Kinships and Marriage in Singapore*
(London: Athlone Press, 1965), pp. 41–42; by Rosemary Firth for Malays in other parts
of Malaysia in *Housekeeping among Malay Peasants* (New York: Humanities Press, 1966),
pp. 26–27; and by Hildred Geertz for Java in *The Javanese Family* (New York: Free Press
of Glencoe, 1961), pp. 124–125.

5. Personal communication from Christine Wilson, 15 April 1977.

6. The Federation of Family Planning Associations, Malaysia, *Women Today in
Peninsular Malaysia*, 1976, p. 35.

7. Ibid., p. 35.

8. Clifford Geertz, *Agricultural Involution* (Berkeley: University of California Press,
1963), p. 35.

9. Ester Boserup, *Women's Roles in Economic Development* (London: George Allen and
Unwin, 1970), p. 25.

10. Federation of Family Planning Associations, p. 20.

11. Ibid., p. 20.

12. Forty-four percent of females between the ages of 13 and 21 attended secondary
and postsecondary educational institutions in 1975 compared to 35% in 1966. See
Heather Strange, "Education and Employment Patterns of Rural Malay Women in
1965–1975," *Journal of Asian and African Studies* 2, 1977.

13. The value of Malaysian dollars in terms of United States dollars has fluctuated
between and during the research periods, from more than M$3.00 = U.S.$1.00 to less
than M$2.50 = U.S.$1.00. For many things, there is rough equivalency in purchasing
power of the currencies in the respective countries.

14. In "Continuity and Change" I discussed the ritual, social, and economic aspects
of ceremonial events in some detail. See also Heather Strange, "The Weavers of Rusila:
Working Women in a Malay Village," unpublished Ph.D. dissertation, New York
University, 1971.

15. See Neil Smelser, "Modernization of Social Relations," in Myron Weiner, ed.,
Modernization: The Dynamics of Growth (New York: Basic Books, 1966), p. 111.

16. See Neil Smelser, "Toward a Theory of Modernization," in George Dalton, ed.,
Tribal and Peasant Economics (New York: Natural History Press, 1967), pp. 30–33.

17. Bernard Berelson and Gary A. Steiner, *Human Behavior: An Inventory of Scientific
Findings* (New York: Harcourt Brace Jovanovich, 1964).

18. Boserup, p. 53.

19. It was not possible to get comparative figures for mats and basketry in 1975
because sales of all goods were included in any day's gross.

6   Women in Indonesian Politics: The Myth of Functional Interest

Stephen A. Douglas

> Because Indonesian women are different from all other
> women, Indonesian women portray the spirit of
> Indonesia. One cannot describe Indonesian society
> without knowing the Indonesian woman.—Sukarno[1]

Traditional Views of Women in Indonesia

In spite of stereotypes deriving largely from China and India, most
Southeast Asian societies traditionally have accorded a high degree of
freedom and respect to their female members. Generally, the Southeast Asian woman is a busy and confident manager of her family, and
often she is a more active participant in community life than is her
husband. Of course there is substantial variation from society to
society, but in the majority of Southeast Asian social systems—and this
fact has come as a surprise to most Western observers—there is an
absence of norms that severely proscribe the opportunities and status
of women.[2]

Just as the area as a whole includes ethnic and cultural groups that
vary in terms of the position of women, Indonesia, the most populous
Southeast Asian nation, consists of numerous cultural communities,
some of which are considerably less egalitarian in their treatment of
the sexes than others. In fact, the country is so culturally diverse that
an article of moderate length simply cannot treat the full range of
cultural standards and their impact on any particular dimension of
social or political life.

The foregoing generalization concerning the status of women in
Southeast Asian societies, as it applies to Indonesia, affords a good
vehicle for explanation of the treatment of the ethnic or cultural
variable in this chapter. In the first place, the fact of cultural variation
is undeniable. The *adat* (customary law) of the matriarchal society of
the Minangkabaus in West Sumatra obviously differs in its regard for

the rights and obligations of females from the *adat* of, say, Lampung, Tapanuli, or Bali, all of which allocate most property rights to men only. Beyond this kind of extremely broad comparison, however, it is difficult to specify the nature and degree of variation in women's political participation attributable to cultural influences. Part of this difficulty stems from the incomplete and dated character of the scholarly literature on the *adat* as it relates to sex roles. The more important point is that in Indonesia, as in most transitional sociopolitical systems, different levels of loyalty and activity, which might be called local, regional, and national, are not neatly interrelated and mutually reinforcing. In the case of women's social and political status, the consequence is that the *adat,* important as it might be in the thousands of relatively isolated villages throughout the country, should not necessarily be expected to be of direct relevance to political behavior at the national level.

For the most part, there is little indication that *adat* prescriptions have shaped the views of educated, nationally oriented Indonesians toward women in politics. Most of the men and women interviewed in the course of researching this chapter identified in some degree with an ethnic group, but expressed both lack of interest and uncertainty about the customs of their own ethnic groups as these related to women's rights and obligations.[3] Standards of behavior more relevant to these urbanized citizens are rooted in the content of their (and perhaps their parents') Western-style education rather than the steadily receding *adat.* Although such people constitute a minority of the population, clearly they dominate the national political process. Furthermore, although parochial and regional influences obviously are caught up in national politics in complex and important ways, this study is concerned primarily with government and politics at the national level.

This national focus does not suggest that *adat* norms have no significance in determining opportunities and actual participation of Indonesian women in national politics. It may be true, as argued above, that traditional attitudes toward women are not *directly* carried over into the modern politics of bureaucracies, parties, and differential economic interests in the capital and other urban centers. On the other hand, popular and preferred thinking regarding the role of women in Indonesia provides an excellent example of the selective utilization of the *adat* in the formulation and propagation of a sociopolitical myth—a myth not in the sense of an erroneous belief, but rather in the sense of a belief widely enough shared and highly enough valued that it helps integrate the political culture. The point is not merely that most Indonesians feel that both sexes should be accorded equal treatment and respect. The more interesting (and mythical) feature of popular thought on this topic is the belief that the norm of equality has been realized in government and politics, the belief that Indonesian women do in fact have opportunities for extensive and meaningful political activities and, further, that they have exploited these opportunities.

The belief in female activism and participation is not shared by all, however. There are cynics and skeptics, and there is a need for repeated legitimation and confirmation. It is at this point, consistent with the general tendency of nationalists in postcolonial societies to infuse national ideology with concepts and language derived from the indigenous culture, that political spokespersons invoke tradition and *adat*.[4] In a series of lectures to trainees in the Ministry of Foreign Affairs, one prominent woman claimed, "Aside from the general fact that the position of women according to the *adat* of each region was completely independent, we should also note that women became good kings, regional chiefs, and so forth."[5] The first part of the statement is misleading. In fairness it should be noted that the lecturer subsequently gave a more detailed and realistic appraisal of variations in *adat* as it applied to the sexes. In general, however, the oversimplified comment regarding women's independence under *adat*, along with some mention of female leaders, represents typical ways in which Indonesians explain the high degree of social and political participation of women today. Cultural communities in which young girls were bought and sold as brides and in which women had no property rights whatsoever are conveniently ignored.

A survey of traditional orientations toward women does seem to suggest that there is a basis for social and political equality and participation of Indonesian women. The *adat*, with some exceptions, generally sanctions an egalitarian approach to sex roles. The emancipation of Raden Adjeng Kartini, a young Javanese heroine, from what she and more recent writers have seen as an alien, Dutch-inspired system of discrimination against girls and women is regarded as the beginning of a movement and tradition that began at the turn of this century.[6] And the religious mythologies, especially of Java, furnish an ethical basis for female activism.

This sort of argument can never be entirely convincing, however. One must maintain at least two reservations. First, there are limitations on the generality of these proposed forces for progressive treatment of the sexes. There are areas in which the *adat* is quite unfavorable to women, other areas in which Kartini's solution of practical schools for girls has yet to be attempted, and models of feminine behavior other than Srikandi in the *wayang* stories.

Of all the female characters in the *wayang,* Srikandi is the one whose name is most often invoked in discussions of the capabilities and disposition of Indonesian women. In *wayang* mythology Srikandi is the wife of Arjuna, perhaps the most nearly perfect male figure. Yet in spite of Arjuna's awesome qualities that make him irresistible to all women, Srikandi is vigorously independent. She is a competent warrior whose life is so exciting that some commentators, including Sukarno, suggested that Srikandi probably was a male in an earlier version of the story.

Regardless of that possibility, there is no confusion now with regard to her sex and her behavioral attributes. As Benedict Anderson has put it, "For the Javanese, Srikandi is the honored type of the active, energetic, disputatious, generous, go-getting woman."[7]

Second, none of these features of traditional cultural patterns are directly indicative of the actual attitudes and behavior of men and women in contemporary Indonesia. The same could be said of an exegesis of Islamic doctrine as it applies to the social position of women. Most Indonesians are quick to point out that restrictive treatment of females in Near Eastern Muslim societies is the manifestation of cultural standards not inherent in Islamic doctrine and that, excepting the thorny issue of polygyny, Islam is more just and egalitarian in its pronouncements on status and treatment of the sexes than are the other major world religions.[8]

The point is, however, that exegesis of doctrine, or legend, is inadequate when one's objective is an understanding of behavior. A detailed analysis of Sukarno's speeches would disclose a massive hortatory exploitation of all elements of traditional culture that enhance the status of women. Clearly this was an effort on his part to mobilize as much support as possible from the feminine half of the population. The facts that much of Sukarno's elaborate ideology now has been thoroughly discredited and that women displayed no particular inclination to preserve "guided democracy" when it began to collapse demonstrate the lack of any necessary link between tradition (treated-as-doctrine) and behavior.

Tradition in itself may provide a sort of framework within which sex roles evolve, but it cannot explain the role of women in contemporary Indonesia. This explanation requires a more direct examination of norms pertaining to women's social and political participation and of the forms which that participation has taken.

A Survey of Attitudes toward Women and Traditional Values

As a mode of investigation, the sample survey affords more direct evidence of relevant attitudes and values, making it a useful supplement to studies of a literary or structural nature. The quantity and quality of social research of this type in Indonesia is limited, however; only one survey bearing directly on the question of perceptions and evaluations of sex roles has been completed. However, it was confined to a specific region and ethnic group.[9] The sample consisted of 1500 rural residents of West Java, and cannot be regarded as representative of any larger population. On the other hand, the respondents were drawn from five types of living area—remote agricultural, agricultural with access to urban centers, agricultural with light industry, fishing and coastal, and estate. Thus it would be difficult to demonstrate that the sample was especially biased or unrepresentative of the agrarian segment of Indonesia's population.

The results of the survey provide a reasonably accurate profile of the views of one of the most traditional sectors of Indonesian society. Assuming that modernization brings with it a more liberal set of

Table 1. Area of Choice in Which Parents Have Most Right to Decide for Their Children and to Expect Obedience*

	For Male Children	For Female Children
Occupation**	16.2%	12.3%
Education	18.3	16.9
Religion	45.0	44.4
Spouse Selection	10.2	16.6
Morals	2.4	2.4
All areas of choice	4.7	4.5
No areas of choice	2.2	1.7
Total	99.0%	98.8%

*Figures given in this and the following six tables are percents of the total sample of 1500 respondents. The percents usually do not add up to exactly 100 because of unrecorded "don't know" and "no answer" responses and because of multiple answers by some respondents.

**This category seems to refer to chores and part-time work of various types by young people, as well as to career selection.

Table 2. Steps that Should Be Taken against a Disobedient Child

	Male Child	Female Child
Initiate legal proceedings	3.4%	3.1%
Force, coercion	5.4	6.8
Advice and persuasion	86.0	86.0
Simply drop the matter	2.8	1.8
Total	97.6%	97.7%

Table 3. Obligations of Children to Help Support their Parents*

	Of Son	*Of Daughter*
Obligated if child has a job	64.2%	45.2%
Not obligated if child is married	7.7	12.5
Obligated if parents are destitute	9.5	13.7
Not obligated if child is poor	9.3	14.9%
Total	90.7%	86.3%

*Apparently the respondent was expected to select the alternative that he liked best or felt was the most important determinant, disregarding the fact that the reasons given for obligation and nonobligation are not mutually exclusive.

Table 4. Best Age for Entry into School

	For Boys	*For Girls*
5 years old	3.9%	4.5%
6 years old	25.9	25.1
7 years old	52.3	53.7
8 years old or over	18.3	16.1
Total	100.4%	99.4

Table 5. Best Age for Child to Stop Attending School

	For Boys	*For Girls*
12 to 15 years old	2.8%	19.5%
16 to 19 years old	4.9	9.8
20 years old	6.3	6.5
Depends on child's capabilities	85.2	70.7
Total	99.2%	106.5%

Table 6. Best Type of School for Child to Attend

	By Boys	*By Girls*
General public school	32.2%	20.9%
Vocational school*	19.8	22.7
Religious school	11.1	11.1
Depends upon omens	31.1	36.7
Other	4.8	6.1
Total	99.0%	97.5%

*Includes teacher-training schools for high-school level.

Table 7. Optimum Terminal Level of Formal Education

	For Boys	For Girls
Grade school	2.7%	10.6%
Junior high school	2.9	8.6
Senior high school	5.9	7.6
University or other tertiary-level institution	11.1	6.7
Depends upon child's capabilities	75.9	64.2
Total	98.5%	97.7%

values relating to the rights of women, the attitudes of farmers and fishermen of West Java should represent a sort of baseline against which changes can be measured. If this is the case, the 1967 survey reveals strikingly little room for improvement. As shown in Tables 1 to 7, the baseline that the survey establishes appears to be relatively free from any sharp and persistent pattern of discrimination against young girls and women.

Without commenting in detail on the data in Tables 1 through 7, the most accurate general conclusion is that responses are quite similar for boys and girls. They are especially similar for questions involving standards of obedience and punishment. Opinions about the age at which children should begin their formal schooling also do not vary with the sex of the child. Other questions about education evoke less thoroughly egalitarian responses: A small number feel that girls should not stay in school as long as boys, and there is a tendency to see general education as more appropriate for boys than for girls. In each of these cases, however, the category of responses most frequently selected applies to both sexes. Substantial majorities feel that the age and level at which the formal education of a child should be terminated should be determined by the capability and, presumably, the performance of the child. As for the selection of the type of school a child should attend, it is interesting that parents are slightly more inclined to base this decision for their daughters on signs and omens than for their sons. But the facts are that this difference is slight and that signs and omens apparently play a major role in this kind of parental decision regardless of the child's sex.

Admittedly, these data cover only a limited part of the range of values and norms that would be relevant to this inquiry. For example, it would be helpful to have information on relative degrees of independence deemed appropriate for boys and girls, approved roles for boys and girls in the home and community, extent of participation by children of each sex in family decisions, and the like. In the absence of such information, however, the available data provide at least some insight into the real meaning of the prevailing myth of equal treatment of the sexes in Indonesia. While equal treatment has not been realized in the area of occupation and career, in the minds even of people in very traditional parts of the country the worth and potential of women and girls is generally assessed as highly as that of men and boys.

The Role of Women in the Nationalist Movement

As the Dutch East Indies entered the twentieth century, the ingredients were present for a feminist movement in which women, at least some classes of women in some areas, would consciously seek to improve their status by organizing to compete for roles, including political ones, that society tended to allocate to men. The colonial experience up to that time had gradually introduced a new set of roles, mostly administrative and economic, that were both highly prestigious and exclusively male. To the elite or socially mobile Indonesian woman the process of acculturation, while it meant participating in a more universal and probably a more intellectually satisfying set of values, paradoxically meant a loss of the independence and status that the *adat* and traditional norms had afforded her.

This was precisely Raden Adjeng Kartini's dilemma. She and her peers had the mental benefits of exposure to Western literature and science and the social benefits of membership in the exclusive modern segment of the indigenous population. As Kartini saw it, the price she was being asked to pay for these intellectual and symbolic gratifications was too high, namely any opportunity for meaningful self-expression through active participation in the modern sectors of society. The absence of opportunities for such women was partly inherent in the unique circumstances of colonialism, including the persistent role of coercion or the threat of force in Dutch-Indonesian relations and the relatively small numbers of Dutch women. In addition, the fact that feminist movements were growing in the Netherlands, Germany, England, and other countries at this same time suggests that the general content of European sex-role conventions was less than egalitarian.

Indeed, the early ideology of the movement sparked by Kartini seemed typically feminist, with women challenging their cohorts to struggle against suppression and inequality. Any such feminist spirit was short-lived, however, for a new sentiment was catching on among Indonesians. This was the idea of national independence and self-government, and it was to dominate the political consciousness of women as well as men for the first half of the twentieth century. There was no place for militant profemale activity because among Indonesians the only test of the legitimacy of each organization came to be whether that organization was committed to the overarching goal of nationalism. This priority did not mean, as it might have in a setting where women had never known or expected active social roles, that Indonesian women postponed their organizational efforts or merely tagged along in their husbands' activities. The test of being pronationalist was easy to pass, and during the drawn-out period of the struggle for independence there was a proliferation of women's organizations, differing in their specific purposes and techniques but alike in their opposition to the continuation of the Dutch colonial government.

The first associations of Indonesian women extending beyond local community boundaries were formed in the 1920s. Few of these organizations were independently established and managed by women. One of the earliest and most successful, for example, was Aisjah, a sort of woman's auxiliary of Muhammidijah. Although Muhammidijah was founded in 1912 as an educationally and culturally oriented organization, by the time Aisjah was formed a decade later Muhammidijah "was a still, but deep, tributary of the stream of political nationalism and quietly but sustainedly nourished and strengthened that stream."[10]

Through Aisjah and similar organizations women were represented in the early stages of the nationalist movement, but their role clearly was subsidiary. Recognition of this fact and dissatisfaction with it inspired several individuals and groups to advocate greater unity and cooperation as a means to achieve more autonomy and influence for women. The result of this line of thought was the event that must rank as the most significant milestone in the history of the Indonesian women's movement—the first Congress of Indonesian Women in 1928.

Specifically, the Congress of Indonesian Women was sponsored by seven major organizations—Wanita Utomo, Wanita Taman Siswa, Puteri Indonesia, Aisjah, Wanita Katolik, and the women's sections of the Jong Islamieten Bond and Jong Java. Of these only Puteri Indonesia, an association of schoolgirls, was not tied to a men's organization. Most of the individuals participating in the meeting, which was held in Jogjakarta, were from Central Java, and most of the organizations represented were stronger in Central Java than elsewhere. Thus the seven sponsoring organizations had an advantage in establishing themselves as the leading component of the national women's movement, and they capitalized on this advantage by dominating the board of directors of the new federative organization created by the Congress, the Association of Indonesian Women's Organizations. The nationwide Congress was successful enough to be repeated the following year and thereafter became institutionalized (though not on an annual basis) as the authoritative, legitimate manifestation of the women's movement.

Perhaps the activity of women during the colonial period can be summarized as formative in the area of attitudes and values. Their deliberations at national conferences helped to define the areas about which women were concerned and the general position that women held on certain issues. Such meetings also helped to establish women as a part of the nationalist movement and therefore as legitimate participants in the emerging political processes.

On the other hand, this period was not formative from the point of view of the organizational structure of the women's movement. No firm pattern of large-scale associations emerged. Actually, even if such a pattern had existed in 1941, it is doubtful that it would have survived the extensive social changes and dislocations of the Japanese occupation and the ensuing political and military struggle against the re-imposition of Dutch sovereignty.

For all practical purposes the women's movement was dormant, if not dead, during the years of the occupation. The Japanese authorities created a single, nationwide association for women, the Fuzenkai. From the perspective of the occupation leaders, this organization was intended as one of several channels of access that would enable mobilization of the population in support of the Japanese war effort. Like the occupation in general, however, the Fuzenkai was not popular, and the Japanese had neither the resources nor, as it turned out, the time to persuade Indonesian women to accept the organization as their own.

If the Japanese had found in Indonesia a well-developed and widely popular set of women's organizations, perhaps they could have exploited them and achieved some success in their effort to mobilize this sector of the population. In the absence of such an organizational structure at the beginning of the occupation, the Fuzenkai had little chance for success over the three-year period. Given the failure of the Fuzenkai, the growing realization in early 1945 that Japan's defeat and the end of the occupation were impending was accompanied by a recognition of the organizational vacuum in the women's movement. The Indonesian independence movement was entering its final phase, a period as romantic as it was difficult, and one during which women were to engage in vigorous acts of courage that now constitute the most recent installment of the Indonesian legends of female heroism.

A small but ostensibly national meeting of female leaders held in Klaten, Central Java in December 1945, set the tone for women's participation in the revolution. By this time, some four months after the Indonesians had proclaimed their independence, the leaders of the new nation could see that the Dutch would employ force in their bid to reestablish the colonial relationship. The Congress of Indonesian Women thus was approving and publicizing acts that already had occurred spontaneously when it resolved that women must prepare to use weapons in defense of the nation, be alert for enemy spies, establish "defense kitchens" and "public kitchens," gather clothing for combat units, arrange nurseries in order to free more mothers for service to the country, and aid with evacuations of battle zones. This list accurately indicates the nature of the bulk of revolutionary activity carried on by women.

There were other, more spectacular, forms of feminine participation, including espionage and liaison work in areas occupied by the Dutch and actual combat operations in guerrilla and Republican army units. These often dramatic exploits were appropriate for incorporation into the myth of full and equal female participation in Indonesian society, but tasks such as maintaining the "public kitchens" that served both military and civilian personnel in communities where households and routines had been disrupted probably were substantially more significant.

The meeting at Klaten was followed by five more national conferences before peace finally was restored to the archipelago in December 1949. Such conferences had not been held nearly so frequently in the past, but this was a period during which there was a continuing need, both for mobilization of as much of the population as possible and for repeated expression of the intense public commitment to nationalism.

Furthermore, it was a time of considerable political jockeying in anticipation of the day when Indonesians would organize and operate their politics for themselves. At least one of the meetings during the revolution, the Congress of Indonesian Women (Kongress Wanita Indonesia or KOWANI) at Solo in August 1948, was convened specifically for the purpose of ironing out political dissension and splits among the burgeoning women's organizations. The immediate object of contention was the Renville Agreement, which many felt should not have been signed by the government of the Republic. Already the nationalist movement was losing some of its solidarity, and, as was to be the case in the postrevolutionary period, the women's movement faithfully reflected the new schisms and factions in the national political system as a whole.

To some extent the appearance of conflict within the women's movement was simply a consequence of the increase in the number of women's associations interested in politics at the national level. Whereas national congresses in pre-independence years rarely attracted more than twenty organizations, the conference of Indonesian Women in Jogjakarta in August 1949 involved delegates from 82 organizations. Among these, several had grown to be truly national in scope, with memberships numbering in the tens of thousands.

Although many of these organizations held conflicting views on specific issues and even represented quite different ways of life, the proliferation of organizations committed to the one cause of overriding importance—national independence—created a strongly felt need for coordination and cooperation. Thus the second major organizational development in the women's movement during the revolution was the emergence of an effective and relatively stable federative structure, the Congress of Indonesian Women (KOWANI).

Officially, the women's movement was 30 years old in 1958. It was rooted in traditions and attitudes that went back into history much further than that, but until the revolution the movement was relatively unstructured and intermittent. The pattern of organizations and activities that emerged toward the end of the struggle for independence was consolidated 'and slightly modified during the next several years.

First, the end of colonial rule brought new opportunities for overt articulation of interests and women's organizations collectively tried to capitalize on this situation by making repeated demands for more governmental attention to such problems as employment opportunities for females, marriage legislation, growing threats to public morals, and the like.

Second, the women gradually expressed more interest in foreign affairs, and, reflecting Indonesia's role in hosting the Afro-Asian Conference at Bandung and her general aspiration to international prestige, they began to send delegates to a variety of international meetings.

Third, with respect to the structure of the women's movement, there was some consolidation of associations and a tendency to distinguish sharply between groups that were local and those that were genuinely national. Of course, groups of the latter type came to dominate the movement. For example, of the scores of women's organizations in Indonesia in 1953, only nineteen were invited to make public statements commemorating the twenty-fifth anniversary of the women's movement. These same organizations were the most active and most powerful in the consultative council, or secretariat, which had replaced the large-scale convention as the primary locus of both policy formulation and internal politicking for the entire women's movement.

Finally, the mid-1950s witnessed some efforts, though not particularly successful ones, to elaborate the interorganizational structure of the women's movement through the establishment of agencies and organizations subsidiary to KOWANI, such as the Women's Cooperative Bank and the Children's Welfare Foundation.

Political Participation under Guided Democracy and the New Order

If during the early and mid-1950s the women's movement appeared to be generating groups potentially capable of participation in an open and rational political process, this development was consistent with the evolution of the formal structure of the entire Indonesian political system toward constitutional democracy. Accordingly, a major feature of the blueprint that the nation's political designers were preparing was an electoral system. After protracted preparations, both administrative and political, nationwide elections were held in late 1955. Since more than 39 million voters, or 90 percent of all persons registered, went to the polls, women apparently made extensive use of the franchise.[11] In some measure this participation was the payoff of the agitation for female voting rights and the more recent voter-education campaign that many women's groups had carried out.

However, the elections of 1955 did not usher in a stable parliamentary system. The ensuing governments were too fragmented to cope with the pressing problems of national development, much less with the basic political problem of national unity. As representative institutions failed, competing centers of political power, specifically President Sukarno and the army, gained in political prominence. The 1958 rebellion of dissident civil and military elements in Sumatra and Sulawesi finally confirmed for many Indonesians their feeling that political arrangements borrowed from the West were unworkable in their country. Now the opposition to the far-reaching structural revisions that Sukarno had been advocating for some time was greatly reduced, and the country entered a regime to be remembered as "guided democracy," or, by the unsympathetic, as the "old order."[12]

Perhaps the most conspicuous, if also the most superficial, connection between Sukarno's political ascendancy and the role of Indonesian women lay in the president's personal predilection for enjoying women's company. Just as the sexual prowess of the god-kings of the old Javanese kingdoms inspired a great deal of gossip among the peasantry and thereby helped link the court with the outlying agrarian society, so did Sukarno's reputed amorous adventures become a favorite subject of eager speculation during 1958 through September of 1965, the years of guided democracy.

Some of the talk focused on the relative merits of Sukarno's many wives and his treatment of them, but this was a secondary topic. The more compelling items of discussion were the president's extramarital activities. Rumors of these adventures implicated not only special stewardesses of international airlines, special geisha girls in Tokyo, special girl friends in Italy and elsewhere, but also daughters of some of the leading families in various parts of Indonesia. Sukarno did little to discourage such stories, and, like all rumors, they grew to exaggerated proportions.[13]

All this womanizing may have alienated at least part of the feminine sector of Indonesian society, and when Sukarno suddenly tumbled from power after the events of late 1965 a large number of women did begin to state publicly that they had long been offended by the palace atmosphere of *la dolce vita.* Yet in 1964 the delegates to the KOWANI conference had voted without dissent to bestow upon Sukarno the title of "Supreme Leader of the Women's Revolutionary Movement." Generally, before his political decline there were no signs that Sukarno's personal behavior with women was important either as a political liability or a political advantage. Nor were his wives or girlfriends very significant as political actors.

It was through his public acts and pronouncements, rather than his private behavior, that Sukarno influenced the changing position and role of women's organizations under guided democracy. As early as 1947 he wrote and published a book entitled *Sarinah,* a treatise on the status of women in Indonesia. On the basis of some comparisons with other countries, Sukarno concluded that while Indonesian women still were being treated unfairly, they were on the threshold of the final stage in the inevitable progression of male-female relations, the stage of equal and fully cooperative participation in social and political life.[14] He affirmed his own belief that attainment of this final stage was desirable, and as president he took some measures that he said were intended to put women on an equal plane with men.

Most of these measures were purely symbolic. For example, in his 1960 Mother's Day speech, President Sukarno announced that he was choosing a number of persons to officially represent various sectors of the national society at the forthcoming dedication of an exhibition hall in Jakarta, and that he already had decided that approximately 50 percent of these participants would be women.[15] Similarly, he often boasted that his government was the only one that invited as many women as men to diplomatic receptions and other official functions. In the later years of guided democracy, Sukarno was especially attentive in his speeches to the *sukarelawati*, female military volunteers. First in the West Irian crisis, then more extensively during the campaign to crush Malaysia, many women participated in military training and drill exercises. To Sukarno this was glorious evidence of cooperation between the sexes—a key to the success of the ongoing Indonesian revolution.

President Sukarno's oratorical exhortations reflected his self-professed romanticism, and, like his scandalous private behavior, probably served primarily to sustain women's interest in national politics, broadly defined. However, the impact of guided democracy on women's political participation was not the consequence of presidential symbol manipulation alone. Guided democracy involved certain transformations in the political structure in order to avoid the narrow, intensely competitive politics of the earlier parliamentary system, which Sukarno labeled "free-fight liberalism." The president's corrective was to establish guaranteed and direct (that is, not via a political party) representation for farmers, youth, businessmen, journalists, armed-services personnel, intellectuals, workers, and all other important population categories. One of the functional groups, as these social groupings were called, was women.

That women, but not men, should be recognized as a functional group seems an implicit recognition of the inability of women to achieve genuinely equal status with men. In principle, women could have been represented through the other functional groups—the representatives of the intellectuals, the workers, and all the others might have included women as well as men. In reality, however, only a handful of women were represented in the upper levels of the governmental hierarchy.

Since independence, Indonesian politics had witnessed the formation and dissolution of numerous cabinets, and under guided democracy the size of the cabinets swelled to more than one hundred members. Yet by late 1965, when the regime was about to be replaced by the current military government that has displayed much less interest in the status of women, only four women had held cabinet posts, and only two of these during the guided-democracy period.[16]

Very few women had attained high positions in judicial or legislative institutions; only two had been designated as ambassadors; and only one had become the mayor of an important city, Pontianak. From the point of view of women aware of this underrepresentation and interested in having more opportunities become available for women in government and politics, the inclusion of women as a functional group was a small but welcome step in the right direction.

Of course a listing of the formal governmental positions held by women would not constitute a complete picture of their political role. The ideology of continuing revolution justified administrative shortcuts, ad hoc political arrangements, and a personalistic political style, all of which meant that informal political processes were especially important under guided democracy. In these circumstances it is not surprising that some women became important politically without holding high political office.

One such person was Mrs. Utami Suryadarma, a leading crusader against American and British motion pictures and chairwoman of the committee opposing foreign military bases. Mrs. Suryadarma became more vocal and prominent as Sukarno's government drifted leftward, but, like all other women activists, she was overshadowed by Mrs. Hurustiati Subandrio, the wife of the foreign minister.

Not only did Mrs. Subandrio become an important political figure, but also, to a large extent, the story of the women's movement during the guided-democracy period is the story of her expanding role in that movement and her eventual control over KOWANI. Born into a Javanese family more prestigious than that of her husband, Mrs. Subandrio gave every impression that, in the absence of a presidential wife who had the skill or the desire to secure the title, she intended to become Indonesia's first lady.

Gradually she took on a number of projects that testified both to her energy and to her support of increasingly radical policies. When training of women volunteers began in 1962, Mrs. Subandrio was in charge. By becoming the titular director of family planning for the entire nation she was able to dominate planning and programs in this politically sensitive area. In 1964, after a United Nations official had spoken of malnutrition and starvation in South Central Java, she assumed the role of spokesperson for the Ministry of Health (she was a deputy minister) and publicly announced that Indonesia was rejecting all future gifts of powdered milk made available by UNICEF.

That same year, Mrs. Subandrio had become the general chairwoman of KOWANI. In a sense, Mrs. Subandrio had captured KOWANI from the top, even though technically she had followed regular channels as a representative of an organization called University Women. Mrs. Subandrio had increased her participation in the University Women organization in the early 1960s and by 1963 had effectively converted it from an intellectually oriented society to a radical leftist political organization. Mrs. Subandrio brought many of her friends in as active members, and this maneuver produced a split that was reflected in the rather peculiar development which found this single organization supporting two more or less competing universities for women—Sarinah University, sponsored by the older and less radical segment of the organization, and Kartini University, established by Mrs. Subandrio and her supporters.

While Mrs. Subandrio was thus engaged, there was occurring simultaneously in the structure of KOWANI a change that reinforced the leftward political drift of the organization. The Communist Party's women's organization, Gerwani (Gerakan Wanita Indonesia or Indonesian Women's Movement), was establishing itself as the largest and most vigorous of the women's groups. Its growth had paralleled that of its parent organization, the Indonesian Communist Party (PKI) having grown to a claimed membership of three million women over the decade and a half ending in 1965. Although that membership figure was surely inflated, Gerwani was able to mobilize large numbers of women for militant demonstrations and was by far the noisiest and most visible of the women's organizations in support of the ideology of guided democracy.

Gerwani's strength was both reflected in and enhanced by the fact that another mass organization, Wanita Marhaenis, the women's affiliate of the Indonesian Nationalist Party (PNI), increasingly emulated Gerwani policies and tactics. Marhaenis, the adjective form of a fictitious proper name (Marhaen) concocted by Sukarno, defies translation. Sukarno's Marhaen was a typical peasant—struggling, simple, and generally virtuous. A third mass organization for women, Perwari (Persatuan Wanita Republik Indonesia or Indonesian Women's Association), tried until late 1964 to preserve its largely apolitical posture, and as a result it lost much of its influence within KOWANI.

In September 1965, the women's movement thus was a mirror image of the national political system in two respects: It was dominated at the top by a single powerful individual, and its political policies and policy machinery were falling into the control of Communist-oriented groups.

But the entire framework was very unstable. Guided democracy was an impermanent arrangement because its smooth operation depended upon the magical balancing and integrating capacities of President Sukarno. The system fell apart, partly because Sukarno's health appeared to be failing in August of 1965 and partly because neither the PKI nor the army was willing to submit to the balancing off process any longer.

The Communist version of the so-called coup of September 30 is that a group of progressive-minded military men took action to forestall an impending seizure of power by a right-wing council of generals. The army's version is essentially that the attempted coup, although it involved certain army officers and units, was arranged by the PKI. One of the facts of the affair that has made the army's argument difficult to negate is the role of some Gerwani members in the 30th of September Movement. In 1964 and early 1965 Gerwani had participated in several demonstrations aimed at capitalist bureaucrats, including Adam Malik, then Minister of Trade, and foreign subversives. The content of hostility in these demonstrations steadily escalated, and in retrospect it seems that this growing hostility, much of it directed toward government officials, reflected a combination of frustration among the Communists over being held at bay by the guided-democracy balancing act (Sukarno had appointed very few PKI members to high governmental positions) and confidence among the Communists that Indonesia's political future was theirs.

On September 27, 1965, a large group of demonstrators, primarily women from Gerwani, broke into the governor's house in Surabaja. In the process of demanding that diplomatic relations with the United States be severed and that the governor appoint some women to his provincial economic department, the demonstrators did considerable damage to the house, grounds, and furnishings. Depending upon one's political sympathies, their excesses could be regarded as either patriotic or extremely unpatriotic, but the action clearly was drastic.

It was the forerunner, however, to a far more violent move. Three nights after the demonstration in Surabaja a contingent of specially trained young women from Gerwani participated in the assassination of six of the top generals of the Indonesian army. Exactly how and why Gerwani was involved is not clear, and none of the murders can be attributed to specific young women who were present. In the eyes of the Indonesian public, however, Gerwani was firmly associated with the murders and, perhaps worse, the torture and humiliation of the generals before their deaths.[17]

The political crisis that followed the 30th of September Movement touched off a process of social reorganization that cut deeply into the women's movement. The most immediate change was elimination of Gerwani as a leading force within the women's movement. In Jakarta and in many other cities, the organization's leaders were imprisoned without trial. In some areas Gerwani members were among those singled out for execution in the wave of killings which swept Java, parts of Sumatra, and Bali. As an organization, Gerwani was among the first victims of Sukarno's new inability to continue in his role of final political arbiter.

For some months, however, Sukarno did manage to retain many formal advantages of office. Before they had generated the confidence and strength which they felt they needed for a direct confrontation with the father of guided democracy, the new-order forces, mainly student groups working closely with some military leaders and units, directed their fire at Sukarno's right-hand man, Dr. Subandrio. As Subandrio came under vicious public attack in early 1966, there was growing agitation within KOWANI to eliminate Mrs. Subandrio's influence. With her husband becoming the whipping boy of Indonesian politics, Mrs. Subandrio found herself unable to elicit support or sympathy within KOWANI. When the government put her under house arrest in March 1966, she was effectively deposed as the leader of the women's movement in Indonesia.

Within KOWANI, then, the new order meant abrupt reversal of the two basic trends that had emerged during the guided-democracy period. To protect against future domination of the federation by a single individual, the position of general chairwoman was abolished and a periodic-chair scheme was introduced. Under this system, which also is employed in several member organizations, KOWANI is governed between national congresses by a nine-member executive council, each member of which takes her turn as chairwoman for a four-month period. Albeit the procedure creates discontinuity in leadership, most women now contend that this is a small price to pay for a structural guarantee against one-woman rule.

As for the reversal of the political shift to the left that had occurred during 1958–1965, the most decisive development was the complete disintegration of Gerwani. In spite of occasional warnings of clandestine Communist reorganization in the months after the 30th of September Movement, there were no apparent remnants or revivals of the Communist women's organization during the decade following the coup.

Surprisingly, however, other organizations (including any which might be termed right-wing) did not seem to benefit very immediately or directly from the change in regime. The two largest organizations remaining, Perwari and Wanita Marhaenis, entered a rather cautious competition for the support of former members of Gerwani, but neither appeared to make significant progress. In fact, by the summer of 1967 Wanita Marhaenis, far from being in a position to capitalize on Gerwani's bad fortune, was struggling to avoid becoming the second women's organization to fall victim to the new order.

Aside from Gerwani's rapid fall, the realignment within KOWANI was gradual and slight. As the general denunciation of the PKI gained vigor, however, that party's closest ally, the PNI, came in for severe criticism. Wanita Marhaenis was closely tied to the PNI and even reflected the ideological split that had practically separated the party into two distinct hierarchies. Therefore it was inevitable that as the party was forced, often through intimidation and violence, to discontinue its operations in various localities, Wanita Marhaenis lost considerable support both within and outside the organization. As of the summer of 1967, leaders of the organization in Jakarta had not heard from many of its 250 branches for nearly two years. Whereas Wanita Marhaenis had claimed nearly three million members in 1965, the organization's officers were unwilling to make even the roughest estimate two years later.

Perhaps mainly to impress other groups of their anticommunism, the Wanita Marhaenis leaders spoke as much of the danger of infiltration by former Gerwani individuals as of a membership campaign. It seemed unlikely that Wanita Marhaenis would be able to retain its previous position as one of the three leading women's associations within KOWANI and in the nation.

Perwari, with an estimated membership of one million women, was the third largest organization for women in 1965. One reason that Perwari apparently has not enjoyed a big rise in membership and prestige as Gerwani and Wanita Marhaenis lost power within KOWANI may be Perwari's apolitical stance. Unlike Gerwani and Wanita Marhaenis, both of which are affiliates of political parties, Perwari is independent. This is not to say that Perwari eschews politics; the organization's constitution states its objectives as follows:

To safeguard the implementation of Human Rights in general, Women's Rights in particular.

To encourage women to participate in every aspect of public life such as becoming members of
  1. The consultative People's Congress.
  2. Parliament.
  3. Provincial and local legislative councils.
  4. Other important posts, both legislative and executive.

To educate women about their rightful place and their duties as responsible citizens.

To promote women's interests in social, economic, educational, health, and legal fields.

To promote active relations with foreign (international) organizations having the same ideals as Perwari.

Politics clearly is important to Perwari, but only as a means toward fulfilling the rights and interests of women. Actually the leadership of

Perwari has, since the organization was founded in 1945, consisted of women with a variety of political leanings, plus others who dislike politics. Such an organization is unlikely to be prepared for the kind of political maneuvering that might have permitted Perwari to capitalize on the misfortunes of Gerwani and Wanita Marhaenis. Yet the continuing restructuring of the political party system and the containment of parties by the regime give Perwari an advantage over the party-affiliated associations.

These benefits accrue to Perwari more than to other nonparty organizations because the other independent women's organizations tend to be relatively particularistic. Nearly one-third of all organizations in KOWANI are restricted in membership to wives of men working in a particular field or institution, and many of the rest are limited to certain geographical areas, in spite of their formal qualification for KOWANI membership under the rule requiring several branches in various regions. Since there is considerable disparity among the member organizations with respect to size and importance, the larger groups are guaranteed the greater influence through permanent representation on the KOWANI executive council, the nine-member body from which the periodic chairwomen are selected.

Initially the most visible features of the gradual reshuffling of political organizations that accompanied the new order were the decline of the Communist Party and the emergence of several anticommunist federative organizations. These action fronts, as the latter were called, stole the political show not only from the parties but from other organizations as well. The Indonesian Women's Action Front (Kesatuan Aksi Wanita Indonesia or KAWI) temporarily eclipsed KOWANI in late 1966.

The founders of KAWI insist that it was the spontaneous product of women's participation in the struggle against the Sukarno regime. When university and high-school students took to the streets demanding political and economic reform in early 1966, KOWANI, like most organizations, was unable to come to their support. Two reasons were Mrs. Subandrio's continuing influence and the stipulation in the organization's by-laws that KOWANI policies must be approved unanimously, that is, by each member organization.

At first as individuals and then in groups, a number of women decided to assist the young people without waiting for KOWANI. Their first large-scale action, and the one most valued by the students, was preparation and transmission of food packages for activists in the Students' Action Front (Kesatuan Aksi Mahasiwa Indonesia or KAMI), many of whom were living at a temporary and embattled camp on the main campus of the University of Indonesia in Jakarta. According to some women, and a few students corroborate this, KAWI grew out of the need to coordinate the delivery of food packages and to protect this operation from infiltration and sabotage. The spirit of the times was reflected in student leaders' indignant rejection of food from "old-order" sources. They sent back one thousand packets of rice delivered by Mrs. Chaerul Saleh, the wife of Sukarno's second deputy prime minister.

KAWI was officially formed on March 6, 1966. As its name implies, the organization professed to be action-oriented, but not as a feminist movement. That is to say, KAWI's goals were in no way particular to females but were those shared by all militant action fronts in the new order: dissolution of the Communist Party, complete expulsion from the government of old-order politicians, reduction of prices, and, more recently, eradication of corruption.

The principal technique of political expression by KAWI was participation in street demonstrations, the more conspicuous because the representatives of other action fronts always insisted, out of chivalrous deference, that the KAWI ladies be given the leading positions in marches and demonstrations. Unfortunately for KAWI, however, the apparent consolidation of political power by the army meant increasing limitations on militant political activity, and the organization rapidly became little more than a symbol of the political confrontation of 1966.

KAWI was a federation, and this fact is vital to an understanding of its rapid rise and decline. The action front was formed at a time when, for reasons already mentioned, KOWANI was politically paralyzed. Many organizations in KOWANI saw that joining KAWI would enable them to side with the new order without forcing a showdown in KOWANI, and therefore several of them, including Perwari and most of the party-affiliated organizations, became members of both federations. This affiliation meant in the long run that when KOWANI was rid of Mrs. Subandrio and was subsequently reorganized by an extraordinary congress held May 31 and June 1, 1966, in a way that strengthened its identification with the new order, most of KAWI's two dozen member organizations shifted their interests and support to the less militant, less radical, and more familiar and comfortable framework of KOWANI. If KAWI had been competing with KOWANI for influence and prestige as the coordinating body of women's organization, it was clear by August of 1967 that KOWANI had met the challenge.

The competition between KAWI and KOWANI was confused by the fact that the political success of the army in 1966 gave added prestige to a third federative structure, the Women's Section of the Joint Secretariat of Functional Groups. The Joint Secretariat had evolved during the guided-democracy years in ways that are obscure but that suggest how the military continued to fare well politically during those years in spite of the Communist Party's more visible progress. The Joint Secretariat was a creation by and for the army, with the ostensible purpose of providing an organizational framework for coordination of functional-group activities in representative bodies of the government. Since the functional groups, being little more than descriptive categories of the population, generally lack effective organization of their own, the army through the Joint Secretariat has been able to manipulate the formula for the distribution of functional-group representation and even has dominated the process of selecting individuals as functional-group representatives. It is only natural that the expanding political role of the army, in convergence with preliminary preparations for national elections, would cause nonparty women's organizations to be at least mildly interested in what transpired in the Women's Section of the Joint Secretariat.

However, the Women's Section of the Joint Secretariat is not likely to replace KOWANI either. For one thing, all parties and party-affiliated organizations are excluded from participation in the Joint Secretariat. Moreover, the number of seats reserved for all functional groups in parliamentary elections is around 8 percent of the total, and the number of seats reserved for women is a mere fraction of that. The reward for expenditure of energy in the Joint Secretariat cannot be very great. Furthermore, the Joint Secretariat provides a mechanism only for formal representation in governmental bodies; it would be irrelevant to the organization and expression of women's interests in other ways like demonstrating in the streets or organizing a fund-raising bazaar for a school for retarded children. Finally, the thoroughness of the army's control over the Joint Secretariat has discouraged women from viewing the Women's Section as an alternative to KOWANI.

In itself, the division of the women's movement into three federations at the beginning of the post-Sukarno era thus was not an insurmountable barrier to effective organization and action. It probably was symptomatic, however, of an underlying inability to suppress class and cultural differences. The three federations could agree on joint sponsorship of a ceremony honoring the six generals slain on September 30, 1965. They disagreed bitterly, however, when the symbolism at issue was less universalistic and was linked to world views and life styles, as when the leaders of KAWI pressed for a flamboyant purging from the presidential palace of Sukarno's collection of nude paintings and statues. KAWI proceeded with its plans for the demonstration, but Acting President Suharto forestalled the siege by having many of the paintings removed before August 17. The planned action exemplifies both the militancy and the puritanical bent that set KAWI apart from KOWANI and from most specific organizations.

Many active Indonesian women have been optimistic about cooperation among the various organizations. It is true that the Joint Secretariat's Jakarta focus complements KOWANI's geographical inclusiveness and affords women a welcome increment of organizational strength at the point of greatest importance on the political map. Also, from the point of view of membership, exclusion of party-affiliated organizations from the Women's Section of the Joint Secretariat gives the independent associations an opportunity for political assertion which they might not find in KOWANI.

The Women's Action Front, KAWI, was considered divisive by groups attuned to respectability, but in many ways it was a progressive and innovative force. For example, although KAWI was open to women's sections of political and religious organizations, it discouraged participation of the sort of wives' organizations, such as railroad employees' wives, that had come to be prominent in KOWANI. The overall movement thus obviously lost some of its vigor when KAWI faded out of existence in the late 1960s. KOWANI now is the only structure that even approximately manifests the history and scope of the women's movement and is the vehicle to which most activists have attached their hopes for improvements in the social and political roles of women. The fact that KOWANI incorporates many wives' organizations is just one indication of the movement's difficulties.

Conclusion

Paradoxically, if Indonesian women had attained the full and equal status to which their leaders claim to aspire and if the national society really had entered the third and final stage of relations between the sexes as described by Sukarno in *Sarinah*, KOWANI would have ceased to be important. If the Indonesian women's movement were fully successful in opening politics to women in the same way that political life is open to men, there would be no need for separate organizations for women; they could work in the same political institutions and processes as men. This paradox suggests that strength in women's organizations, and especially in a strong KOWANI, far from being the ultimate objective of the women's movement, may at some point be an obstacle to real freedom and equality of the sexes.

Some women have recognized this dilemma, as revealed in occasional reminders to their peers that the practice of reserving legislative seats to females under the functional-group system should be abolished as soon as political opportunities and participation are the same for both sexes. The dilemma is not especially troubling, though, and few women are concerned about the possible dysfunctionality of a strong KOWANI. In their more realistic moments the leaders of the women's movement know that the myth of vigorous and coordinated female political activity is far from an accurate picture. Women are relatively inactive and have few opportunities for political expression. There apparently are some sex-linked aspects of the sociopolitical structure and norms that inhibit political participation of women, and as long as there are, KOWANI and other women's organizations undoubtedly serve to provide channels for women's political activity, however minimal, that might not be possible in the absence of these organizations.

Three broad categories of evidence confirm the lack of progress by women in their quest for political equality in Indonesia. The first of these, a dearth of women in high public office such as the cabinet and governorships, has already been mentioned. In legislative bodies the record is equally poor: in 1967 the national parliament of 350 members included only 26 women and the Provisional People's Consultative Council of 661 members had only 42 women. In both cases the proportion of female representatives was 7 percent, nearly all of which can be attributed to the functional-group scheme. A decade of military domination of Indonesian politics has done little to remedy this situation. In 1971, for example, of 460 members of parliament 33 were women. Under the Suharto regime women have continued to do well in the legal profession, however. In 1973 approximately 16 percent of lower- and appeals-court judges were women, and one woman sat on the Supreme Court.

Second, women have been even less successful in acquiring leadership positions within parties and other political organizations. Few of the major political institutions are limited to men only, yet most of them do have separate organizations for women. To some extent this development may result from women's frustration at being virtually excluded from important positions within the organization. In most cases, however, the separate organizational hierarchy, which is a sort of shadow of the real structure of the organization, was set up with good feeling all around. The women saw a certain opportunity for formal status, apparently overlooking the possibility that participation in the shadow hierarchy might effectively eliminate women from consideration for real leadership positions within the organization.

Unfortunately, this formal separation of the sexes does not appear to be an old-fashioned arrangement that may die out in the near future; thorough compartmentalization of female officers and members was especially common among the organizations of the generation of 1966, the student and youth groups that played such a dramatic role as champions of the new order.

An interesting variation of the shadow-hierarchy phenomenon is the wives' organizations. Of course, most of these are mainly social in nature. Still, in spite of their lack of any basis other than the common occupation of husbands, some of these groups are quite active in the federations, especially KOWANI, and seem to have the total effect of introducing quite a bit of confusion into the women's movement.

One of the current points of dissension within the movement, for example, centers on allegations that Persit (Persatuan Istri Tentara), the army officers' wives' group, has been blessed with funds and facilities the likes of which no other organization can hope to obtain. If this sort of grumbling corresponds to the heightening tension in civilian-military relations throughout Indonesia, it also reinforces the conclusion that wives' organizations function mainly to demonstrate and promote status emanating from their husbands' careers. Although neither the shadow hierarchy nor the wives' organizations probably represent a conscious effort by men to limit the effectiveness of public activities of women, both of these characteristic features of Indonesian organizational life do have that effect.

The third type of evidence bearing on the lack of success of the women's movement has to do with the inability of women to realize the specific claims and demands they have been expressing ever since the first national congress in 1928. Foremost among these is the demand for marriage legislation. Prior to 1973 nearly every national meeting of women's organizations produced a strong statement urging a basic law that would give women equal rights and protection in matters of marriage and divorce. Yet the law finally adopted in that year, Marriage Bill No. 1, is a compromise that still allows polygyny if the man can show that his wives will be treated equally.

Opposition to a more thorough law was quiet but apparently firm. This issue is one that tends to unsettle relations between most political organizations and their women's sections. Marriage legislation has had a great deal of symbolic importance to Indonesian women, and, although the 1973 legislation may be reassuring enough to reduce the salience of the issue, it seems more likely that the law's compromises and less than vigorous enforcement will be continuing matters of contention. In fact, Marriage Bill No. 1 did not take force until an implementation regulation took effect in late 1975, and the implementation regulation affects only portions of the original bill.

By any objective standards, then, and certainly in contrast to popular mythology about the position of women, the role of women in Indonesian politics is deficient. Aside from the mythology, however, and from a broader perspective, there is no reason to expect Indonesia to be far ahead of the rest of the world in this respect. On the basis of his cross-national survey for UNESCO, Maurice Duverger concluded, "One fact, at least, seems beyond doubt—the existence of great inequality between the sexes in the actual exercise of political rights."[18] Actually, many of Duverger's findings, such as the fact that the proportion of women in national legislative bodies rarely exceeds 5 percent, do make female participation in Indonesian politics appear slightly higher than it is in the politics of most other countries.

The reasons for the failure of women to achieve full and equal representation in politics and government are perhaps even less clear in Indonesia than elsewhere. Duverger's emphasis on the actual exercise of political rights, setting behavior apart from legal standards, is appropriate for Indonesia, because under the law women do have equal political (if not marital) prerogatives and opportunities. The educational system is nearly completely coeducational in practice as well as in form, and therefore does not appear to constitute a barrier to entry into politics by women. Certainly most of the national societal norms about sex roles are favorable to independence and equal opportunities for the sexes, and the more parochial beliefs and traditions generally appear to be consistent with these. Almost all public pronouncements on this topic by individuals of both sexes are reaffirmations of the myth that women do not merely have equal opportunities in politics but that they actually wield about as much political power and influence as do men.

Economic circumstances undoubtedly prevent many women from participating in politics, both in the sense that most of them find keeping house without any electrical conveniences a full-time job, and also in the sense that the structure of the Indonesian economy tends to make it difficult for women to enter modern careers that might provide a basis for political interest and activity. These economic factors, along with the universal image of women as the weaker sex, probably contribute to a private attitude which, though it rarely is articulated publicly, may be the major explanation for the lack of female political activity.

It seems not unreasonable to suspect that the Semarang newspaper *Tanah Air* was expressing a bias common in Indonesia and throughout the world when it finished its editorial saluting twenty-five years of the Indonesian women's movement with the statement, "We have intentionally avoided discussing the matter of politics, because in our opinion the fields in which the women's movement can most appropriately participate are those of social work and education."[19]

In the past such sentiments have not often been expressed openly, even though many Indonesians, women as frequently as men, would readily agree to them in private. Of course under his guided democracy the women's movement, and particularly KOWANI, were used by Sukarno as instruments for mobilization of support for his government and policies. In invoking the myth of equal female participation for this purpose Sukarno brooked little dissent. The present reaction against Sukarno's style and ideology therefore might entail some feeling that women should stay out of politics.

At least one incident occurred in August 1967 that seemed to reveal such a feeling. Acting President Suharto, addressing the All-Indonesian Congress of Catholic Women, reminded the delegates that under guided democracy the natural differences in character and style of all organizations had been obliterated by the imperative that all of them become mass political organizations supporting the revolution. The dangers in this process were most vividly manifested, Suharto went on, in the role of Gerwani in the 30th of September Movement.

The audience took this reminder to heart and the Congress of Catholic Women, as reported in the Jakarta press, decided that "political slogans should be abandoned, divisive statements and activities should be eliminated, and deliberations and programs should focus on improvements in social welfare." This was seen as a restoration of proper functional specialization to the women's movement.[20]

The resolutions of the All-Indonesian Congress of Catholic Women may typify nothing more than a transitional phase through which attitudes toward women in politics must pass before guided democracy is forgotten; and even if General Suharto is not enthusiastic about the political role of women he probably has neither the will nor the ability to alter the prevailing mythology on this subject. If the mythology has been persistent, however, so has the behavioral pattern of minimal political participation by women. There is little reason to expect, especially with politics increasingly dominated by the military, that the political role of Indonesian women will expand in the foreseeable future.

180   Stephen A. Douglas

Notes

1. Sukarno, *Wanita Indonesia Selalu Ikut Bergerak Dalam Barisan Revolusioner (The Women of Indonesia Always Are Active in the Forefront of the Revolution)*, speech before the 10th Congress of Indonesian Women, 24 July 1964, Jakarta (Jakarta: Departemen Penerangan R.I., Penerbitan Chusus, 1964), p. 11.

2. The generally favorable position of women in Southeast Asia is noted in Lucian W. Pye, *Southeast Asia's Political Systems* (Englewood Cliffs: Prentice-Hall, 1967), p. 16; and Robbins Burling, *Hill Farms and Padi Fields: Life in Mainland Southeast Asia* (Englewood Cliffs: Prentice-Hall, 1965), pp. 2 and 99.

3. Some Indonesians, especially younger ones, disavow any ethnic identity whatsoever, asserting that they are of mixed parentage and/or that they regard themselves only as Indonesians.

4. For the argument that the traditional content of the national ideology is a crucial aspect of political dynamics in Indonesia see Donald E. Weatherbee, "Traditional Values in Modernizing Ideologies: An Indonesian Example," *Journal of Developing Areas*, October 1966, pp. 41–53.

5. Dr. Jetty Rizali Noor, "Peranan Wanita Indonesia Didalam Sedjarah Pergerakan Kemerdekaan" ("The Role of Indonesian Women in the History of the Independence Movement"), series of four unpublished lectures delivered to trainees in the Ministry of Foreign Affairs, June 1967.

6. Raden Adjeng Kartini was the daughter of a Javanese regent. A collection of her letters was published, and it is usually cited as the cornerstone of women's emancipation in Indonesia. See Raden Adjeng Kartini, *Letters of a Javanese Princess* (New York: W. W. Norton, 1964), tr. from the Dutch by Agnes Louise Symmers. Kartini's birthday is a national holiday, and her image as a progressive advocate of women's rights is second to none.

7. See Sukarno, *Srikandi Tjut Njak Dhien—Pahlawan Nasional (Srikandi Tjut Njak Dhien—National Hero)*, speech commemorating the anniversary of Tjut Njak Dhien's martyrdom, 8 December 1964, Jakarta (Jakarta: Departemen Penerangan R.I., Penerbitan Chusus, 1965), pp. 5–6. See also Benedict R. O'G. Anderson, *Mythology and the Tolerance of the Javanese* (Ithaca: Monograph Series, Modern Indonesia Project, Southeast Asian Program, Department of Asian Studies, Cornell University, 1965), p. 22.

8. For an especially vigorous argument that women have greater freedom under Islam than other world religions, see A. N. Rani, *Wanita Dalam Islam (Women in Islam)* (Surabaja: Penerbit RADJA-PENA, 1965).

9. R. A. Santoso Sastrohamidjojo, *Pendapat Rakjat Djawa Barat di Pedesaan Tentang Tata Masjarakat Jang Diinginkan (Opinion of People in Rural Areas of West Java Regarding the Desirable Social Order)* (Jakarta: Lembaga Ekonomi dan Kemasjarakatan Nasional, 1965).

10. See George McTurnan Kahin, *Nationalism and Revolution in Indonesia* (Ithaca: Cornell University Press, 1952), p. 88.

11. Precise data on voter turnout by sex are not available, but the author is aware of no evidence suggesting that women made substantially less use of the franchise than men.

12. For a concise history of this period, see J. D. Legge, *Indonesia* (Englewood Cliffs: Prentice-Hall, 1964), pp. 144–153.

13. Sukarno's views on marriage and women are presented in *Sukarno: An Autobiography* (New York: Bobbs-Merrill, 1965).

14. The previous stage is that of "feminism," during which women seek to improve their status through militant competition with men. See Sukarno, *Sarinah: Kewadjiban Wanita Dalam Perdjoangan Republik Indonesia (Sarinah: Women's Duty in the Struggle of the Republic of Indonesia)* (Jakarta: Panitya Penerbit Buku-Buku Karangan Presiden Sukarno, 1963).

15. Sukarno, *Peranan Wanita Indonesia Dalam Pembangunan Semesta Berentjana (The Role of Indonesian Women in Planned Development)*, speech at the Mothers' Day Ceremony, 22 December 1960, Jakarta (Jakarta: Departemen Penerangan R.I., Penerbitan Chusus, 1961), pp. 3–4.

16. They were Maria Ullfah Santoso, Social Welfare, 1945–47; Mrs. S. K. Trimurti, Labor, 1947–49; Mrs. Rusiah Sardjono, Social Welfare, 1964–1966; Mrs. Artati Marzuki, Basic Education and Culture, 1965–66.

17. See John Hughes, *Indonesian Upheaval* (New York: David McKay, 1967), esp. Chapter 4.

18. Maurice Duverger, *The Political Role of Women* (Paris: UNESCO, 1955), p. 10.

19. Cited in *Buku Peringatan 30 Tahun Kesatuan Pergerakan Wanita Indonesia (Book commemorating 30 years of United Indonesian Women's Movement)*, n.d., p. 103.

20. *Kompas,* 28 August 1967, p. 2.

7 Expanding Women's Horizons in Indonesia: Toward Maximum Equality with Minimum Conflict

Ann Ruth Willner

The thesis I wish to advance is that there may be greater potential for the rapid development of the position of women in technologically underdeveloped Indonesia than there may be for the improvement of the position of women in many technologically overdeveloped countries of the Western world. This thesis is not based upon comparisons of legal codes or of the relative growth rates of numbers of women receiving higher education, gaining public office, or entering high-status occupations. It is rather derived from impressions of underlying cultural values and attitudes that can influence the success or failure of attempts to change roles and patterns of behavior of and toward women.

Consider for a moment the confining connotations of the phrase "Woman's Role in . . . ," stipulated in the singular number. Does this not imply such questions as "What is *the role* of women?" or "What should be the *appropriate role* for women?"[1] Where it is taken for granted that many roles are simultaneously open to women, a statement in the singular would be singular indeed. Evoked by this phrasing are the dichotomies of limited choice, the kind of cultural conditioning by American media that defines existence for many American women in such terms as career *versus* home, nurturer *or* competitor, sex symbol *or* mother figure.

The notion of the development of the position of women, as employed here, broadly relates to an increase in the range of life possibilities amenable to women's exercise of preference as individuals. It can equally be viewed as a decrease in the limitations upon women's options that are imposed by sexually defined prescriptions.

More specifically, I would suggest, as a rough framework for estimating levels of development, three related indicators and two dimensions of the range of choices open to women in a society. The first indicator refers to the availability, or lack of availability, of a variety of roles and a multiplicity of spheres of activity. The second relates to the relative costs of choosing or emphasizing one role or activity rather than another. The third indicator, dealing with modes of enacting or performing activities, is one which, for want of a more precise term, I shall call personal, expressive, or emotional style.

The two dimensions, equivalence and identity, refer to comparisons with the range of choices open to men. One might examine, for instance, whether the number of roles or spheres of activity accessible to women is equivalent to that accessible to men, even though different in type, or whether it is less. Thus a type of separate-but-equal argument might be advanced to the effect that women are not disadvantaged in a society in which their range of choices is as extensive as that of men, despite culturally prescribed limitations upon both men and women on the basis of sexual differentiation.

There are those who would assert, however, that numerical equivalence does not constitute equality. Consider a situation in which family food preparation is an activity exclusively allocated to women and prohibited to men while legal advocacy is the exclusive domain of men and prohibited to women. Proponents of this point of view might argue that family food preparation tends to be monotonous, unchallenging, and restricted in locus as compared with the variety, mental stimulus, and movement afforded by the practice of law. The identity dimension is here employed to encompass the qualitative aspects of role or activity and the point of view that equality of choice is achieved through equal access by women and men to the identical range of activities and roles.[2]

In examining the range of choice, it is perhaps fitting to exclude those choices that are limited by biological factors, for instance, the ability of a male to procreate beyond the age of sixty whereas a female cannot. More to the point are choices that are culturally rather than biologically determined. In our society, for example, what is commonly called a "May-December" marriage or romance is culturally acceptable when the December partner is the male and the May partner the female, but the reverse is regarded as ridiculous. In Java, however, there is no differentiation by sex in this respect, marriage generally being frowned upon between those differing greatly in age[3] and men with considerably younger paramours are no less sniggered about than women in this position.

Economic and Political Roles of Javanese Women

The preceding framework is only partially employed here, for my data are not the result of a systematic investigation of women in

Indonesia. Data of this kind are just not available at this time. Thus what I have to say is based upon my occasional observations and those of others made in the course of research on other subjects. The observations are largely restricted to women in Java, since this is the area in which I have had the most opportunity for direct observation.

Since the emphasis here is on the range of roles and activities available to women, attention will not be given to the domestic roles widely available in all societies, except as they affect other roles. Thus in many societies the exclusive or primary allocation to women of the tasks of homemaking and childrearing limits their undertaking other activities or is held to be a limiting factor that justifies or rationalizes their exclusion from many other activities.

This limiting is decidedly not the case in Java, where the options open to women have traditionally been many and where they are increasing in the contemporary period. Of primary importance is the fact that women have never been economically dependent on men by virtue of restrictions on holding property or engaging in entrepreneurial pursuits through which income and wealth can be accumulated. It might be noted here that in this respect the Netherlands was considerably more backward than her former colony. There, until fairly recently, the woman lost property rights by virtue of marriage, unless otherwise stipulated in a marriage contract, and could not engage in some types of financial transactions without the written permission of her husband.

In Javanese *adat*, or traditional customary law, and in that of most other Indonesian ethnic groups, each partner in a marriage retains exclusive rights to some categories of property. A woman retains title to property that she inherits, acquires from her family in advance of inheritance, or receives as a marriage gift. She keeps title to property she may have acquired before marriage just as her husband keeps title to that which he acquired before marriage. Property gained by the couple in the course of the marriage is jointly owned.[4] In case of divorce, each party withdraws from the joint household that which was his or her individual property. Property that has been jointly acquired during the marriage is divided between the two. In Java, among the so-called *santri,* those who follow the tenets of Islam fairly closely, a husband's share of joint household property is twice that of the wife; however, among many families with syncretist orientations the pre-Islamic tradition of equal division is observed.[5]

Islam is the dominant religion in Indonesia, and Islamic law governing inheritance favors male over female heirs. However, in many regions customary inheritance laws have prevailed over or modified Islamic prescription and some of these customs give equal, and even favored, rights of inheritance to females.[6] In Atjeh, a stronghold of Islam, parents first provide a house and residential land for each daughter and, if able, a rice field as well; only thereafter is the remainder of the estate divided among sons and daughters in accordance with Islamic regulations for division.[7]

In central and east Java, much of the irrigable land is owned communally by villages. Rights to shares of such land are held by a certain number of so-called core families and are inherited by one member of each successive generation in each family. Women as well as men can inherit such shares, although a higher proportion of shareholders are men. In two villages in a rural area in which I did research in the 1950s there were, respectively, 12 women out of a total of 61 shareholders and 11 out of a total of 81 shareholders.

Since land is in short supply in Java, not only the landless in rural areas but also many landholders need other sources of income and engage in other primary or subsidiary occupations. I would not go so far as Hildred Geertz, who has observed that "Javanese women may do almost any kind of work that a man can do,"[8] for, in the course of fairly extensive investigations of industry I did not encounter even one woman smith, stone mason, foundry worker, or welder. It is true, however, that a wide variety of artisan, entrepreneurial, and industrial occupations have traditionally been open to women and practiced by women. In rural areas, women not only work as paid agricultural laborers but also own and operate cottage enterprises and small shops. Alice Dewey has amply documented the range of women's activities in the marketplace in her impressive study of marketing in Java.[9] Women are employed in large-scale mechanized industry, although they are rarely in supervisory or managerial posts over men.[10]

As compared with village women and those of lower social strata in towns and cities, women from gentry and other upper-strata background traditionally were relatively uninvolved in occupations and activities outside the home. This differentiation has changed considerably in recent years. First, such women have become enthusiastically involved in organizational life and in voluntary activities relating to social welfare, political action, and other causes. Moreover, younger women especially are acquiring in greater numbers skills and higher education and entering government, business, and the professions.[11]

This shift has resulted in part from increased educational opportunities, official encouragement, and personal inclination to become modern. Another factor, however, and one that is likely to facilitate the trend, has been inflation and continued economic hardship.

Inhibitions about engaging in gainful occupations on account of family status have had to give way to economic necessities. It is no longer unusual for women of aristocratic background and wives of men with prestigious but poorly paid posts in government or at universities to undertake a variety of entrepreneurial activities to augment the family income.

There are still relatively few women in such professions as medicine, dentistry, law, journalism, and higher education, and in the top echelons of government. From none of those I have known in these fields, however, have I heard accounts of opposition from their families to their entering such occupations or of discrimination or hostility from male colleagues and fellow professionals. A woman I encountered who is an active partner in a shipyard, perhaps the only woman in this occupation, also did not experience difficulty on account of her sex.

It would be premature, however, to conclude that there are few obstacles to the entry of increasing numbers of women into fields dominated by men. The women I have known in the professions and in the higher echelons of public service have generally been from the country's leading families. Since family status and family ties play a large part in anyone's opportunities, they may have been major factors in the relative ease of acceptance of these women. In countries where ascriptive criteria are still important, women may have an edge over more qualified men with less influential connections.

In decisions concerning domestic affairs, women decidedly play the major role. The wife's voice is dominant not only in matters related to childrearing but also in nearly all matters of household expenditures. Observations of rural life in Java by anthropologists indicate that women control the domestic purse strings and men are often dependent upon them for cash disbursements.[12] Moreover, among agrarian families, decisions concerning transactions and obligations with respect to land, market, wages, and harvest involve, at minimum, consultation with his wife by the husband; he may formally negotiate, but hers may frequently be the decisive voice. Jay notes that "more enterprising wives contract for land rights and market crops virtually on their own."[13]

That these are not recent phenomena is evident from similar observations made in the eighteenth and nineteenth centuries. Raffles noted:

> In the transactions of money concerns, the women are universally superior to the men, and from the common laborer to the chief of a province, it is usual for the husband to entrust his pecuniary affairs entirely to his wife.

The women alone attend the markets and conduct all the business of buying and selling.[14]

I do not have sufficient data to estimate whether this traditional and contemporary rural pattern of women's dominance in financial affairs prevails among urban and upper strata families. My own research on factory workers suggests that when the sources of a man's income are far from the locus of his household, his wife tends to have less control over it.

If women's economic roles are many and pronounced, their political roles are fewer and more subdued than those of men. Interestingly enough, in the precolonial period there were some women rulers of kingdoms. Of thirteen rulers of the Singasari-Madjapahit dynasties in medieval Java, two were women; the Atjanese throne was occupied by women between 1641 and 1699; at least three women were the supreme rulers of Sumbawa in the seventeenth and eighteenth centuries; and many women reigned over small kingdoms of southern Sulawesi.[15] Among a number of ethnic groups, women traditionally have participated in local family and village councils. In Bali, for example, membership in the *bandjar*, the hamlet council, requires a male and female pair, generally a married couple.[16]

Although elective and appointive offices are open to women in the contemporary period, women have not been markedly prominent here.[17] The proportion of women in the national parliament has generally been under 10 percent. In parliament and other national bodies, the committees chaired by women have generally been the welfare committee. There have been no women in the top leadership of any of the major political parties. With the exception of the secretary-general of the Ministry of Foreign Affairs, the few senior ministerial posts held by women have been in the areas of health, education, and welfare. During the period of my observations of rural villages in Java, I did not encounter any women village or district heads or officials, nor have I heard of any, although this experience does not mean that there may not be some. Village women would express themselves on public affairs in private; they were shy about speaking out in public meetings.

Nonetheless, it would be incorrect to infer that women do not exert considerable influence on public affairs, although the degree of such influence would be exceedingly difficult to measure. Not only are there numerous women's organizations exerting pressure upon public officials, but in addition nearly all political parties have active women's auxiliaries. Moreover, women exercise what might be described as indirect or concealed influence. The stories that circulate in the political rumor mill of Jakarta attributing this or that political figure's decision to the persuasion of his wife and the hints that one or another public figure might best be persuaded or influenced through the women around him are too numerous to have no basis in fact.

Extending Women's Roles

Several factors suggest the probability of further and more rapid extension of role possibilities for women in Indonesia. Not the least of these is the encouragement that women receive. One might say that the position of women has improved considerably since Raden Kartini at the turn of the century rebelled against the seclusion of upper-class women and the lack of educational facilities. Yet Indonesians, both men and women, tend to emphasize the gains less than the distance women still have to go. So village women are exhorted by local government officials, for example, to keep their daughters as well as their sons in school and to interest themselves more in public affairs.

There are religious leaders and devout Muslims who deplore the sexually mixed social and recreational activities of adolescents and younger men and women on the ground that these lead to sexual immorality. It is interesting to note, however, that the Orthodox Islamic Party has elected women members to parliament. Apart from such reservations, however, I have encountered no overt or latent attitudes among men or women tending to discourage women's interests in a variety of roles. Admittedly, Indonesians are extremely polite and are not likely to express such attitudes to an American woman political scientist or in her presence.

Another factor encouraging a broad range of choice is that for many Indonesian women selection of one role or emphasis on it does not necessarily involve the sacrifice of another. Household help in the form of servants or dependents and the relative ease with which children can be placed with or cared for by relatives for brief or extended periods mean that mothers with young children need not be confined to their homes. Even though child-care centers did not yet seem necessary to enable women to work in factories that I studied, the men leaders of some unions included such centers for working mothers among their expressed goals.

Widows, divorcees (of which there are many for divorce is frequent), and women who have never married do not appear to be penalized by relative social isolation and loneliness. Much of social entertaining appears to be done on the scale of the extended family group or the surrounding neighborhood residents and includes the unattached as well as married couples with or without their children.

The woman physician, the woman who operates a shipyard, the woman who enters parliament, the woman who travels abroad by herself to attend an international congress have all assumed roles formerly not held by women. Yet they have not been made to feel that by so doing they have become somehow desexed, have diminished their marital possibilities, or have somehow emasculated their husbands. For, as far as I could ascertain, such activities are not considered unfeminine.

Perhaps the most important indicator for the potential development of the position of women relative to that of men in any society is what I have referred to as personal, expressive, or emotional style. This includes culturally defined notions of valued and denigrated personality attributes and affective or emotional states as well as the appropriate modes for their expressions and/or control.

I suspect that if a psychologist were to give the same list of personality attributes and modes of behavior to a group of Javanese men and women and to a group of American men and women and ask each group to classify these as either masculine or feminine, the Javanese respondents would have far greater difficulty in so doing. In the course of my many years of residence in Java, I have yet to encounter reference to a woman as having a "masculine" mind or an aggressively male style, comments that are not infrequent in American society. I have indeed heard Javanese women described, either favorably or critically, by other Javanese women and men as logical, strong-willed, direct, and outspoken, but the adjective masculine was not appended to such comments. Nor have I heard any man described by Indonesians as possessing an almost feminine intuition or as expressing himself in an oblique feminine or catty feminine manner. Indonesian culture, or at least the Javanese and Sudanese subcultures with which I am most familiar, do not seem to distinguish qualities and styles as properly masculine or feminine.

There are, of course, recognized categories of contrasting behavior and style. One of the most frequently noted distinctions in Javanese culture is that between *haloes* (refined, subtle) and *kasar* (crude, direct). Another is between self-control and a calm demeanor on the one hand, which are valued, and impulsiveness and an agitated demeanor on the other, which are frowned upon. It is significant, however, that these are not, by and large, dichotomized along sexual lines. Such distinctions are associated with social origins and status. Thus *kasar* behavior tends to be associated with peasant villagers or urban workers of either sex and *haloes* mannerisms with men and women from the gentry and officialdom.

This lack of cultural assignment of specific styles in accordance with sex has significance for the future development of both women and men in Indonesia. In contrast with societies such as ours where the dichotomy of psychological attributes as male or female and the corresponding narrowing of approved choices have long impoverished the possibilities of fulfillment for both men and women, the future possibilities for women in Indonesia seem very rich, indeed.

Notes

1. One need not be a member of Women's Lib to wonder about the relative lack of research entitled "Men's Role . . ." or "The Role of Men in . . ." one or another context or society.
2. See Stephen Kelman, "Sweden's Liberated Men and Women," *New Republic*, 13 March 1971, pp. 21–23 for a description of the emphasis in Sweden on identical sex roles, including part-time work for both sexes to give time to each for family responsibilities and a high-school curriculum in which home economics, woodworking, sewing, and baby-care are compulsory for both boys and girls.
3. Robert R. Jay, *Javanese Villagers: Social Relations in Rural Modjokuto* (Cambridge: M.I.T. Press, 1969), p. 129.
4. Ibid., pp. 56, 63–65, 88. See also Barend ter Haar, *Adat Law in Indonesia*, translated from the Dutch (New York: Institute of Pacific Relations, 1948), pp. 187–194, especially for the variations and limitations upon individual ownership or transfer in accordance with different kinship regulations.
5. Jay, pp. 64–65.
6. Ter Haar, *passim*. Also see Cora Vreede-de Stuers, "Indonesia," in Raphael Patai, ed., *Women in the Modern World* (New York: Free Press, 1967), pp. 367–370.
7. James Siegel, *The Rope of God* (Berkeley: University of California Press, 1969), pp. 51–52, 138–140.
8. Hildred Geertz, "The Vocabulary of Emotion," *Psychiatry* 22, no. 3 (August 1959): 229.
9. Alice G. Dewey, *Peasant Marketing in Java* (New York: Free Press of Glencoe, 1962).
10. Ann Ruth Willner, "The Adaptation of Peasants to Conditions of Factory Labor," *Asian Survey* 3, no. 2 (February 1963).
11. See Hurustiati Subandrio, "The Respective Roles of Men and Women in Indonesia," in Barbara Ward, ed., *Women in the New Asia* (Paris: UNESCO, 1963), pp. 229–242, for a personal account of the changes that have occurred in three generations for women of elite background.
12. Geertz, p. 229. Also Hildred Geertz, *The Javanese Family* (Glencoe, Ill.: Free Press, 1961), pp. 123–125. Also: Jay, pp. 61, 87, 92.
13. Jay, p. 62.
14. Thomas Stamford Raffles, *The History of Java* (London, 1830), 1: 394. See also *Adatrechtbundels* (The Hague, 1910–1930), 34: 388–392.
15. Daniel G. Hall, *A History of Southeast Asia* (London: Macmillan, 1961), p. 745; Peter R. Goethals,'*Aspects of Local Government in a Sumbawan Village* (Modern Indonesia Project Monograph. Ithaca, N.Y.: Cornell University, 1961), p. 114; Vreede-de Stuers, p. 362.
16. Hildred Geertz, "Indonesian Cultures and Communities," in Ruth T. McVey, ed., *Indonesia* (New Haven: HRAF Press, 1967), p. 56.
17. See also Stephen A. Douglas's chapter in this book for a more detailed discussion of the political roles of Indonesian women.

III   South Asia

The cultural, historical, and religious burdens that affect the status of women everywhere weigh most heavily on the women of South Asia. When we examine the Indian subcontinent, we find the status of women at its lowest in both real and ideal terms.

A strong patriarchal family system, reinforced by caste division, Hindu and Muslim religious ideals, and total or near-total absence of opportunity for economic activity outside the home, has served to place women at the bottom of the South Asian status ladder. This picture appears even more depressing in the light of the research presented in the following chapters. Most of the data offered here indicate that the process of modernization has brought little change in the status of South Asian women. What benefits have accrued have gone to a very small minority of elite women. Only those in this group have managed, in some degree, to escape the status trap of history, caste, religion, economic order, and cultural tradition. Little, if any, of the increasing status of this small elite has trickled down to the majority.

As we have seen, in East and Southeast Asia certain factors—either inheritance patterns, important economic roles, or kinship systems—in part counterbalance those variables that tend to depress female status. Unfortunately, mitigating factors apparently do not exist in South Asia, where all these things that affect women's status are mutually supportive in the direction of female inferiority.

To say this is not to suggest that no changes are taking place. Increasing educational opportunities, factory work for women in urban environments, national efforts toward population control, and other factors that must come with the industrialization of India and Pakistan must in time affect female status. However, the effect of these factors will occur later and the process of change will be slower here than in the rest of Asia. Clearly, the patience with events bred into South Asian women through centuries of yielding to fate will serve them well during the slow movement to a higher status level over the long and difficult years ahead.

In Part III we focus on women in the Hindu and Islamic cultures of South Asia. Here, as noted in the Introduction, the burdens of class reinforce caste behavior. Under these conditions we would expect that female status would be highest and role activity greatest for Hindu women such as Indira Gandhi, who came from upper-caste and class families, and for women such as the members of the All Pakistan Women's Association, who come from upper-class Muslim families.

In regard to the latter groups much research has shown that these women have played a significant role in Indian Muslim politics. Although these findings are in sharp contrast with images of Muslim women as shadowy, veiled figures kept out of circulation and certainly out of politics by the custom of *parda,* the sequestration of women, there is some disagreement about the future implications of this political activity.

On the one hand Gail Minault argues that historically parda has not been as restrictive to women taking an active part in the political process, especially in the early twentieth century, as previous observers have indicated. The women, many of them wives of leaders in the Khilafat movement, operated within the bounds of traditionally regarded feminine roles, yet nonetheless stretched the interpretation of parda, thus setting the stage for their daughters and granddaughters to challenge parda itself. Bi Amman, and others like her, helped pave the way for other women like the Begum Liaquat Ali Khan and the ladies of the All Pakistan Women's Association and their limited form of political activity.

Sylvia A. Chipp, on the other hand, looks at a group of elite women in Pakistan but finds very little evidence of a feminist spirit and virtually no claim to "equality." In working for improvements in social, economic, and political conditions, the All Pakistan Women's Association operated entirely within the context of Islamic culture and socially acceptable behavior.

Rounaq Jahan, analyzing the results of the national elections of 1973, discusses the political attitudes and behavior of urban women in Bangladesh. She finds that men are significantly better educated, better informed about the political process, and more active in it. However, the situation is reversed when she turns her attention to the 15 women holding the "reserved seats" in the Bangladesh National Parliament in 1974. They are significantly better educated and wealthier than their male counterparts. Interesting differences in attitudes toward important political issues are revealed.

Finally, Manjulika Koshal takes a look at how and why Indira Gandhi—as the daughter of former Prime Minister Nehru and of high caste and upper class—was able to escape the status position of most Hindu women and was chosen as the leader of what has been called the world's largest democracy. Koshal sees Gandhi as a strong-willed woman who ruled India for more than ten years with the firm conviction that she could deal effectively with the nation's overwhelming problems. She suggests that one can find examples of political elites in other countries that were faced with similar situations, but nowhere is the boldness of personality revealed so strikingly.

8   Political Change: Muslim Women in Conflict with Parda: Their Role in the Indian Nationalist Movement[1]

Gail Minault

In recent years, the questioning of the dichotomy between the concepts of "tradition" and "modernity" had led to a number of studies of the role of traditional figures as political communicators.[2] While working on one such study concerned with Indo-Muslim politics in the early twentieth century, the present author came across the following comment by a British administrator in India: "The priests and the women are the most important influences in India . . . and I am not very much afraid of the politicians until they play on these two."[3] The observation was astute, for not only did the "priests," or ulama, play a significant role in Indian Muslim politics at that time, but so too did Muslim women. This may seem surprising, for Muslim women are usually pictured as shadowy, veiled figures, kept out of circulation and certainly out of politics by the custom of parda, or the sequestration of women.

Working backward from the fact that Muslim women were involved in Indian politics in the early twentieth century, several interesting questions arise. The most obvious is: How, given the institution of parda, were they able to participate politically? Secondly, how was this involvement outside their homes accepted by Indian Muslim society? The conflict between parda and politics would seem to be absolute. The women, in challenging parda, were presumably risking their honor and hence the honor of their men. In bringing shame upon their men, they would thus, again presumably, render their men less effective politically. But this expectation was not the case. To explain these phenomena—the very real political influence wielded by the Indian Muslim women, and the increased effectiveness they brought to Muslim political activity—one must examine the institution of parda in general, particularly as it is practiced in North India, and then go on to an individual case study of political involvement. One will find that within their traditional roles Muslim women had a great deal of influence. This feature of the tradition will help explain how, even without leaving parda, women were able to exercise attitudinal influence within a wide social context. Once such influence had been exerted, and accepted, the way was open for some women, whose traditional status permitted them a certain liberty, to challenge the outward forms of parda bit by bit. The particular case to be cited will show that the women were not, strictly speaking, in conflict with parda. Their importance on the political scene was not so much in spite of parda as it was because of their traditional roles.

The institution of parda is found to a greater or lesser degree in all Islamic societies. The sanction for it is found in the Qur'an, in a verse that posits the superiority of men over women: "Men are the managers of the affairs of women, for that God has preferred in bounty one of them over another, and for that they have expended of their property. Righteous women are therefore obedient."[4] Male supremacy was nothing new in Mediterranean society. It antedates Islam, and it has been argued that Islam actually improved the lot of women, giving them rights of inheritance and limiting polygyny, at least theoretically, to four wives. Others disagree, claiming that women in pre-Islamic tribal society were relatively free, that the harem and the veil were adopted as means for the men to safeguard their honor by cutting their women off from the sexual temptations of city life.[5]

In any case, the observance of parda varies as much according to locale and social class as it does according to degrees of religious orthodoxy. In tribal societies, women may move about unveiled with relative freedom.[6] In villages, the poorer women who work in the fields will also be free of the veil, out of economic necessity.[7] As one moves up the social ladder in settled societies, however, seclusion is observed as a sign of social status. Lower-middle-class wives in villages will observe parda, indicating that their husbands earn sufficient income to permit their wives to stay at home. In urban areas, seclusion is observed for reasons both of status and security by those who can afford it. But the custom decreases among those most able to afford it, the westernized elite, since education of women—another status indicator—militates against it.[8]

Just as there are wide variations in the observance of parda in the Islamic world, so too are there variations in the degrees of seclusion. In North India, one finds large households where there are separate men's and women's quarters, and sufficient numbers of servants so the women never have to leave their own domain. The following passage describes parda in such a household:

> In the zenana [women's quarters] things went on with the monotonous sameness of Indian life. No one went out anywhere. Only now and then some cousin or aunt or some other relation came to see them. . . . Mostly life stayed like water in a pond with nothing to break the monotony of its static life. . . . The world lived and died, things happened, events took place, but all this did not disturb the equanimity of the zenana, which had its world too where the pale and fragile beauties of the hothouse lived secluded from outside harm, the storms that blow in the world of men. The day dawned, the evening came, and life passed them by.[9]

In contrast to this affluent model are the one-room dwellings of the urban poor out of which women seldom ventured, even for sunlight and air.[10]

Should she wish to go out, a secluded woman resorts to the portable parda of the burqa, a garment that effectively hides her face and figure. Again there are variations in style, ranging from the flowing, ghostlike tent of homespun cotton with only two small eye holes to a capelike coat of silk or rayon that permits freedom of the hands and has a separate headpiece, permitting the wearer to cover or uncover her face. A burqa, while designedly formless and obviously inconvenient, may nevertheless be viewed, by the wearer, as a liberating garment. It permits her to move about in public and still remain relatively invisible.[11]

This wide variation in the observance and styles of parda indicates that the reasons for the institution are much more complex than can be explained by quoting the Qur'an. Starting from the assumption of male superiority—whether Qur'anic or not—certain other assumptions follow: Women, as physically weaker and as socially and economically inferior, are vulnerable and need to be protected. The corollary of this assumed weakness is that women are also weaker emotionally, hence unable to control their sexual desires, and in need of strict governance by the male—her father before marriage and her husband thereafter. A man's honor is thus inextricably bound up with his ability both to provide economically for his wife and family and to protect his womenfolk from the sexuality of other men. The emphasis on male honor and virility leads to a cult of female chastity, whether virginity of the bride or faithfulness of the wife.[12] The point of view of the Muslim male may be summarized by quoting an Algerian revolutionary leader:

> Social life, manners, customs had as their essential objective the jealous safeguarding of the women's sex. They [the men] consider this as inalien-

able, and their honor was buried in the vagina as if it were a treasure more precious than life.[13]

Parda, then, is a complex of social values, sanctioned by religion but based on belief in the female's social inferiority and inherent sexual promiscuity. She must be protected, that is, segregated, so that the man's honor, the family, and the whole social order may be preserved.

Within this social order, marriages are arranged; thus there is no need for social contact between the sexes—and the promiscuity that implies—prior to marriage. Romantic love in such a society is viewed with suspicion, if not total dismay. Marriage is a contract that joins two families as much as it joins two individuals. The custom of cousin marriages further limits the element of chance in the choice of mates, and also keeps the family property together by limiting the kin group. After marriage, the woman gains status as the mother of sons and her proper fulfillment of the roles of wife and mother adds to the honor and status of her husband. Should she become a widow, she can inherit some of her husband's property, thus attaining independent economic status, albeit probably still under the direction of her sons or other male relatives. She can even remarry. The position of the Muslim widow stands in significant contrast to the position of her Hindu counterpart, who can have no individual status independent of her conjugal family, and who can neither inherit property nor acceptably remarry.[14]

The consequences of the custom of parda for the society are also many and varied. For purposes of this study, however, only one needs to be considered in detail, and that is what Hanna Papanek has termed the "separate worlds" of men and women in a parda society. These different worlds involve both a sharp division of labor and a high degree of interdependence. It is obvious that the man's work is outside the home and woman's inside, but there is also a moral division of labor. Just as the man provides the external shelter and protection for his wife and family, so the wife provides the emotional shelter. She is undeniably the queen in her own realm. She is the locus of affection for the children, the early molder of personality, the instructress in basic religious observances and cultural attitudes.[15] Perhaps the power of women in the home can best be illustrated by an excerpt from the biography of the Munshi Zakaullah of Delhi, a pioneer in Muslim educational reform in the nineteenth century:

Although the influence of his father and his grandfather in moulding Zaka Ullah's religious life was great, undoubtedly the strongest influence on his character and his daily conduct . . . came from his mother. . . . From his very earliest childhood Zaka Ullah clung to his mother with a child's ardent and impetuous affection. She was a woman of very strong will, and she ruled her children as well as loved them. She would never allow a fault to be passed over, and her least displeasure was greatly feared by her sons. . . . Zaka Ullah would relate the incident, how, some years before the Mutiny, the family had been in straitened circumstances, and it was very hard indeed for his father to support his six young children. But his mother sold all her ornaments and household things and purchased with the money the books that were needed for her children's education.[16]

This account of a mother's intervention to save the children's schooling indicates another result of the separation of male and female worlds. That is, women are not dependent on the approval of men for their self-esteem. Thus in a situation directly related to her sphere of influence, such as a decision regarding a child's education, the woman's voice may often prevail, even over considerable male opposition. Similar to the case of Zakaullah's mother is a later example of a young widow who needed all the resolution she could muster against united family displeasure. Muhammad Ali, an important Muslim political leader of the early twentieth century, thus described his mother, Bi Amman, and her struggle:

> Unlike most of our cousins whose parents were averse to endangering their salvation by subjecting them to "the Godless influence of English education," two of my brothers had already been sent to the school at Bareilly by our mother. She had become a widow at the age of 27. . . . She refused to remarry, and . . . told those who advised her to do so that she had had a husband to look after her long enough and now she had herself five husbands and a wife to look after, referring, of course, to her five boys and one girl. . . . When the younger of these two brothers of mine, Shaukat, was selected by her for a course of English education, the uncle who was managing our property refused to sanction an allowance for his school expenses, remarking . . . that one "infidel" was bad enough in the family! But our mother was determined and secretly pawned some personal jewelry of her own with the help of the maid-servant of a Hindu neighbour, who was a banker, and packed off the second would-be "infidel" to Bareilly. . . . When our uncle had been thus outwitted by a resolute woman whose self-reliance . . . had only been equalled by her trust in the bountiful providence of God, he got her trinkets released from pawn and paid for the schooling of both his nephews. When yet another "infidel" sought perdition, he accepted the inevitable and I proceeded to Bareilly.[17]

Bi Amman, introduced in this adulatory account by her equally headstrong and energetic son, was obviously a woman to be reckoned with. She had an unassailable position as a widow, a mother of many sons, and a woman of some property, even though she had to pry it loose from her reluctant brother-in-law by pawning her jewelry, an action that reflected on his honor as her protector.

In parda society, the woman was also important as a religious preceptor. Sheltered from the outside world, she represented cultural continuity. If she was given any education at all, it was in learning to read the Qur'an; thus the sacred book had a special importance for her. The children's early religious training was in their mother's hands. They followed her example in praying, and she saw to it that they too were tutored in the Arabic of the Qur'an. Muhammad Ali reminisced about his mother's saintliness, relating how, having learned to read the Qur'an in Arabic, which she could barely understand, she then learned to read Urdu (written in a script similar to Arabic) by having a nephew read novels to her. She would virtually memorize these stories and then reread them in secret. After that, she got an Urdu translation of the Qur'an, and would read it along with the Arabic original. Bi Amman, relates Muhammad Ali, was also a marvelous storyteller. She undoubtedly retained many of the yarns she had learned in her quest for the scripture.[18]

A Parda-nashin[19] Enters Politics: Bi Amman and the Khilafat Movement

Bi Amman was like many Muslim women at the end of the last century in her desire to see her children well-educated in British-style schools, and in her anxiety to assure that such education did not cut them off from their religious and cultural heritage. The major center for such English education for Muslim boys[20] was Sir Sayyid Ahmad Khan's Aligarh College, where the Ali brothers went to school. Shaukat and Muhammad earned their B.A.'s and were the best orators on the debating team. Shaukat was also idolized as a winning cricket captain and later became a well-known figure in fund-raising and alumni affairs for the college. Muhammad went on to Oxford from Aligarh and returned to India hoping to teach at his alma mater, but he was turned down. He went on to an administrative post, but later turned to political journalism. In 1911 he started the English weekly *Comrade,* and a year later its Urdu counterpart *Hamdard.* With his brother, Muhammad was active in Aligarh alumni affairs and increasingly, especially through his eloquent editorials, in Muslim political affairs.[21]

The Ali brothers' growing involvement in Indian politics culminated in 1911-1913 in a flurry of religiopolitical activity, centered on opposition to British policy in the Middle East and toward Indian Muslims. These years saw the Balkan wars against Turkey, which excited Indo-Muslim suspicions of a Christian conspiracy against the Ottoman Empire, the seat of the Islamic Caliphate. In addition, the British government in 1911 revoked the partition of Bengal, a blow to

Muslims who had seen in Eastern Bengal a source of Muslim administrative jobs and political influence. Further, in 1912 the government
turned down the request by the Aligarh College administration and
graduates that the college be made into a Muslim University. These
blows to Muslim self-esteem in India, combined with what was seen as
an attack on Islamic religion in the institution of the Turkish
Caliphate, led to a spate of organizational activity on the part of
articulate young Muslims, most notably Shaukat and Muhammad Ali.
In these efforts, they were ably assisted by Bi Amman. Meetings of
protest were organized for women only, at which Bi Amman spoke,
urging the women to support the cause of Islam by giving money to
help the Turkish Caliph withstand the onslaught of Christian Europe.
In these beginnings of parda politics, the Ali matriarch was joined by
Muhammad Ali's wife and the wives of other prominent Muslim
leaders.[22]

Later, Bi Amman became more involved in Muslim politics at the
national level. During World War I, while Britain was at war with
Turkey, the Ali brothers were interned for their pro-Turkish activities and writings. In 1917, Bi Amman helped lead an appeal to the
viceroy for their release, which ultimately failed. In anticipation of his
release, Muhammad Ali was chosen president of the 1917 annual
Muslim League meeting. Since Muhammad was still in detention at
the time of the meeting, however, the presidential chair was graced by
his photograph, and Bi Amman spoke briefly to the assembled
Muslim Leaguers from behind the veil of her burqa.[23]

After the war, when the Ali brothers were released, they became
the most prominent Muslim political leaders during the Khilafat
movement. This movement, building upon some of their prewar
efforts, was designed to pressure the British government to preserve
the defeated Ottoman Empire and its ruler, the Caliph of Islam.
Genuine religious faith learned at their mother's knee, combined with
their political acumen, led the Ali brothers to a form of political
activity that could mobilize a Muslim constituency united by means of
religious and cultural symbols meaningful to all strata of the community. The Khilafat movement gained added significance because it
took place simultaneously, and cooperated fully, with Mohandas
Gandhi's first nonviolent noncooperation movement against British
rule. Muslim and Hindu were thus engaged in a parallel political
effort: the broadening of national political participation from the elite
to the mass through new techniques of organization and communication.

In this organization and communication, the women had a
significant role to play. With feminine support, the political leaders

had potential contact with every hearth. The indefatigable Bi Amman was one of the most active women in the movement. She toured the countryside with her sons, appearing on the platform at political meetings in her burqa, but then lifted her veil to speak to the crowds, explaining that all present were like her sons and daughters, and thus there was no reason to maintain parda before them.[24]

Bi Amman, because her high status as the mother of respected men, and as a widow with a high degree of independence and self-confidence, was able to challenge customs forbidding political activity for women. She began in a small way by venturing out in a burqa to attend ostensibly religious meetings of women only. As these meetings became politicized, thanks largely to her efforts, the image dichotomy between what respectable women do and political activity began to break down. She then was able to attend a mixed political meeting, the 1917 Muslim League, though still veiled. During the Khilafat movement, with religious fervor at a high pitch, she was finally able to lift her veil to speak to mixed groups. She justified it by including all present within her family; others may have accepted it as an act of religious devotion.

Bi Amman had opened the way for others to become involved in politics. Her daughter-in-law, Begum Muhammad Ali, also traveled constantly with her husband during the Khilafat movement, and helped organize a women's branch of the All-India Khilafat Committee in 1921. She was Muhammad Ali's bookkeeper and as good at fund raising as he. Muhammad Ali commented in his memoirs:

> On 14th September 1921, I was arrested at the railway station of Walthair, when we were travelling on our way to Madras. . . . We parted company once more, but it has been a source of consolation to me, not unmixed with some amusement, that my wife is still travelling . . . and has collected large amounts for the Khilafat Fund and the National Muslim University. Mahatma Gandhi had insisted more than once on her addressing a few words to gatherings of ladies and had assured her at the end of her speeches that she was a better speaker than myself.[25]

The Ali women and many others furthered the Khilafat movement at meetings where women were exhorted to do their duty to God by supporting their men and by imbuing their children with religious faith and patriotism. They were told to economize on household expenses in order to support the cause. They responded with small gifts of cash and larger gifts of gold bangles, anklets, and earrings.[26] The women were also active in Gandhi's *Swadeshi* campaign to boycott foreign-made cloth and to wear homespun. They propagandized use of the spinning wheel and gave piles of imported cloth to feed *Swadeshi* bonfires.[27] Both Hindu and Muslim women knew that many politicians were saying that self-rule for India could not be won by politics alone. It had to begin in their homes, in renewed pride in their religion and culture.[28]

Bi Amman, Begum Muhammad Ali, and other wives of Khilafat movement leaders, while engaging in a limited form of political activity, nevertheless remained within the bounds of traditionally regarded feminine roles. They continued to observe parda, even though they stretched its limits to include unveiling of the face under certain conditions, as mentioned above. Most of their work was done among women, and their appeals treated themes especially relevant to women's experience: moral training, religious observance, cultural pride and continuity. These were also themes that were politically relevant in the Gandhian era of resurgent national self-respect and quest for cultural autonomy. Furthermore, these women, though remaining within traditionally sanctioned limits, and thus gaining social acceptance, opened the way for their daughters and grand-daughters to begin challenging parda itself.[29]

Notes

1. This paper was prepared for presentation at the Berkshire Conference of Women Historians, Douglass College of Rutgers University, New Brunswick, New Jersey, 3 March, 1973.

2. See, for example, Lloyd Rudolph and Suzanne H. Rudolph, *The Modernity of Tradition* (Chicago: University of Chicago Press, 1967); Donald Eugene Smith, *Religion and Political Development* (Boston: Little, Brown, 1970).

3. Gail Minault Graham, "Islam and Mass Politics: The Indian Ulama and the Khilafat Movement," in Donald E. Smith, ed., *Religion and Political Modernization* (New Haven: Yale University Press, 1974). The quotation is from Sir Harcourt Butler to Lord Harding, 16 January 1916, Butler Papers, Mss. Eur. F 116/53/II, India Office Library.

4. Qur'an IV: 38, tr. by A. J. Arberry, *The Koran Interpreted I* (New York: Macmillan, 1950), p. 105.

5. For the pros and cons of this argument, see Ameer Ali, *The Spirit of Islam* (London: Methuen, 1965), pp. 227–230; Fazlur Rahman, *Islam* (London: Weidenfeld and Nicolson, 1966), p. 38; and Germaine Tillion, *Le Harem et les Cousins* (Paris, 1966), quoted in David G. Gordon, *Women in Algeria: An Essay in Change* (Cambridge, Mass: Harvard Middle East Monograph 19, 1968), pp. 6–9.

6. Gordon, pp. 15–18.

7. Eglar Zekiye, *A Punjabi Village in Pakistan* (New York: Columbia University Press, 1960), pp. 33–34; Raphael Patai, *Society, Culture and Change in the Middle East* (Philadelphia: University of Pennsylvania Press, 1969), pp. 117–118.

8. Patai, pp. 119–120; Elizabeth W. Fernea, *Guests of the Sheik* (Garden City, N.Y.: Doubleday Anchor Books, 1969), Chs. 2, 3, 7; Hanna Papanek, "Purdah in Pakistan: Seclusion and Modern Occupations for Women," *Journal of Marriage and the Family* 33, no. 3 (August 1971): 520–523.

9. Ahmed Ali, *Twilight in Delhi* (Bombay: Oxford University Press, Champak Library, 1966), pp. 39–40.

10. Cora Vreede-de Steurs, *Parda: A Study of Muslim Women's Life in Northern India* (Assen: Van Gorcum, 1968), pp. 59–64, 73–76.

11. Hanna Papanek, "Purdah: Separate Worlds and Symbolic Shelter," *Comparative Studies in Society and History* 15, no. 3 (June 1973): 289–325.

12. Patai, pp. 474–477.

13. Mouloud Feraoun's *Journal,* quoted in Gordon, p. 52.

14. Patai, pp. 125, 135; Papanek, "Purdah: Separate Worlds and Symbolic Shelter"; Sylvia J. Vatuk, "Trends in North Indian Urban Kinship," *Southwestern Journal of Anthropology* 27, no. 3 (1971): 289–292, 305.

15. Patai, pp. 439–444; Papanek, "Separate Worlds and Symbolic Shelter"; Mrs. Meer Hasan Ali, *Observations un the Mussalmauns of India* (London: Oxford University Press, 1971), pp. 167–168.

16. C. F. Andrews, *Zaka Ullah of Delhi* (Cambridge: W. Heffer & Sons, 1929), p. 52.

17. Muhammad Ali, *My Life: A Fragment* (Lahore: S. M. Ashraf, 1966), pp. 4–5.

18. Ibid., pp. 12–16.

19. A woman who observes parda.

20. Education for girls at Aligarh came later. A school for girls was started there in 1906, in the face of much public outrage. A boarding hostel was added to the girls' school in 1914. Vreede-de Steurs, pp. 54–55.

21. For a detailed treatment of the academic and political issues centered at Aligarh, see David Lelyveld and Gail Minault, "The Campaign for a Muslim University, 1898–1920," in *Modern Asian Studies* 8, no. 2 (April 1974): 145–189.

22. Begum Muhammad Ali was her husband's second cousin, the daughter of the nephew, mentioned above, who helped Bi Amman learn to read. Notice of a Ladies' Meeting of the Anjuman-e-Kaaba, 6 November 1913, Abdul Bari Papers, Firangi Mahal, Lucknow.

23. Mazhar Ansari, *Tarikh-e-Muslim League* (Delhi: Maktaba-e-Jamia, 1940), p. 189.

24. *Independent* (Allahabad), 28 September 1921; Tufail Ahmad Manglori, *Musulmanon ka Raushan Mustaqbil* (Delhi: Maktaba-e-Jamia, 1945), pp. 531–532.

25. Muhammad Ali, p. 140.

26. Collections through Begum Muhammad Ali, Central Khilafat Committee, Bombay, n.d., Muhammad Ali Papers, Jamia Millia Islamia, New Delhi; *Bombay Chronicle,* 20 January 1922.

27. *Independent* (Allahabad), 10–11 January and 2 May 1920; *Bombay Chronicle,* 11 April and 21 July 1921.

28. Speech by Sarojini Naidu reported in *Bombay Chronicle,* 25 April 1921.

29. For an interesting account, by a woman of the succeeding generation who left parda and was involved in the Muslim League and the Pakistan movement, see Shaista Ikramullah, *From Purdah to Parliament* (London: Cresset Press, 1963).

9   The Modern Pakistani Woman
in a Muslim Society[1]

Sylvia A. Chipp

"It is the woman who can do the most to make or break a nation. . . ."
Based on this belief, the All Pakistan Women's Association (the
APWA) was founded by Begum Ra'ana Liaquat Ali Khan in 1949 in
the aftermath of the Partition of the Indian subcontinent. In Pakistan,
an Islamic society, the law gives women equal status with men in legal
matters, but their full participation in public life is still largely
restricted by custom and tradition. The formation of this organization
was an attempt to bring the women of Pakistan out of their symbolic
shells.

The APWA is a small group of women, many of whom have led
active lives in politics, social service, and the professions. Most are the
wives of prominent civil servants, politicians, and professional men.
The stated objective of their activities, which are still confined mainly
to the urban areas, is the "informed and intelligent participation of
the women of Pakistan in the growth and development of the country
and the advancement of the welfare of the Pakistani women through
the improvement of their legal, political, social and economic status."

Specific projects directed by the APWA include health and family-
planning clinics, hospitals, industrial homes, schools, and colleges.
They have also acted as an interest group to pressure the government
of Pakistan to pass laws aimed at improving the status of women. The
rationale for the organization is their belief that "it is the duty of
educated women, as much as that of men, to come forward and bend
their energies to make Pakistan flourish economically and socially." It
was argued that young women must accept the challenge of the social
changes that are taking place in order to facilitate the process of
adjustment.

The APWA faces what would appear to be a problem typical of
modernizing societies—difficulty of communication between the so-
called new elites—that is, the "APWA ladies"—and the masses. This

problem is made even more difficult by the influence of the traditional elites, that is, the ulama (Muslim religious leaders) and the
village elders. Although the power of the religious leaders gradually
declined on the national level when General Mohammed Ayub Khan
and the military elite assumed control in 1958, their influence remains
strong with the rural population. Ironically, the Basic Democracies
system of the Ayub regime tended to perpetuate the power and
influence of the traditional elites on the local level.

Elites are not necessarily motivated to seek social change. The
ulama and village elders, for example, do not want to surrender
power to the younger, more Westernized and secularized elite, particularly if that elite includes women. In Pakistan, the gap between the
secularized groups—military, business, wealthy, educated—and the
masses remains significant and is perpetuated by the religious leaders
with whom the masses understandably have more empathy. The
ulama charge that the APWA is attempting to lure the women of
Pakistan away from the true Islamic path into the corrupt realm of
Western thought and practices. "This organization is working for the
avowed purpose of drifting the women out of purdah and to make
them blindly follow the life of Western women and society."[2]

The process of social and economic change is cultural as well as
material. Inevitably, such change involves promoting, establishing, and
maintaining new norms and new roles for women. It is the privileged
elite of a society who would appear to be best suited to perform these
functions and to "convince both men and women, by example, that
the elevation of women is necessary for the development of a society."
In order to achieve this elevation, a United Nations Seminar concluded that the elite have the responsibility "to see that some of their
rights and privileges are extended to women in the lesser social and
economic ranks." Educated women should encourage "civic education
and participation among women" and arouse them to "greater responsibility and participation in public affairs."[3] The members of the
APWA are thus in an ideal position to promote the necessary social
and economic changes in their society, but it is doubtful that they, in
fact, reach this goal. In their efforts, they are led by the dynamic
widow of Pakistan's first prime minister, the Begum Ra'ana Liaquat
Ali Khan, or "Begum Sahiba" as she is called. Hers is an interesting
story.

Born in the small hill station of Almora in the United Provinces of
India, she received her early education at the Wellesley Girls' High
School in Naini Tal, United Provinces, and later attended the Isabella
Thoburn High School and College in Lucknow. After receiving her
Bachelor of Arts degree from Isabella Thoburn she studied at

Lucknow University, where she was the only female in her class. Standing first in the university's Master of Arts examination, she was awarded a master's degree in Economics and Sociology. Her master's thesis, "Women Labour in Agriculture in the United Provinces in India," reflected her early interest in the status of women.

The following year she entered the Diocesan College in Calcutta for the graduate teachers' training course and passed Calcutta University's Licentiate of Teaching examination, again standing first in her class. For six months she taught at the Gokhale Memorial School in Calcutta, after which she went to Indraprastha Girls' College in Delhi, where she remained as professor of economics for a year and a half.

In April 1933, she married Nawabzada Liaquat Ali Khan, who later became Pakistan's first prime minister. In addition to raising two sons, Begum Sahiba assisted her husband in the Muslim League Movement and later during the Partition assumed the leadership of Pakistan's women's movement.

Three years after her husband's assassination, the Begum was sent as Pakistan's ambassador to the Netherlands, where she remained until June of 1961, when she assumed the ambassadorship to Italy and Tunisia. Although she retired from this post in March of 1966, she continued to serve as a member of the United Nations International Labor Organization's Committee of Experts on the Application of Recommendations. She is the founder of numerous organizations and the recipient of several awards, including the Jane Addams Medal in 1950 and the International Gimbel Award in 1962. She more recently served as the governor of Sind.

The National Executive Committee

At the time of my visit to Pakistan in 1969, Begum Sahiba had resumed her position as the driving force behind the All Pakistan Women's Association after several years in Europe. With her assistance, I administered a questionnaire of approximately eighty questions to twenty-two members of the National Executive Committee. The questionnaire served as the basis of this study.

The National Executive Committee (located in Karachi) was made up of the Founder Life President (Begum Sahiba), the national chairman (a liaison position in Rawalpindi, the nation's capital at that time), the chairman, the senior vice-chairman, five vice-chairmen, two vice-chairmen ex-officio (the presidents of APWA-West Pakistan and APWA-East Pakistan), the treasurer, twenty-one sectional secretaries, fourteen joint (or assistant) secretaries, four members of honor, and seven consultants. (Even though all of these positions were held by women, they used the title of chairman.)

For the purposes of this study, the questionnaire was administered only to those women (national chairman, chairman, vice-chairmen, treasurer, and sectional secretaries) who were most actively concerned with the work of the organization. Of this actively involved group only the Founder Life President, one vice-chairman, and seven sectional secretaries, three of whom were out of the country during my stay in Karachi, did not participate in the study. The other six did not wish to participate. The members of honor, consultants, vice-chairmen ex-officio, and joint secretaries were not included in this study. Members will be referred to throughout this study as Begum or Miss A, B, C, and the like. Data are reported to the nearest whole percent or to the nearest tenth of one percent.

Most were very cooperative, although a few seemed to be uneasy about the personal nature of some of the questions. Their doubt may have resulted partly from the political unrest in the country during this period, or it may reflect their lack of experience with studies of this kind.

Studies of elites must, of necessity, include consideration of such factors as age, family and educational background, religious affiliation, and previous experience in civic and political affairs.

Age and Family Background
Most sectional secretaries and all chairmen and vice-chairmen were born in India before 1930. Only four women were born in what is now Pakistan. With few exceptions, all had joined the APWA in its early years between 1949 and 1954. Only three members had joined the Executive Committee between 1955 and 1966, while Begum Sahiba was out of the country, perhaps indicating her close supervision of the organization. In an attempt to bring "new blood" into the organization, Begum Sahiba asked several younger women to join the Executive Committee after her return to Pakistan in 1966. All of the women but one, a Parsi, were Muslims. The Parsi lady had been brought up in the Zoroastrian faith.

Marital Status
Of the 22 members of the APWA Executive Committee who submitted to the questionnaire, 16 (73 percent) were married, two (9 percent) were widowed, and four (18 percent) were single with no immediate plans for marriage. None was divorced. Only 39 percent of their marriages had been arranged, while 33 percent reported their

Table 1. Number of Children of APWA Members and Parents

Number of Children	APWA Members		Parents	
	Number	Percent	Number	Percent
0 (unmarried)	4	18	—	—
0	1	5	0	0
1	0	0	0	0
2	5	23	0	0
3	6	27	2	9
4	4	18	6	27
5	2	9	3	14
6 or more	0	0	11	50

marriages were "semiarranged" or contracted with their parents' consent. The marriages of 28 percent were not arranged, including the Parsi's, who said that her community has no official institution of arranged marriage. Of those whose marriages were arranged, one had actually met her husband before the marriage took place. This couple had known each other from childhood. Those of nonarranged marriages had met their husbands in college; through family, friends, or neighbors; and in one case, "at a badminton court." These kinds of meetings would seem to indicate a lessening of the tradition of arranged marriages among this particular segment of upper-class urban society.

Of the 18 married or widowed, only one had no children. The families of the APWA ladies tended to be much smaller than those in

Table 2. Education Attainments of Respondents' Mothers and Fathers, "APWA Husbands," and Respondents

Highest Level of Education Attained	APWA Members		APWA Husbands		Mothers		Fathers	
	No.	Percent	No.*	Percent*	No.	Percent	No.	Percent
No formal schooling (educated at home)	1	4.5	—	—	9	41	2	9
Primary school	—	—	—	—	5	23	—	—
Middle school	4	18	2	11	3	13.5	4	18
Intermediate college	1	4.5	1	6	2	9	2	9
Degree college (B.A.)	3	13.5	5	28	—	—	6	27
University (no degree)	—	—	—	—	3	13.5	3	13.5
University (M.A.)	8	36	6	33	—	—	2	9
University (Ph.D.)	2	9	—	—	—	—	—	—
Special training (LL.B.)	2	9	3	17	—	—	—	—
Other	1	4.5	1	6	—	—	1	4.5
Not known	—	—	—	—	—	—	2	9

*$N = 18$.

which they had been raised. Most had 4 or fewer children, perhaps reflecting a recent tendency of the more educated upper classes to have smaller families. Only 2 (9 percent) had as many as 5 children. This family size was in sharp contrast with that of the 64 percent of their mothers who had 5 or more children.

Education

The importance of education for the development of future generations cannot be overemphasized. Historically, men have been more highly educated than women. It is interesting to examine the educational achievements of the APWA ladies and their families. A large proportion (41 percent) of their mothers received no formal schooling, receiving a limited education at home.[4] The others received various levels of formal education up to and including the university (see Table 2). Most of the mothers (55 percent) spoke at least a little English, including one mother who spoke mostly English. Several also spoke one or two other Western languages, indicating a higher level of education than usual. Most also spoke Urdu, the official language of Pakistan.

Reflecting the nationwide picture, the fathers of the APWA members were generally more highly educated than were their mothers. Only two (9 percent) did not receive formal schooling. One received only religious instruction at the Sind Madrasa. A much higher percentage received a college or university education, including one who earned his M.A. in English at Cambridge in England. Two respondents had no knowledge of their father's educational attainments, having been very young when their fathers died (see Table 2). A much higher percentage (91 percent) of the fathers were able to speak English, compared to 55 percent of the mothers. Most (68 percent) spoke at least two other languages.

In contrast to the mothers of the respondents, 41 percent of whom received no formal schooling, only one APWA lady did not attend school. However, she was educated at home up to the intermediate college level. All were educated beyond the primary school level, and over half (54 percent) attended the university, including Miss Q, who earned her B.A. secretly, that is, unknown to her father, while in purdah at Aligarh University where her mother's family "had connections." Miss T received her Ph.D. in adult education and community development from an American university. Begum B completed all requirements except the dissertation for a Ph.D. in social psychology from an Indian university. Eight, or 36 percent, had received Master's degrees in a variety of fields: history, Persian, mathematics, English, and political science. Two, Begum E and Begum U, received law degrees and are practicing attorneys in Karachi. Begum U also received a Master's degree in comparative law. Three (13.5 percent) received B.A. degrees in domestic science, history, and political science. Miss I was an M.A. student in adult literacy. Three (13.5 percent) received their advanced degrees from American institutions—two from Columbia University in New York and one from Southern Methodist University in Texas.

Of the eighteen "APWA husbands," none had earned a Ph.D., but six (33 percent) had earned M.A. degrees. Three of these men had also earned the LL.B. degree. Five (28 percent) had received B.A. degrees. One finished two years of college; another received his education at a military academy; two completed middle school.

All the APWA ladies were able to speak at least a little English and at least two other languages. In fact, most handled the language with a high degree of proficiency, characteristic of the highly educated person of this generation. For most (59 percent), Urdu was the first language they had learned as children. Four (18 percent) learned English as their first language, although in all four cases it was actually learned simultaneously with Urdu. For the others, Punjabi, Gujarati, Hindustani, or Kanarese were the first languages learned. Most of the APWA husbands spoke English. Only one husband spoke no English, but had spent 18 years living and teaching in Japan and spoke fluent Japanese. Most spoke at least two languages.

Ability to use the English language with facility would appear to be a mark of the educated classes, especially in Asian countries with a British colonial background. It is interesting to note that among the APWA ladies and their husbands there is not so wide a gap in educational level or language skills as appears in the parents' generation. In fact, the women actually show a slightly higher level of educational achievement.

Travel

Travel, and thus experiencing cultures different from one's own, is generally considered to be an important aspect of the education of elites. It is difficult, of course, to measure the extent to which such travel brings about changes in the individual since it is entirely possible to travel without being changed very much. However, there are probably very few substitutes for the awareness and the understanding of other cultures that travel can bring to the traveler.

Only two (9 percent) of the respondents had spent no time abroad. Most had spent less than one year abroad, but several others had spent more than five years abroad, including Begum S who had spent

18 years with her husband in Japan. Miss T had spent about eight years studying and working in the United States.

Of those who had traveled, most had represented the APWA at various international conferences held in different parts of the world. Five (23 percent) traveled abroad for the purpose of education or employment. Several had also taken trips mainly for pleasure. Most had visited Western Europe, the United States, and at least one other country in Asia, or the Middle East. Two had also visited the Soviet Union.

Employment

The traditional role of the Pakistani woman had not included employment or any other activities that have required the woman's extended absence from her home or her unrestricted participation in mixed society. In this light, it is interesting to examine the occupations of the APWA ladies and their mothers and compare them with those of their husbands and fathers (see Table 3).

As expected, a large proportion (86 percent) of their mothers were housewives, although one of these also did social work and another also ran a small family business. Of those who claimed to be career oriented, one was a teacher and one was a professional social worker. Another combined several careers: social worker, teacher, and writer. Her daughter was following the same basic pattern of social work, teaching, and writing, although she had received much more specialized training in these fields than had her mother. One mother, although primarily a housewife, had been very active in her commu-

Table 3. Occupations of APWA Ladies, Their Husbands, Mothers, and Fathers

Present Occupation	APWA Ladies		Husbands		Mothers		Fathers	
	No.	Percent	No.	Percent	No.	Percent	No.	Percent
Agriculture	—	—	—	—	—	—	1	4.5
Business	—	—	10	55	—	—	7	32
Education	1	5	—	—	1	5	2	9
Engineering	—	—	2	11	—	—	1	4.5
Government Service	—	—	—	—	—	—	9	41
Housewife	10	45	—	—	19	86	—	—
Law	2	9	—	—	—	—	—	—
Medicine	—	—	1	6	—	—	—	—
Military	—	—	—	—	—	—	2	9
Social Work	7	32	—	—	2	9	—	—
Other	2	9	—	—	—	—	—	—
Retired/Deceased	—	—	5	28	—	—	—	—

nity as a member of the Women's Division of the Muslim League, the All India Women's Conference, and the Red Cross. She served as a member of the United Provinces Legislature and even though more than 80 years of age continued to serve as head of the local school board in her community. These women all served in fields which, for the most part, allowed them to adhere to traditional feminine roles.

The occupational fields that the APWA fathers pursued were far more varied. The largest number of fathers (9 or 41 percent) served in government posts. Several others were businessmen. The rest were about evenly divided among agriculture, education, engineering, and the military.

It is interesting to note that the occupational choices of the APWA ladies have expanded somewhat beyond those of their mothers. Fewer than half considered their principal occupation to be house-wife, and many of them were also active in other fields. For example, Begum L was a former teacher and principal with 18 years experience in India, Pakistan, and London. Begum K occasionally wrote scripts for the Pakistan government television network. Several others con-sidered their principal occupation to be voluntary social work, in-cluding one former teacher and one lecturer of international repute. Significantly, only four (18 percent) of the respondents were engaged in full-time paid employment. Begum E and Begum U were practic-ing lawyers; Begum U also taught comparative law. Both were par-ticularly concerned with women's legal status. Begum F was employed by CARE, and Begum J was the principal of Karachi's APWA College for Women. Miss I was an M.A. student (see Table 3).

Only five women could not recall anyone who had actively encouraged them toward their occupational choice. Begum U's deci-sion to become a lawyer was her own idea, although her husband's family did not approve. Only 4 percent reported any opposition to their occupational choice, including Begum C, whose husband was afraid she would get too involved.

Not all of the APWA ladies had always been limited to their current social-work/housewife roles. Many (50 percent) had held government posts at the local, provincial, and national levels. Begum G, who held an elective post in the city government, had tried unsuccessfully for election to the National Assembly in 1962. Begum A, the APWA's national chairman from February of 1968, when the position was created, until March of 1969, had served for two years as West Pakistan's deputy minister of education. Of the two lawyers, Begum E served on the West Pakistan government's panel of advocates and Begum U was an assistant public prosecutor. Begum J, Begum L, and Miss Q had been teachers in government schools and colleges. Miss Q had also served as a government inspectress of schools. Miss T worked several years on a project with UNESCO and the government of Pakistan's Ministry of Social Welfare. Begum F had held various positions with the Central Government's Industrial Development Program and the Village AID Program. Both Begum B and Begum D had held several posts in education and social welfare at all three levels of government. Even though their horizons had obviously broadened, they still operated well within the bounds of the acceptable "women's world."

Like their wives, half of the "APWA Husbands" had served in a government post. All had since retired from these posts and had taken up other work. Upon his retirement from the Indian Civil Service, and later the Civil Service of Pakistan, Begum A's husband was the personal adviser to President Ayub Khan until March of 1969, when Ayub was removed from office. Three had served in the army. The rest had held a variety of positions, such as professor of surgery in a government hospital, press commissioner, pilot for the governor of West Pakistan, commissioner of excise taxation, and project director of the Oil and Gas Development Corporation. Most of the APWA husbands were now businessmen (56 percent), and two (11 percent) were engineers. Begum U's husband retired from his former position to become a writer. Begum G's husband was a doctor, and Begum J's husband was retired.

Voluntary Organizations

For the most part, members of the APWA Executive Committee were also active in a variety of other organizations. Only four (18 percent) of the respondents did not belong to any other groups. Most belonged to at least two organizations, and all but one have held at least one executive office in organizations, such as the Ladies Horticulture Society of Karachi, the Gul-e-Ra'ana Nusrat Club, the International Federation of Women Lawyers, the United Nations Association, the Girl Guides, the Federation of University Women, the Pakistan Association for the Blind, the Business and Professional Women's Club, the Inner Wheel of Rotary, and the Red Cross.

Summary

The "typical" member of the APWA's National Executive Committee in the late 1960s was more highly educated than her mother, with at least a B.A. degree, and she spoke at least two languages fluently, including English. She was married and the mother of three or four children. Although she was not usually currently employed, she considered her chief occupation to be that of social work. She belonged to at least two organizations in addition to the APWA and had traveled to foreign countries, particularly to Western Europe, for business as well as pleasure. Her husband was also likely to be well-educated and was usually engaged in business. In short, the "APWA lady" was unusual in her society, but she was still forced to operate within the constraints of rather narrowly defined role expectations.

The Social-Work Elite

In an Islamic society in which women were not expected to assert themselves, indeed were frequently discouraged from participating in a public capacity, why did some women make every effort to educate themselves and to take an active part in community life, in this case by working for an organization such as the APWA? From talking with fewer than 25 executive-committee members of the APWA in the city of Karachi, one certainly cannot come to any definitive conclusions. However, it soon became evident that "voluntary social work" is a safe and somehow more respectable occupation for the woman than working at a salaried position when her husband already earns a more than sufficient income to support his wife and family in comfort. In fact, many of the older women seemed to regret the increasing difficulty of attracting young women to voluntary work. They deplored the tendency of the younger generation to seek only paid employment. It is interesting to note that, for the most part, the older daughters of the present members of the APWA were not particularly interested in following their mothers' footsteps into the field of social work.[5]

An important factor that may have contributed in large measure to the motivation of this group of women to pursue advanced education was the active encouragement of their parents. Only three women (13.5 percent) reported their mothers as unconcerned about their education, including one mother who stipulated that her daughter could study only until her marriage. Another reported that even though her mother had "vehemently insisted" upon her education, she had to study for her M.A. through Lahore College for Women as her parents did not want her to go to the coeducational university. They did not even want her and her sister to live in the girls' hostel at the college, but she and her sister insisted. Begum E said that she was encouraged to finish her education after her marriage by a friend who insisted that "every girl should be a B.A. or you are nothing!" None reported that her parents had actively opposed her educational goals, but a few reported that relatives or the community did not approve of higher education for women. One woman's grandmother was opposed to her attendance at an English Convent school; another woman's family did not approve of her seeking advanced degrees.

Thus in most cases opposition seemed to be directed against a *type* of education rather than against education per se. The prevailing attitude seemed to be that girls should have a certain basic education, but that one's education should not interfere with marriage "at the proper time." For example, Begum H, who emphasized that she had come from an orthodox family, said that her parents allowed her to study at home but insisted that she "get married in time." After several years of marriage, however, she decided to continue her education at least to the B.A. level.

When asked how their formal education had contributed to their present activities or way of life, most responded in very general and idealistic terms. Begum A said that she had learned the spirit of social service in her college days. Begum F spoke of broadening her horizons and becoming more broadminded. Miss I, who had studied economics and political science, said she learned the value of internationalism. She felt that everyone should contribute to the development of the country. Begum J, Begum L, and Begum V each spoke of having gained greater self-confidence and self-reliance. Begum O claimed that her education had enabled her to become more socially enlightened. Miss T's education gave her a more scientific approach to basic social problems—both rural and urban. Begum U said her education taught her how to think. She explained, "It is through thinking that I am what I am."

No doubt joining the APWA and other similar groups provided an opportunity to act upon this idealism. Most reported that they had been asked personally to join the APWA by Begum Sahiba, the Founder Life President, by another member of the National Executive Committee, or by friends. The rest joined basically on their own initiative.

Specific reasons for joining the APWA varied greatly. For example, the national chairman, Begum A, admitted that it was actually through her husband's position as commissioner of Lahore that she originally was asked to join. It was customary for the wife of a city's commissioner (or deputy commissioner) to be elected to the post of president of that city's branch of the APWA. Begum A served in that capacity until 1968, when she was elected to the newly created post of national chairman of the APWA. Once again, her husband's position as adviser to President Ayub Khan would appear to have been the motivation for her appointment. Her residence in the capital city greatly facilitated the organization's contact with government officials.

Since the change in government in March of 1969, she has resigned from that post and returned to Lahore.

Begum D pointed out that she never would have gone into social work had it not been for the circumstances in which Pakistan was founded. "One had to help," she stated. Begum L wanted to do some social work after her children had grown up and she had some free time. Begum M joined after the death of her only son "for something to do." Others claimed to have joined the APWA for such ideals as service to humanity and out of a feeling of duty to help those less fortunate. Another found herself voted into membership on the National Executive Committee without even being asked first!

Approximately 55 percent of the National Executive Committee's members have had relatives who had at one time or another belonged to the APWA. However, only three or four APWA members had obviously been influenced by their families and early life experiences. Begum B had been president of her university's student union and had been involved in social work since the Partition. Ever since she could remember, her mother had been active in Muslim League politics and in social work. Begum C, as a young girl, had also been active with her parents in their political and social work as well as in the Muslim League movement. Miss Q reported a long family history in the field of social work but that her relatives objected to her walking on the streets in the pursuit of her social-work activities. Begum S also came from a family long active in social welfare and politics, including the Khilafat movement. She worked in the All India Women's Conference during the early 1930s before going to Japan with her husband.

It soon became obvious that without the consent of the "APWA husbands" there would be very few APWA social workers. Begum E and Begum H reported that their husbands generally approved of their APWA activities, but they were not too happy when they were away from the house too much. Begum J added that her husband, who was retired, did not object to her working. In fact, with his background in journalism, he had helped her write numerous articles concerning the APWA for the press.

Begum F acknowledged that her husband was "a great believer in women working." His own background in social work had been an especially important influence. "Without his support," she said, "I could not have done this." In fact, she reported, "My husband has often pushed me into things I would not otherwise have done." Begum M also reported that it was her husband's idea that she do social work for the country when the children were grown up. Begum O said that her husband allowed her to do whatever she liked. Begum

P's husband apparently objected to her joining the APWA at first, as he had heard unfavorable stories about the APWA, but eventually he approved. "However," she added, "he wants me first to be a good housewife." Although several respondents made it clear that their husbands did not want them to work in paid employment, none reported any particular opposition to her doing voluntary social work in the APWA.

In an effort to ascertain the respondents' feelings about voluntary social work, I asked them the following questions: "What do you feel is the most satisfying aspect of voluntary work?" and "What do you feel is the least satisfying aspect?" Most were quick to respond concerning the positive aspects of their work, but, not surprisingly, many seemed rather reluctant to engage in what might be construed as criticism of their co-workers if they revealed their feelings about the least satisfying aspect of voluntary work.

Few admitted to any dissatisfactions. One respondent objected to the "traditions and old customs against women being able to work." Begum A said she enjoyed seeing institutions grow up and people become trained but deplored jealousies and unjust criticism. Begum C expressed satisfaction in the "feeling that one has helped the under-privileged." Begum D, however, was discouraged by "the same problems—disease and poverty—coming up again." Miss R said that she could "do something useful without spending the whole day in the office." Begum U observed that her satisfaction came from "improving the lot of others and making others happy." Such satisfactions are obviously well within the bounds of feminine expectations.

The "Second Sex"?

What was the "APWA lady's" self-image? Did she have any sense of belonging to an elite? Did she feel that she was in any way special? Did she see herself as an individual apart from her role as wife and mother? Did this woman have any sense of unusual or unique achievement? Had she a sense of pride in this achievement? Did she see herself as a leader in her community? Did she feel that there was a necessity for change in her society, and did she feel any personal responsibility for bringing about that change?

One can give no conclusive answers to these questions, but it is possible to gain an understanding of this particular group of women. However, one should take care not to generalize too freely for all highly placed women in Pakistani society.

It was interesting to note that when asked what they considered their most important achievement, only two women, both very young,

Table 4. Most Important Achievement of Respondents

Achievement	Number	Percent
Social welfare work	9	41
Educational status	3	13.5
Role as wife and mother	5	23
Employment	1	4.5
Personal development	1	4.5
None	3	13.5

could give no answer. Most answered in terms of their social welfare activities, education, or employment (Table 4). A few felt that their most important achievement had been their roles as wife and mother, including Begum M, who revealed that her four years of living in France gave her greater self-confidence. Begum B referred to herself as "a group work trained person," explaining that she did not think in terms of individual achievement.

Begum A took special pride in the fact that she was the first girl from her family to earn a Master's degree. Attendance at a Christian college for her B.A. and at a predominantly men's college for her M.A. did not make her task an easy one. She did, in fact, meet some opposition, which she overcame largely by ignoring.

Begum L said it was her own will and her brother's understanding that helped her get her education, pointing out that "not many women in my family are highly educated." She was faced with extensive resistance, especially from relatives. Explaining that "thirty years back, things were different," she reported that there were "only five girls when I did my 'matric,' and I was the only girl who did M.A. in math." In fact, girls made up less than 10 percent of the university at that time.

Begum D at first answered that she felt her most important achievement was learning the self-discipline to put personal interest aside. Due to her early Theosophical training, she had attained a "universal or cosmopolitan attitude—to know oneself as a human rather than as a Hindu, et cetera." Then after thinking a moment, she decided that being a mother had been even more important to her.

Begum J was particularly proud of the progress that the APWA College had made since she had taken charge. However, she seemed somewhat disturbed by the largely negative response from the parents of her students to her attempts to introduce vocational subjects such as nursing into the college curriculum. In the three years since nursing had been taught at the college, the number of girls enrolled had slightly more than tripled: from four to five to thirteen. She talked to the girls about nursing as a useful subject, but she felt that the prejudice against nursing as a career for Muslim girls remained firmly entrenched and was not likely to lessen in the near future.

Begum F felt her study of Islam and social work enabled her to influence people to have faith in the common man. She declared, "The educated, intelligent class does not feel the common man is capable." Although she had no real way of telling whether she had actually changed attitudes, she stressed the fact that the government had allocated funds for her social-work projects.

The Working Woman

Although a few spoke of customs and traditions against women's education and work, it is interesting to note that very few women, including several high achievers, felt that discrimination against women was a particular problem. For example, Begum E, a trained lawyer, pointed out that as a woman, "You must prove yourself to lawyers, most of whom are men." She added, "Some are *more* accommodating to women." Begum F reported that she had received encouragement as a woman up to a certain point. However, when she reached the senior level in government, she felt some resistance. Begum B, who had held many honorary government positions and was a prominent figure nationally and internationally, felt that it was "more important to feel you were a human being rather than to have a chip on your shoulder as a woman."

In an effort to determine attitudes concerning the role of the Pakistani woman, I posed several questions dealing with such issues as the type of education appropriate for women, independent careers for women, and involvement of women in government or politics. All of the APWA ladies stressed the need for women to have at least a basic education. Most felt that it should be left to the girl's aptitude and her own interests to determine her field of study and to what level she should pursue her education. Only a few suggested that she should pursue that kind of education that would specifically equip her with the skills of a wife and homemaker. For example, Begum A observed, "She should have all types [of education], with emphasis on things which would help her to remain a woman and would help her to be a good wife and mother." The more generally held attitude seemed to support the necessity of an education that would enable a woman to become a good wife and mother, to run her home well, and also to contribute something to society.

In explaining the liberal view of the education of the modern Pakistani woman Begum B observed:

> Education is enjoined in the Qur'an and becomes a matter not of opinion but of obligation. This education should not only be text-book centered, but

also education of the total personality. The woman has been liberated 1,400 years ago from playing a secondary role in society. It has been custom which has prevented her from taking on her full responsibilities. Islam has in no way prevented the woman from playing her full role in society. Rights such as the right to education involve responsibilities and, therefore, if women want rights they must accept responsibilities and help to develop a morally, mentally and physically healthy society. This process begins in the home.[6]

This statement illustrates the apologetic tone of the modern Muslim intellectual's explanation of the status of the Muslim woman throughout history and in modern society. Furthermore, this statement reflects the widespread belief, even among highly educated women, that the woman's primary responsibility is in the home as wife and mother. In fact, the woman's role in Islamic society is complementary to that of the man within the basic unit of Islam, the total family. It is, therefore, not a question of an equal role but rather one of a complementary role. "The woman can accept professional responsibilities," maintained Begum B, "but she must see that she can adjust her dual role of homemaker and wage earner." She really has no other option.

The Begum Ra'ana Liaquat Ali Khan agreed with Begum B's contention that the woman's role is complementary to that of the man, explaining what would appear to be the underlying philosophy of the women's movement in Pakistan:

I am neither ultra-conservative nor ultra-modern in my views, for I believe very sincerely that women should take an active interest and part in public life, *but mainly within the sphere of their own specific interests, capabilities, and limitations, and not to the detriment of their homes and families or their own intrinsic strength and finer qualities as women.* I am one of those who believes that it should be possible for a woman to retain her femininity, as well as do an efficient job of work, assume public responsibility and otherwise participate in public life.[7]

Maintaining that she was "quite happy with the way women are coming out," the Begum added:

It is old fashioned, and should no longer be necessary for a woman to ape a man in order to prove her capability. This is the sign of an inferiority complex. . . . The rights we demand are on *our own specific merits, and not on any artificial basis of a questionable equality.* If a woman is capable to doing a job, *as a woman,* as well as a man can, then she has a just claim to equal consideration, on her own merits and not as a mere comparison with man's merits.[8]

In her view, therefore, the woman has her *own* dual role to play. "As

Table 5. Respondent's Opinions Concerning Women's Involvement in
          Employment, Government, and Politics

Question	Yes		No	
	Number	*Percent*	*Number*	*Percent*
Should women have an independent career?	20	91	2	9
Should women become involved in government?	19	86	3	14
Should women become involved in politics?	17	77	5	23

a housewife she must be trained in skills such as cooking and sewing; but every woman should also have a profession before she marries so that she can stand on her own feet and gain confidence in herself and seek employment *if necessary*."[9]

Of the 22 respondents, 20 (91 percent) favored a woman's having an independent career. Several, although generally in favor, qualified their answers, saying the married woman with children should not work or that the woman should work only when necessary. Only two of the women were not inclined to view careers for women favorably (see Table 5). Begum A generally favored work for women, but warned that women should not work with men because "men don't like women in their fields." Begum J, who is herself a working woman, felt that women should work if necessary, but that the sole aim of a woman is to get a good husband. She added that women should not be passive but ended by saying that it is hard for women to face difficulties and failures.

Begum P agreed that the women should work only if necessary because they have full-time jobs at home, adding that she did not want to "mix the spheres of men and women." Begum C pointed out that the woman's home comes first but that the affluent should help the less fortunate. Begum D agreed that for the married woman, home and family are the most important, but suggested that pursuit of a profession was permissible for the single woman. Begum E maintained that only because she had hired help for the household chores was it possible for her to work. The career woman, she concluded, has a double responsibility, a point of view not unfamiliar to American women.

Begum H saw the proper role for the woman as one of preserving Islamic values through which one can find every solution for every problem. "But, the time is coming," she admitted, "when women will have to work." Begum M stressed the importance of being a good housewife and bringing up one's children in the Islamic way. Begum S thought that the woman should place more emphasis on the house. "If she has extra time she can do social welfare work, but the first social work is in the house." It is interesting to note that in spite of her rejection of marriage for herself, Miss Q still saw marriage as *the* proper role for the woman, adding that one needs a companion in later years.

Women in Government and Politics

A slightly smaller proportion of respondents (86 percent) agreed that women should be free to seek government posts (see Table 5). Only three women rejected the idea of a woman's serving in government, for three entirely different reasons. Begum P felt that men and women have their separate spheres. "Government posts should be reserved for men," she maintained, "for they have superiority in thinking and physical strength." Government service is inappropriate for the woman who has "superiority in love and affection." Women are considered to be "too sensitive and sentimental for government service." Miss R vehemently rejected government service for women because "one has to kow-tow too much to the person in charge. One is not allowed a free hand." Begum U was inclined to feel that women did not generally have the necessary background in government to serve.

Several women, while agreeing to the principle of government service for women, would limit their service to certain fields. For example, Begum M felt that female government servants should take the "lighter side" such as health, rehabilitation, social welfare, or education, but not "the heavier aspects." Begum C agreed, adding that foreign affairs should be run by men. Miss Q pointed out that women should not serve as city commissioners or deputy com-missioners because the duties of these officers include going to the scenes of riots. However, Begum J would not limit the woman's sphere. "Women are needed in government," she observed, "and they should serve in any post including the foreign service."

There was more disagreement concerning the role of women in politics. While 77 percent (17) felt that the woman should be able to enter into politics, the rest would prohibit such activity by women for a variety of reasons (see Table 5). Begum H contended that one must know what is happening in the country but should *not* get actively involved. Begum J was not convinced that politics was a good field for either men or women. "Very few men or women can cope with politics," she contended. "It is better for the woman to influence intelligently. If she has a flair for politics then she can come." Begum

P stated, "The woman should know how and what to vote, but not beyond this," explaining that "if you trust the men, they will do everything for you." She added, "Islam gives women their rights, so what is the point of fighting the men?" She questioned the utility of five or six seats in the National Assembly since "the men are still in the majority and will do what they want to." Miss R emphatically rejected a role in politics for the woman, declaring, "The political climate is too shady!"

On the other hand, Begum D observed, "Without her, politics won't be right. She can influence ideologies, as a mother, for the benefit of the people. In her partnership with men, she can influence what is good for men." Begum M admitted that there is a role for the woman in politics if she is capable, adding, "Sometimes the woman can make better decisions." Miss Q suggested that there is a special need for women's participation in the struggle for the rights of women.

Behind the Veil

Observation of purdah may be considered symbolic of the traditional woman. It is interesting to note that when attempting to define purdah, most of the women drew a sharp distinction between wearing the veil and modest behavior. No one claimed to wear the veil currently, although eight women had worn the veil in the past. Of the 14 who said they had never observed purdah, Miss Q said that she had observed purdah since the age of eight but not in the sense of covering or seclusion. Her mode of purdah consisted of covering her head and modest behavior, but this did not prevent her from going out. She continues to observe purdah in this broader sense (see Table 6).

In fact, several defined the correct meaning of purdah as "modest behavior." However, when asked if they had ever observed purdah, they were inclined to say no, indicating an inclination to define purdah as wearing the veil. Begum C defined purdah in terms of the character of the woman and at least partial segregation of the sexes. She argued, "There should not be free mixing with men but only when necessary." Begum P defined purdah as it is defined in Islamic

Table 6. Observance of Purdah (Wearing the Veil)

| | Respondents | | Mothers | |
	Number	Percent	Number	Percent
Yes	5	23	11	50
No	14	63.5	9	41
Occasionally	3	13.5	2	9

doctrine, that is, in terms of providing protection for women and making society "more clean from bad elements."

Of the eight women who had actually worn the veil, all were encouraged by their husbands or in-laws at the time of their marriage to give it up, including Begum P, who reported that she had observed very strict purdah. Upon her marriage, however, her husband said it was useless to wear the burqa. Begum H said that her in-laws did not want her to wear the veil, but that she still maintained values gained from earlier observation.

Approximately half of the respondents reported that their mothers had observed purdah, that is, had worn the veil, at one time or another. Begum F said her mother wore a burqa only in certain communities. Begum C reported that her mother wore the veil for about ten years after marriage until she became involved in social work but that her grandmother had never worn the veil. A fairly large number reported that so far as they knew neither their mothers nor their grandmothers had ever worn the veil. However, Begum M indicated that her mother and grandmother observed a semi-purdah, which meant that while they did not wear the veil they did not participate in mixed groups. Two respondents reported that their grandmothers had worn the veil but that their mothers had not. Begum B's mother had worn the veil only until marriage to her father, who was against the veil (see Table 6).

Begum B expressed concern over what she saw as the Western scholar's preoccupation with purdah. "This is a most difficult concept for Westerners to understand," she observed. "Wearing the veil," she contended, "is immaterial." She had no objection to anyone wearing the veil if it gives them a feeling of security. She was far more concerned with what goes under the veil: "Is it an educated or uneducated mind?" She continued, "There can be illiterate women who do not wear the veil and highly educated women who do." Therefore, she concluded, "It is not the veil but the degree of education which counts." Citing a recent survey, she reported that it was found that only 4 percent of the total population wore the veil because in the rural areas where most of the population is located, the burqa is not worn in the extended family. In fact, she added, "The burqa is often worn as a cloak or coat."

This figure of only 4 percent of the total population who wear the burqa seems low even when it is realized that the burqa is only one aspect of the practice of purdah. In the cities, the orthodox woman would rarely have occasion to go out of her house, as the men do all the necessary errands. Many women of the lower classes cannot afford to own a burqa. Even so, the proportion of those who wear the veil is surely higher. Such a survey is essentially meaningless as a measure of the practice of purdah.

The tone of the above discussion reflects a rather ambivalent attitude toward purdah. It is important to note that the actual wearing of the burqa may not be the most significant aspect of the observation of purdah. It is, perhaps, the mental attitude that results from this custom and from the segregation of the sexes that is more significant. Even the woman who did not wear the burqa saw her role as limited to something separate and different from that of men—complementary, perhaps, but definitely not equal. It would be difficult to find a Pakistani woman who could conceive of a role other than that of wife and mother for herself or for other women. This attitude, of course, did not preclude the more sophisticated woman's participation in activities outside of her home *as long as those activities did not interfere with her role in the home.* At no time did the APWA directly attack the observation of purdah or attempt to ban the wearing of the burqa. To do so would have, without question, destroyed their effectiveness in other areas.

In general this group of women seemed to accept their established role. They did not seem to worry very much about self-fulfillment, self-realization, or expressing their own individuality. For the most part, this group of women is economically and socially privileged. Their comparatively high level of education, their well-dressed appearance, their well-furnished homes, their servants, their cars, and even the title of Begum are clear indications of their high status. As a group, and in some cases as individuals, they were in close contact with the governing elite. During the Ayub Administration, the President of Pakistan was the official patron of the APWA. The organization's interests were represented in the national and provincial assemblies through women such as the Begum Khudeja G. A. Khan, a founding member of the APWA. In fact, of the six women listed in the "Who's Who" section of *Twenty Years of Pakistan,* a Pakistan government publication, three have been at one time or another associated with APWA. The Begum Ra'ana Liaquat Ali Khan, Founder Life President of the APWA, served as governor of Sind for the Bhutto administration.

The APWA ladies are thus in a unique position to extend their own privileges of education, legal rights, material well-being, health, and general welfare to their less fortunate sisters. However, they seemed reluctant to consider themselves as elites or as activists overtly seeking to change their society. Much of this reluctance seemed due to fear of the power of the ulama, who have been severely critical of the APWA since its inception. The members' attitudes reflect a desire to work through the established traditions and gradually bring about improvements in their society rather than undertake any drastic alterations in the status of Pakistani women or secularization of their way of life.

The APWA ladies are most certainly not revolutionaries. They justify their efforts to improve social, economic, and political conditions in their country on the Islamic teaching of *zakat* or almsgiving. The APWA at no time has engaged in frontal assaults on traditional practices or beliefs, particularly not in dealing with the problem of purdah, which most often is not even viewed as a problem. More often it is considered a completely natural phenomenon in the life cycle of Muslim females. On the whole, there was very little evidence among the APWA ladies of a radical feminist spirit which characterized the women's movements in the United States and Western Europe. There is little claim to equality. The Muslim woman in Pakistan is socialized to know her place.

Notes

1. This chapter is based on a paper prepared for the Southwestern Conference on Asian Studies held at North Texas State University in Denton, Texas, 12–13 October 1973.

2. Ahmad Khurshid, ed., *Marriage Commission Report X-rayed* (Karachi: Churagh-e-rah Publications, 1959), p. 212.

3. *United Nations Seminar on Measures Required for the Advancement of Women with Special Reference to the Establishment of a Long-term Program,* held in Manila, Philippines, 6–19 December 1966. See background paper by Dr. Marguerite J. Fisher, Professor of Political Science, Syracuse University.

4. At the 1966 United Nations Seminar held in Manila it was brought out that generally the Asian woman leader had a mother with more education than usual.

5. It would be interesting to make a study of a group of young women to discover their aspirations for themselves.

6. Interview, February 1969.

7. Begum Ra'ana Liaguat Ali Khan, "The Woman in Public Life" (Utrecht, Netherlands, 1956), mimeographed, p. 2 (emphasis added).

8. Ibid. (emphasis added).

9. All Pakistan Women's Association, Personal interview with the Founder Life President of the All Pakistan Women's Association, the Begum Ra'ana Liaquat Ali Khan, 15 January 1969 (emphasis added).

10 Women in Politics: A Case Study of Bangladesh

Rounaq Jahan

Women's participation in politics is one of the recent research interests in the study of political participation.[1] Data from various countries have shown that though women participate nearly equally with men at the citizenship level, their participation at the elite level is marginal.[2] While the rate of voting for women is almost equal· to that of men, few women contest for public office at the local, state, and national levels. At the higher levels of public office women's participation is nominal, both in the developed industrialized countries and in the less developed countries of the Third World. Data have also indicated certain differential patterns of political participation between the sexes. However, whether or not the sex factor is crucial in explaining these differences is still a debated issue. Obviously we would need some more detailed and sophisticated studies on women's political participation. Cross-national studies are needed to see whether there are cross-cultural similarities in the patterns of women's political participation.

This chapter is an attempt to present some data on women's political participation in a Third World country, Bangladesh. I analyze women's political participation at two levels—at the level of high public officeholders (that is, members of Parliament) and at the level of citizens (that is, voters). At the level of public officeholders, my concern is to find out what kind of women get involved and, more important, what kind succeed in politics. I use data from a 1974 survey of the members of Parliament in Bangladesh.[3] I interviewed 283 members of the Bangladesh parliament out of a total of 315 who were elected in the 1973 national election. Of the 283 members, 15 were women. In analyzing the data on women Parliament members, who obviously constitute the political leadership of Bangalee women, I raise four major questions: What is the early socialization process of women political leaders? How are these leaders recruited to politics?

What is their political ideology and what kind of political issues do
they consider important? And finally, how different are the women
from their male colleagues in their socioeconomic-political
background and their attitude toward political issues? (See Table 1
below.)

To analyze citizen's participation in constitutional politics, I use
data from my survey of voters during the 1973 national election in
Bangladesh. In the survey, we interviewed 1427 voters (941 men and
486 women) in an urban constituency. We also interviewed 225 male
voters in a rural constituency; in the rural constituency we could not
contact the women voters because our women interviewers refused to
go to the rural areas for interviews.[4] In looking at citizens' political
participation, first I analyze citizen's participation in constitutional
politics, and second I describe the pattern of their participation in
mass political movements.

In analyzing the survey data on women's political participation, I
focus on three major issues. First, I describe the demographic
background of women voters. Second, I show the levels of their media
exposure and information on various political issues. And third, I
discuss women's participation in various types of political action. Here
again, as in the case of elite participation, I try to bring forth the
differences between the sexes in various forms of participatory behavior.

I analyze women's participation in movement politics and social and
political organizations because movements and pressure groups have
been more influential in determining the social and political changes
of Bangladesh. Here I raise the basic question: What does a citizen's
political participation really mean in the context of Bangladesh, and
what role do women play in that context? Finally, I analyze some of
the societal and cultural constraints that limit women's participation in
politics in Bangladesh. (See Table 2 below.)

Women in Politics at the Elite Level

In Bangladesh, as in most other countries of the world, few women
participate at higher levels of political decision making. The cabinet
does not have, and never has had, a woman. Only two women worked
as ministers of state, for approximately six months and in typically
women's ministries, that is, education and health.[5] The ruling political
party never had a woman in any significant party office. All political
parties in Bangladesh have separate women's wings, and the highest
party post a woman may aspire to hold is that of the women's
secretary of the party.[6]

The membership of the Bangladesh Parliament comprises 15 women and 300 men. This scant 5-percent representation of women in Parliament is somewhat misleading in that these 15 women were "elected" to the women's reserved seats in the house. Bangladesh's constitution stipulates 15 reserved seats for women in Parliament but these women are not elected by the voters; rather, they are selected by the 300 Parliament members who were elected to the general seats. The Bangladesh constitution does not prohibit women from contesting for the general seats, but the provision of reserved seats for women inhibits parties from giving women nominations for the general seats. In the 1973 election, only two women contested for general seats, and they lost. Bangladesh thus continued the tradition of reserved seats for women that it inherited from the colonial British and Pakistani days. It is interesting to note that while during the Pakistani period the nationalist bourgeoisie in Bangladesh challenged the concept of reserved seats for Hindus and other religious minority communities, they never questioned the provision of reserved seats for women. The Bangladesh constitution abolished reserved seats for religious and other ethnic minorities, but the reserved seats for women continued.

Since only a limited number of women contest for election to public offices, it is useful to take an analytical look at those few women who have succeeded in achieving a leadership position in politics. How does one account for the political involvement and success of these few women? Are the women politicians in any way different from the male politicians in their political outlook? Our survey data on members of Parliament show some clear differences between the men and women in their socioeconomic backgrounds, their patterns of political recruitment, and their attitudes toward politics.

As compared to their male counterparts, the women members of Parliament (MPs) are definitely younger in age, more educated, more urbanized, and come from families who are more educated and more urban-oriented. Fifty-three percent of the women members as compared to 35 percent of the men are less than 35 years of age. Only 13 percent of the women are more than 46 years of age while 27 percent of the men are over 46. Women MPs are also more highly educated; 80 percent of them are college graduates and the remaining 20 percent are at least high-school graduates. Of the male MPs, 69 percent are college graduates and nearly 4 percent did not finish high school.

In spite of their higher education, the women in Parliament are generally full-time housewives with no employment experience. Sixty percent of the women MPs are housewives, and at the time of the interviews they listed politics as their major occupation. Thirty-three percent of the women MPs were teachers before they were "elected" to Parliament. In contrast, the majority of male MPs had an occupation other than politics before they were elected to Parliament; only 13 percent of them listed politics as their major occupation. The two most common occupations for the male MPs are law (26 percent) and business (23 percent). Agriculture is the major occupation of 16 percent of them and 38 percent referred to it as their secondary source of income. None of the women in Parliament listed agriculture as either their major or minor source of income.

The male and female MPs differ significantly with respect to their family backgrounds. The women come from families that are better educated, more affluent, more urban, and more modern than those of male MPs. The fathers of 60 percent of the women MPs were college graduates and had annual incomes of over *taka* 10,000.[7] The fathers of 17 percent of the male MPs were college graduates and the fathers of 43 percent had an annual income of over *taka* 10,000. Most important, the fathers of 46 percent of women MPs belonged to the government service; the rest were mostly professionals, such as lawyers and doctors. The father of only one woman MP was a landlord, and none was a cultivator. In contrast, the fathers of 56 percent of the male MPs were cultivators.

The family background reveals the socialization process of the women in Parliament. As their fathers were generally in government service or in professions, the women MPs grew up and went to school either in small towns or in large cities; they spent little time in village homes. Even in cases where they spent their childhood in villages, they went to towns at puberty either to go to schools or as wives of husbands who worked in urban areas. Since villages did not have separate girls' schools and village society frowned upon coeducation after puberty, women had to go to girls' schools in towns. Additionally, as the fathers were generally college-educated and in government service, they valued education for their children—both boys and girls. The women MPs were married young, as is the custom in Bangladesh, but the husbands were all in a modern occupation with comfortable incomes. They settled in big cities, usually the capital. Thus the women Parliament members grew up in a milieu where agriculture was not the major occupation of the family. They also married into noncultivating families. The women MPs are thus usually a generation apart from the peasant culture of the rural society around them. In contrast, the majority of male MPs were socialized in a rural setting; they grew up in peasant families, went to village schools and small-town colleges, and settled in subdivisional or district towns. Thus they maintained close contact with the rural society and culture around them.

But though the women in Parliament are more educated and come from more affluent family background, they are not excessively rich—only comfortably rich. A mere 6 percent of the women, as against 35 percent of the men, have annual incomes of over *taka* 30,000. Similarly, fewer women MPs have landed property; only 26 percent of them as compared to 70 percent of the men reported owning more land than 6.5 acres. Fifty percent of the male MPs own more than 15.6 acres whereas only 11 percent of the women own that much land. The nonownership of land indicates that the women in Parliament lack a rural basis of support. As has been mentioned, the women MPs belong to families whose major source of income is salary or business, not land. Moreover, women in Bangladesh traditionally give up their land inheritance in favor of their brothers, which partially explains why so few women have land in their villages. In short, women MPs generally do not have any grass-roots contact. They spent little time in rural areas as children and even less in their adult lives. They maintain very minor rural interests—that it, land or house—and as a result very little rural contact. In a country that is only 5 percent urban, these women's lack of a firm rural base is significant. It shows that they have very little identity with rural voters.

When we compare their political backgrounds and patterns of recruitment to politics, we again find a clear difference between the men and the women in Parliament. The women MPs have had very little political experience. Our data show that 60 percent of them had less than 5 years of experience of holding a party office before they were elected. Only 20 percent had more than 15 years of experience. Of the men in Parliament, on the other hand, 40 percent had more than 15 years of experience with the party and only 22 percent had less than 5 years.

Women were recruited to politics either through their involvement in student movements or through women's organizations. The majority of the women MPs were social workers belonging to various women's organizations, since voluntary social work is a socially accepted hobby of the affluent middle-class housewives in the urban areas. The women MPs' involvement with political parties usually started with their work in the women's wings of the parties. The major function of the women's wings is to mobilize and recruit the votes of the women voters, who, after all, constitute half of the electorate. In a purdah society it is impossible for male party workers to contact the women voters; women have to be contacted by women.[8] All the women MPs hold party offices in the women's wing of the party, but none holds office in the top party hierarchy.

Additionally, the women in Parliament have very limited experience in working with the party organization at the village, subdivision, or district levels. The majority of men in Parliament are district party bosses, but women MPs have no such base. Our data show that no woman MP has ever held any office either at the village level or at the subdivision level of the party organization. Only 30 percent of the women MPs held party offices at the district level; 60 percent held party office at the national level. In contrast, only 28 percent of the men in Parliament held offices at the national level of the party organization; 70 percent had held office at the district level, 62 percent at the subdivision level, and 34 percent at the village level.

Thus, compared to the men, the women in Parliament have less grass-roots contact and experience. They are co-opted to the national leadership, albeit in the women's wing of the party, after only a limited period of apprenticeship with the party and after very little experience with party work at the constituency level. Indeed, women Parliament members are much less politicized than are their male counterparts. Their involvement in the various political movements of the country was marginal. Few of them went to prison—the chief criterion of establishing one's claim as a political leader in Bangladesh—and none was in prison for a very long time. Fewer women changed party loyalties—13 percent of the women as against 23 percent of the men. However, this fact seems to be more an indication of the women MPs' noninvolvement in politics than of their party loyalty.

The women's lack of grass-roots politicization is also indicated by their leadership preferences. When we asked the MPs to list three of their ideal leaders, the men generally mentioned the names of Sheikh Mujibur Rahman, the father of the nation (85 percent), H. S. Suhrawardy, the founding father of the ruling Awami League Party to which all the MPs belonged (49 percent), and A. K. Fazlul Haq, the first Muslim populist leader of Bangal (48 percent). Thirty-three percent of the male MPs mentioned the name of one foreign leftist leader, such as Lenin, Mao, Castro, or Che; 29 percent mentioned the name of a foreign democratic leader, such as Lincoln, Kennedy, or Washington. In the case of women MPs, while 92 percent listed Sheikh Mujibur Rahman, only 26 percent mentioned the name of Suhrawardy and 20 percent mentioned Fazlul Haq. Sixty-four percent of the women mentioned at least one foreign democratic leader. That the women MPs generally did not regard two of the great

Bangalee Muslims of the century as their ideal leaders may indicate their noninvolvement in party politics. Since the 1920s, Muslim politics in Bengal has been divided into three factions reflecting a struggle among Fazlul Haq, Suhrawardy, and Nazimuddin. The majority of Bangalee Muslim politicians of the present generation grew up as factional followers of one of these three leaders. Sheikh Mujibur Rahman himself was a follower of the Suhrawardy faction. That women politicians mention the name of a foreign leader more often than that of Haq or Suhrawardy only reflects their lack of internalizing the indigenous political idioms and symbols of the country. Additionally, in comparison to their male counterparts, women Parliament members prefer democratic leadership to leftist leadership. This preference for democratic leadership in part reflects their urban middle-class background. In part it is again an indicator of their ignorance of the dominant political myths and idioms of their society.[9]

Our data show differences between male and female Parliament members with regard to their attitudes toward political issues. In our interviews we asked the MPs to list three major problems facing the country and to suggest three solutions to the problems listed. Women's answers most frequently mentioned population (53 percent), education (46 percent), law and order (37 percent), food (37 percent), and the economy (37 percent) as major problems facing the country. Men's answers, on the other hand, emphasized law and order (41 percent), the economy (41 percent), food (39 percent) and fall in production (15 percent) as the major problems. Only 14 percent of the men perceived population and education as major problems.

The differences in the perceptions of men and women can in part be attributed to their different life experiences. More men than women regarded law and order as a major problem because the male Parliament members usually lived in district and subdivisional towns where law and order constituted a problem. They had to do party work in a milieu of violence. In the first three years after independence five MPs were assassinated and 3000 party workers of the ruling Awami League were reportedly killed. Many MPs had to flee their district homes in order to avoid assassination. The women in Parliament, on the other hand, usually lived in Dacca. They were not involved with party work at the district level, and none of them faced assassination threats. They were aware of the problem of law and order as a general issue, but not as a problem that touched them personally.

Similarly, more women than men regarded population and education as major problems because these issues are specifically linked to women's status in society. Women, as bearers of children, can be expected to be more aware of the problem of population. Since education is a key instrument for raising women's status, women put priority on education. However, there is a consensus among men and women on a number of issues—economy, food, and law and order—which leads me to conclude that once women move up to high public offices, their perceptions of major political issues are not greatly different from those of their male counterparts. They cannot be preoccupied solely by women's issues though they may be sensitive to one or two issues that are directly relevant for raising women's status.

In response to the request for solutions, again there is a consensus among men and women. Both categories of MPs put priority on increasing production in agriculture and industry (75 percent of the men and 69 percent of the women) as *the* solution to the country's problems. Far fewer women emphasized population control (23 percent) or improvement of law and order (23 percent) as solutions to the country's problems. While education was a high-priority problem with women, none referred to it as a solution. In contrast, male MPs listed education as their second-priority solution (24 percent), though fewer mentioned it as a problem. Law and order is their third-priority solution (19 percent), though a much larger number of male MPs mentioned it as a problem. More men listed population control as a solution (16 percent) than mentioned it as a problem.

In response to a question regarding the necessity for amending the constitution, a slightly larger proportion of women (54 percent as opposed to 47 percent of the men) favored the amendment. Surprisingly enough, the proportion of nonresponse was higher among the men than among the women. However, when we asked the MPs to specify the type of constitutional amendment they would prefer, none of the women MPs were able to specify the type. In contrast, 41 percent of the male MPs could specify the amendment they would like to see incorporated in the constitution. By failing to specify the amendment the women parliamentarians were following the general pattern of women's responses to complex and critical questions, to wit, a higher percentage of women than men answer "do not know" to such questions.

In sum, women MPs significantly differ from male MPs in their socioeconomic backgrounds and their levels of politicization, but their orientation toward political issues is not greatly different from that of their male counterparts. As compared to men, women MPs are much more educated and urbanized and come from more modern and urbanized family backgrounds. Their early socialization is different from that of men. They have less contact with the masses. They are less involved in political organizations and movements. This minimal politicization of women MPs, however, is a reflection of the process of their selection. Since women MPs are selected by their male peers and not elected by the voters, they tend to have little grass-roots contact and support. If the women had to face election campaigns and win votes, they would have to be more familiar with the dominant political heroes, idioms, and symbols of the country. The provision of reserved seats for women thus affects the nature of women's political involvement. The underlying assumption behind the concept of reserved seats is that women are still a backward group not competent to face equal competition with men. Political campaigning in a direct election is considered to be too rough for them. The result of this concern to keep women out of the dirty and manly world of politics is that women political leaders tend to have very little experience with party politics and mass political activities, which are the existential realities of politics in Bangladesh. Being in their own cocoons, women political leaders find it difficult to break out of this protected place and claim their rightful equal voice side by side with men.

Table 1. Women in Politics at the Elite Level: Members of Parliament Chosen in the 1973 National Election in Bangladesh

Comparative Background	Men (283)	Women (15)
AGE: (less than 35 years old)	35%	53%
(over 46 years old)	27	13
EDUCATION: (College Degree)	69	80
(High-school degree)	27	20
MAJOR OCCUPATION AT TIME OF		
ELECTION: Politics	13	60
Teacher	—	33
Law	26	—
Business	23	—
Agriculture	16	—
FAMILY BACKGROUND: Education of Father:		
College Degree	17	60
Income of Father: Over *taka* 10,000	43	60
Occupation of Father: Government Service	—	46
Professional	—	46
Cultivators	56	—
Annual Income: Over *taka* 30,000	35	6
Land Owner: Over 6.5 acres	70	26
Over 15.6 acres	50	11
PREVIOUS POLITICAL EXPERIENCE: Less than		
5 years	22	60
More than 15 years	40	20

Table 1 (Cont'd.)

PREVIOUS POLITICAL OFFICE: Village level	34	—
Subdivisional Level	62	—
District level	70	30
National level	28	60
CHANGED PARTY LOYALTIES	23	13
LEADERSHIP PREFERENCES: Sheikh Mujibur Rahman	85	92
H. S. Suhrawardy	49	26
A. K. Fazlul Haq	48	20
FOREIGN LEFTIST LEADER (such as: Lenin, Mao)	33	—
FOREIGN DEMOCRATIC LEADER (such as: Lincoln, Kennedy)	29	64
THREE MAJOR PROBLEMS FACING THE COUNTRY:		
Population ⎱	14	53
Education ⎰		46
Law and order	41	37
Food	39	37
Economy	41	37
Fall in production	15	—
MAJOR SOLUTIONS TO PROBLEMS OF THE COUNTRY:		
Increase production in agriculture and industry	75	69
Population control	16	23
Improve law and order	19	23
Education	24	—
Amend the constitution	47	54

Women in Politics at the Mass Level

It is difficult to measure citizens' political participation at the mass level. Part of this difficulty lies in the multidimensionality of the concept. Participation connotes different things in different political systems. In Western liberal democracies political participation usually refers to "those activities by private citizens that are more or less directly aimed at influencing the selection of governmental personnel and/or the actions they take."[10] Political participation in mobilizational systems (like that of Bangladesh), on the other hand, refers to "support participation, where citizens 'take part' by expressing support for the government . . . by working hard in developmental projects, by participating in youth groups organized by the government, or by voting in ceremonial elections."[11] The majority of available studies on political participation are concerned with participation within the system, that is, elections, party activities, pressure-group activities, and the like. But in most new states of the Third World, significant social and political changes were brought about only by activities outside the system, such as protest actions, demonstrations, mass movements, and revolutions.

In a Third World country, the evaluation of citizens' political participation at the mass level should extend beyond studies of voting and participation in constitutional politics; it should encompass participation in the mass movements and revolutionary activities that more often, and more significantly, influence the selection of government personnel and policies. Indeed, citizens of Third World countries participate at periodic intervals at both levels of political actions—constitutional and extraconstitutional. All-round political activists participate with vigor not only in electoral politics but also in mass movements; both are considered legitimate and necessary political actions.

In this section I shall very briefly evaluate Bangalee women's participation both in constitutional politics and in movement politics. To evaluate women's participation in constitutional politics I shall use data from my survey of the 1973 national election in Bangladesh. Our survey data on voters indicate that apart from the act of voting, women generally do not participate in any other electoral or political activities. They are not involved in social or political organizations or in what could be called activities within the religious community *(umma).* They do not campaign for candidates, and their contact with officials is nonexistent.

It is, however, pertinent to point out that men also generally participate only through the single act of voting. Men's involvement in the various acts of political participation, such as campaigning, community organizations, and political parties, and contact with officials is low. Our data show some differences between men and women in their levels of political information and their involvement in various types of political actions, but it is difficult to judge to what extent these differences are due to demographic differences between men and women. When we compare the responses of urban men, urban women, and rural men, we often find more similarities between urban men and urban women than between urban men and rural men.

Our data indicate differences between urban men and urban women in some key demographic variables. Women are much less educated than men. Their participation in the civilian labor force is also nominal. In the urban constituency, 27 percent of the women voters are illiterate, as against 17 percent of the men. Twenty-two percent of the women and 31 percent of the men attended college.

However, urban women are more educated than rural men; 39 percent of rural men are illiterate and only 13 percent attended college.

Thus while at the elite level women Parliament members are more educated than their male counterparts, at the mass level women are less educated than men. At both the elite and mass levels, women generally tend to be full-time housewives with no occupation. Eighty-five percent of the women in our survey are classified as dependents, and only 5 percent are in a modern occupation. Five percent are categorized as laborers, mainly low-paid workers in factories, and 5 percent as domestic servants.

In comparison, only 7 percent of urban men are listed as dependents. They are mostly students; as the voting age was lowered to 18, a large number of students are enrolled as voters. Forty-three percent of the urban men in our survey are in domestic service, 19 percent in business, and 16 percent are classified as laborers. Three percent of them and 1 percent of the women are reported to be unemployed.

In the rural constituency, 26 percent of men are in agriculture, 28 percent in business, and 8 percent in service. Only 4 percent are classified as dependents.

Another interesting difference between men and women voters is that women appear to be more religious than men. Fifty-three percent of the women and only 33 percent of the urban men reported that they said their prayers regularly. Even rural men, who are much less educated than urban women, follow the religious rituals less rigorously; only 33 percent of the rural men say their prayers regularly. How much of this religiosity has to do with women being full-time housewives and having more time at home and consequently more time to pray is debatable. Since data from other countries also show that women are more religious than men, it is fair to assume that women do follow the religious rituals more strictly.

Differences in demographic variables between men and women are paralleled by differences in their levels of political information. Since women are less educated and spend more time in their home milieu, they receive less exposure to the various organs of the media. Seventeen percent of the women and 44 percent of the men in our urban sample followed the election campaign through the newspapers. Twenty-six percent of the women and 31 percent of the urban men got information from the radio broadcasts; and 12 percent of the urban men attended public meetings before the election as compared with 3 percent of the women. The media exposure of rural men is nearly comparable to that of urban women: 14 percent read the newspapers; 26 percent listened to the radio; and 4 percent attended public meetings. It is significant that urban men depend more on newspapers than on the radio, while urban women and rural men depend more on the radio than on newspapers. It is also interesting to note that though rural men are less educated than urban women, their media exposure is nearly as high as that of urban women.

Additionally, women came into less contact with campaign workers. Nearly 74 percent of the women and 65 percent of the men responded that they had never been contacted by a campaign worker before election.

Given their low level of information, it is not surprising to discover that women have less interest in election politics than urban men. When we asked the voters to list the names of candidates contesting the election from their constituency, 69 percent of the men and 29 percent of the women from our urban sample scored high in their knowledge of the candidates. Nine percent of the urban men and 21 percent of the women scored low. Eight percent of the urban men and 38 percent of the women failed to identify the name of a single candidate. Similarly, when asked to name the parties that put up candidates in the election, 70 percent of the urban men and 35 percent of the urban women scored at a high level of information; 14 percent of the urban men and 7 percent of the women scored at a middle information level; and 7 percent of the urban men and 10 percent of the women scored at a low level of information. Only 9 percent of the urban men could not name a single party, but 48 percent of the women could not.

It is interesting to compare the responses of urban women with those of rural men. In the rural constituency in response to our question regarding candidates, 14 percent scored high, 77 percent scored middle, and 5 percent scored low levels of information about the candidates. Only two percent of the rural men failed to identify a single candidate. In response to the request to name the parties, 13 percent showed a high level of information, 53 percent a middle level and 10 percent a low level of information; 25 percent of the rural men could not name a single party. In the rural constituency the overwhelming majority of voters scored at a middle level of information because the election was mainly a contest between two candidates, though two other candidates also ran. Most of the voters identified the two leading contestants. Thus our data show that as compared to rural men a larger percentage of urban women display a high level of information; but, then again, a larger percentage of women also show a complete lack of information. Urban women are better informed than rural men on general political issues, but their interest in elections is lower.

In response to our question regarding *Mujibbad,* the four guiding principles of state ideology (socialism, nationalism, secularism, and democracy), 96 percent of the urban men, 80 percent of the urban women, and 64 percent of the rural men said that they were familiar with the term *Mujibbad.* However, 39 percent of the urban men, 69 percent of the urban women, and 79 percent of the rural men could not specify a single principle of *Mujibbad.*[12]

It thus appears from our data that women, in spite of having better education, better media exposure, and better political information than rural men, are less interested in elections. Men, both urban and rural, take more interest in elections than do women.

Men, both urban and rural, perform better in response to other questions relating to political participation. The rate of voting for women is generally less than that of men: 89 percent of the urban men, 80 percent of the urban women, and 79 percent of the rural men voted in the election. Furthermore, men appear to be more partisan. When asked if they would vote for a candidate nominated by a party they did not like, 28 percent of the urban men, 18 percent of the rural men, and 15 percent of the urban women replied that they would still vote for the candidate. A larger proportion of women chose not to vote in case of such a dilemma (7 percent as compared to 2 percent of the urban men and 5 percent of the rural men).

Rural men appear to have a greater faith in voting and elections than urban men and women: 40 percent of the rural men as opposed to 30 percent of the urban men and 25 percent of the urban women expected some change in the country as a result of a party's victory in the election. This high level of rural interest in elections is quite typical of small communities around the world.[13]

In sum, our survey data on voters show that women's participation at the citizenship level is limited to the act of voting. Urban men and urban women differ sharply in their levels of political information and their involvement in electoral politics. But since urban men and urban women also differ in their demographic background, it is difficult to judge how much of their differences in participatory behavior is due to differences in the demographic variables. However, when we compare the responses of urban women with those of rural men, who are less educated and less exposed to the media, we find that the latter group is more interested and involved in elections. This leads me to argue that in Bangladesh men, both urban and rural, are more active participants in politics than women.

Women in Movement Politics

If women's participation in constitutional politics is largely ceremonial and at a formal level, their participation in movement politics is even more limited. Although Bangalees have gone through Partition, a national liberation movement, and a mass movement against the

Table 2. Women in Politics at the Mass Level: Voters in the 1973 National Elections in Bangladesh

Comparative Background	*Urban Men (941)*	*Urban Women (486)*	*Rural Men (225)*
EDUCATION: Illiterate	17%	27%	39%
Attended college	31	22	13
OCCUPATION: Dependent	7*	85	4
Laborer	16	5	—
Domestic service	43	5	8
Business	19	—	28
"Modern occupation"	—	5	—
Agriculture	—	—	26
Unemployed	3	1	—
RELIGION: Say prayers regularly	33	53	33
LEVEL OF POLITICAL INFORMATION:			
Newspapers	44	17	14
Radio	31	26	26
Attend public meetings	12	3	4
KNOWLEDGE OF CANDIDATES:			
High score	69	29	14
Middle score	14	12	77
Low score	9	21	5
Failure to recognize a single candidate	8	38	2
KNOWLEDGE OF PARTIES: High score	70	35	13
Middle score	14	7	53
Low score	7	10	10
Failure to name a single party	9	48	25
KNOWLEDGE OF MUJIBBAD:			
Familiar with the term	96	80	64
Unfamiliar with principles	39	69	79
RATE OF VOTING: In 1973 election	89	80	79
Would vote for candidate of party he/she did not like	28	15	18
Would not vote in case of such dilemma	2	7	5
Expect changes from party's victory	30	25	40

*Mainly students.

military dictatorship based in West Pakistan, all in the last three decades, movement politics has involved mostly men, leaving women out. Unlike the revolutions in China and Vietnam (and even to a limited extent the national independence movement in India), which radically changed women's status in society by giving them substantial participation in the liberation movements, the mass movements in Bangladesh did not consciously attempt to integrate women. Women were largely uninvolved in the political movements, in part because of the prevailing sociocultural norm of purdah society which frowns upon women's participation in public affairs.[14] In addition, the low level of women's participation was due to the very nature of the movements, which depended heavily on the mobilized sections of society, that is, students, labor, and the proletariat (rickshaw pullers, small shopkeepers, bus and taxi drivers, and the like). Women's representation in these mobilized groups was marginal.

In the last few decades major political changes were brought about in Bangladesh by mass movements.[15] What is interesting to note is that elections were held at crucial periods to ascertain the people's mandate on these major changes. Such elections had a plebiscite nature. In 1947 India was divided, and the new state of Pakistan was created. Muslim Bangalees not only demonstrated in the streets in favor of Pakistan, but they also voted overwhelmingly in favor of joining Pakistan in the election of 1946. However, soon after Pakistan was born, Bangalees began to feel that they were being treated like a colony by the central government located in West Pakistan. The struggle for autonomy started in Bangladesh in the early 1950s. The language movements of 1949 and 1952 were the major movements of this period. There was an election in 1954, which again had a plebiscital nature, seeking Bangalee opinion on the issue of autonomy. The election results overwhelmingly favored the Bangalee nationalists. The autonomy movements of the 1950s were led by students and professionals. They were restricted to the capital city of Dacca and one or two major urban centers. The movements were generally peaceful, involving strikes, picketing, processions, demonstrations, and mass meetings. Students were the major active participants in these movements and they were unarmed, peaceful, and disciplined. The administration generally used the police force to control the student-led demonstrations, and police violence was minimal. Only once, in 1952, police opened fire on a student procession and four students were killed.

The nonviolent autonomy movements of the 1950s became more militant in the sixties, when the autonomy demands of Bangalees turned radical and leaned toward independence. The 1960s saw the student movements of 1962–1964 against the constitution and education reforms of Ayub Khan, the six-point autonomy movement of 1966, and the anti-Ayub mass movement of 1968–1969, which resulted in Ayub's fall from power. The movements of the 1960s were led by students, but industrial laborers and *lumpen* proletariat were the active participants in the street demonstrations. The movements of the 1960s were not restricted to urban centers but spread to medium-sized and small towns. Picketing, demonstrations, and mass meetings often turned violent. Mob violence, which was absent in the 1950s, was quite frequent in the movements of the 1960s. The administration used armed force to control the movements and the army used instruments of violence more frequently than the police. The mass movements of the 1960s were thus more costly in terms of loss of human lives and property. In the 1950s peaceful student demonstrators had courted arrests by the police; in the 1960s militant mobs faced and battled the armed forces. Mob looting of arms from police stations also started in the 1960s.

At the end of the 1960s, after a decade of mass movements, there was once again an election in 1970, plebiscital in nature, which sought people's mandate on the six points—the radical demands for autonomy. The election results overwhelmingly favored the six points, but the military government at the center refused to honor the election results. Bangalee masses again took to the streets in 1971, and after a year-long armed revolutionary struggle, Pakistan was partitioned and the new state of Bangladesh was born.

Bangalee women sat on the sidelines of the turbulent political struggles of the 1950s and 1960s. In the liberation movement of 1971 their role was more that of victims of war than of active participants in the struggle. The Pakistan movement had not drawn active participation of women—except at the polls—as Bangalee Muslim women were still largely in purdah. Few women were in schools or in the modern occupations. Women's participation in the language movement of the 1950s was also marginal. This movement was mostly a university students' movement, and women constituted a minuscule fraction of the student population. In 1947–48 there were 1593 male students and 27 female students in the university. In 1951–52, the year of the major language movement, there were 2306 male students and 85 female students in the university. Not only were women limited in numbers but moreover the majority of them followed the norms of purdah society, even when they were in coeducational schools. Women students went to the university but spent most of their time in a separate women's common room and reading room. In the classrooms they also sat in their separate assigned seats. They attended classes, went to libraries, took examinations, and earned degrees, but they were not involved in the general life of the university nor were they encouraged to take an interest in general political issues that concerned most of the male students. The separate world of women students revolved around classes, degrees, marriages, and occasionally around jobs. Only a handful of women students participated in the processions and demonstrations of the language movement and theirs was chiefly a token participation.

The movements of the 1960s, especially the education movement of 1963–64, drew a larger number of women students. There was a rapid rise in the enrollment of women students. In 1960–61 there were 3622 male students and 348 female students in the universities; by 1969–70 there were 12,016 male students and 1872 female students in the universities.[16] Women's enrollment in secondary schools also rose—from 66,679 in 1960–61 to 254,472 in 1969–70. The education movement succeeded in getting the active participation not only of university students but also of high-school students. But as the mass movements turned more militant and violent in 1966, in 1968–69 and in 1971, women students withdrew from participating in these demonstrations. The 1966 and 1968–69 movements depended heavily on labor and *lumpen* proletariat participation. These were in the forefront of the *gherao* movement and the breaking of curfew.[17] From 1968–69 onward a number of slum women were involved in street demonstrations and mass meetings, but these women were generally mobilized by the male political bosses to show women's participation in the meetings and demonstrations. Women voted in large numbers—the rate of voting for women was nearly equal to that of men—in 1954 and again in 1970, but they did not participate in the mass movements that gave rise to the great political issues of those two elections.

Even in the liberation movement of 1971, when thousands of young men volunteered to form the *Mukti Bahini* (freedom fighters) and train for armed struggle, not a single women's armed battalion was formed. Only a few hundred women worked as nurses and teachers in the war hospitals and refugee camps. A few women worked in the urban guerrilla force, and there again they were mostly in supportive rather than in combat roles.

It is significant that Bangalee women drew worldwide sympathy and support only as victims of the war when reports were circulated stating that thousands of women—the official figure was 200,000, the unofficial figure even higher—were raped by Pakistani soldiers and later abandoned by their own families as social outcasts. Women and peasants—the two largest unmobilized groups of Bangalee society—

suffered the worst Pakistani atrocities of mass rape and genocide.[18] Their suffering succeeded in creating worldwide indignation against Pakistan and support for the cause of Bangladesh.

However, since women were not politically mobilized, after the war they failed to create any popular movement in support of the raped women. Rehabilitation centers were opened for the victims but the cultural norm of shame and guilt that has forced these women to live the lives of social outcasts has not been challenged.[19] The purdah society's norm of the woman's separate world and the high value placed on the woman's virginity and chastity remained intact even after the liberation war, though the war had amply demonstrated the male-dominated society's failure to protect the woman's sheltered world.

Movement politics almost completely failed to draw women out of their cocoons. Community organizations and political parties were not much more successful. In the 1950s and 1960s we saw a proliferation of community organizations, but women were usually active only in women's organizations. During those two decades, a number of women's organizations were established in the urban centers of the country, most prominent of them the All Pakistan Women's Association (APWA), the Business and Career Women's Club, Zonta, and Women's Voluntary Association (WVA). In addition there were numerous neighborhood groups of *Mahila Samity* (women's associations).

All these organizations were very much like social clubs, where middle-class women met in social and cultural get-togethers and sometimes raised funds for charities. Some of these associations ran schools and handicraft and sewing centers for women. Their major goal was to work *for,* and not *with,* poor women to improve their socioeconomic status.

The APWA, which had branches in all the districts and subdivisions of the country, was very closely related to the power structures. In the subdivisions and districts the wives of the subdivisional and district officers were the presidents of the branch organizations; and in the capital, Dacca, the presidency alternated between the wives of the chief minister and of the governor, depending on their husbands' relative power in the political system. After the birth of Bangladesh APWA was renamed Mahila Samity, but the old leadership pattern continued.

The women's organizations never took an independent position on political issues. Most of them were nonpolitical; some were closely tied with the various political forces and followed the corresponding party lines.[20]

Women's participation in political parties is also restricted. Every political party, including the student parties, has a separate women's wing. The few women who are interested in politics join the women's wings of the parties. The only function of this small number of politically active women is to recruit the electoral support of the masses of women for their respective political parties at election time. Thus the politically active women play the role of intermediaries between the male party leadership and the female electorate. But these women have, so far, failed to exploit their crucial role to the advantage of feminist causes. They did not organize the masses of women on feminist issues nor did they pressure the male party leadership to give women greater participation in the political process.

Women's limited political involvement, especially their nonrepresentation in the higher ranks of political offices, is a worldwide phenomenon. In Bangladesh, however, a number of special constraints inhibit women's political participation.

Women in Politics: Problems and Prospects

The major constraint on women's political participation in Bangladesh is the cultural norm of purdah. The seclusion of women and the concept of a separate world for women, which purdah implies, obviously limit women's participation in politics. Politics, national or local, deals with public affairs—it is concerned with issues outside the home. In a purdah society, a woman's proper place is defined as limited within the four walls of the home.

The woman negotiates the outside world through the intermediary of a male guardian, her father or brother or husband or son. Purdah not only restricts her contact with men, but also makes her association with other women extremely limited. Men, from early childhood on, spend most of their time outside the home and are encouraged to join associations and organizations with friends and colleagues, such as neighborhood and school play groups or clubs, work associations, and community organizations. Women, on the other hand, have to spend their time at home after puberty. Fear of losing virginity and chastity—values on which purdah society places a high premium—is the main reason behind women's seclusion. After puberty, women have only limited opportunities to make and meet friends. Since few women work outside the home, the question of work associations and colleagues does not arise.

While in Islam the idea of *umma* (community) is important, women are excluded from any community celebrations. The religious com-

munity takes little notice of women's existence. Women do not participate in any congregational prayers, specifically the Friday prayer,
the *I'd* prayer, or the funeral prayer. In some of the Muslim countries
of the Middle East, women do participate in separate women's congregational prayers, but Bangalee Muslim women do not. Thus
women are excluded from a sense of community and fraternity not
only with men but also with other women. In nonpurdah societies,
women are at least active in community organizations. In a purdah
society women are not encouraged to form even community organizations. When women are thus segregated with no opportunity for
outside associations and with a cultural norm that disapproves of such
outside participation, it is difficult to mobilize women for any political
action.

While purdah norms make it difficult for women to get interested
in politics, those few women who do succeed in breaking down the
purdah barriers and who do get involved in politics find it hard to
move up the ranks of political offices. Here again, as women they face
two major problems that block their advancement. First, in the kind of
factional political situation that exists in Bangladesh, any ambitious
new entrant into politics needs a factional political leader as a patron.
The younger politicians cannot succeed unless they are in client
relationships with a political leader. For a young woman politician it is
difficult to enter into a patron-client relationship with a political
leader who is a man, for doing so might give the impression that the
relationship extends beyond politics to a sexual relationship. Whereas
a young male politician can publicize to his advantage his close
relationship with the patron leader, for a young woman politician
such publicity would ruin her political career. This dilemma makes it
nearly impossible for women to work through grass-roots politics.
The only women who tend to succeed in politics are related to
powerful politicians and can use that connection without invoking any
suspicion of having loose morals.

All successful women political leaders of South Asia more or less
inherited their position from their politically powerful male relatives.
Indira Gandhi, the prime minister of India, is the only child of
Jawaharlal Nehru, who was one of the founding fathers of Indian
independence and prime minister for eighteen years. She was her
father's political hostess and close confidante, and moved into Congress Party leadership without any grass-roots work. Similarly,
Sirimavo Bandaranaike, the prime minister of Sri Lanka, comes from
a politically established wealthy family and became prime minister
after the assassination of her husband when he was the prime minister.

Male politicians also can utilize the kinship networks for political advancement but, unlike women, are not solely dependent on kinship networks. Men can use the friendship and association networks, too.

The second constraint on women politicians is the problem related to imprisonment and police brutalities. To have experienced imprisonment for a political cause is a long-established criterion of leadership in Bangladesh. Since the days of the independence struggle against the British, the route to leadership positions lay in courting long periods of imprisonment, which are regarded as political sacrifices. No politician could aspire to be a leader unless he had some proof of political sacrifice; and courting arrest and facing police brutalities are indices of political sacrifice. The biographies and resumés of successful politicians list in detail their political sacrifices— the years they spent in prison and the atrocities they suffered at police hands. Without political sacrifice a politician could not achieve a halo of martyrdom, and without that halo it is difficult to win mass support. Sheikh Mujibur Rahman, the charismatic founding father of the nation, always emphasized his sacrifices for the cause of Bangalee nationalism. Sacrifice for a cause implies a claim on political leadership.

It is difficult, however, for women to follow the route of imprisonment to political success. If a woman is imprisoned and "merely" beaten up by police, she could utilize these sacrifices to promote her political career. But if a woman political activist is raped in the process of courting imprisonment and police brutalities, she cannot use her sacrifice as an asset to build up a political career. If a woman politician is raped and killed by police, she might achieve martyrdom and a political movement might be launched in her memory. But if a woman were to be raped and live to tell about it, she would find it nearly impossible to attain the halo of martyrdom.

The most noted case of a woman politician who was raped in prison was that of Mrs. Ila Mitra, one of the Communist leaders of the peasant uprisings of the 1950s. In her statement before the court Mrs. Mitra charged that police atrocities on her included, among other things, rape. Though the publicity of the rape created indignation against the police, Mrs. Mitra's political career faded. The risk of rape and the consequent status of social outcast inhibit women from taking a militant and active part in mass political movements.

The problems of Bangalee women are very similar to those of women in many other Muslim countries. A comparable case is that of women in Algeria. Algeria and Bangladesh have both gone through protracted and bloody political struggles, but the national liberation movements in neither case challenged the basic social structures and cultural norms. Neither political revolution envisioned social and cultural revolution. The leadership in Bangladesh, as in Algeria, defined modernization and development almost exclusively in economic terms, perhaps hoping that modernization would bring with it an improvement in women's status. But the experiences of modern industrial countries have shown that women can be modernized economically and integrated into the modern sector of the economy without becoming equal participants politically, especially in the higher echelons of political decision making.

To facilitate women's political participation one needs to do more than change their economic status. The socioeconomic norms of purdah society must be challenged in order to integrate women fully into the political process. In all other revolutionary societies which have radically changed women's status, such as the Soviet Union, China, and Vietnam, the revolution directly challenged the traditional cultural norm of keeping women isolated and treating them as inferior.[21] In the Western industrial nations, the recent women's liberation movement is again very much a cultural revolution that has raised some fundamental questions about the dominant sociocultural norms and the adverse impact of existing socialization processes and cultural values on women's equal participation.[22] In the absence of such a sociocultural revolution the prospects of equal political participation for women in Bangladesh is very bleak indeed.

Notes

1. Jane S. Jacquette, *Women in Politics* (New York: Wiley, 1974); Jeane J. Kirkpatrick, *Political Woman* (New York: Basic Books, 1974).

2. Maureen Fiedler, "The Participation of Women in American Politics," unpublished paper presented at the 1975 Annual Meeting of the American Political Science Association, San Francisco, 2–5 September 1975; Gillian Peele, "The Role of Women in the British Political System," unpublished paper presented at the 1975 Annual Meeting of the American Political Science Association, San Francisco, 2–5 September 1975.

3. For a fuller report on the survey see Rounaq Jahan, "Members of Parliament in Bangladesh," *Legislative Studies Quarterly*, Spring 1976.

4. In Bangladesh, because of purdah (seclusion of women), women had to be interviewed by women; but no woman wanted to go and live in the villages as the law and order situation was still not regarded as good in early 1973. Women interviewers felt unsafe in the villages so we could complete only male rural interviews.

5. Education, health, and social welfare are regarded as women's concerns. These ministries are regarded as less important than Home, Finance, and Foreign Affairs. Part of this distinction is a legacy of the British Colonial tradition when Education and Health were treated as provincial and hence less important subjects, while Home, Finance, and Foreign Affairs were central and thus more important subjects.

6. The only exception is Mrs. Motia Chowdhury, who was the organizing secretary of the Pro-Moscow National Awami Party (NAP).

7. In 1973 the official exchange was at the rate of 7.10 taka to $1 U.S.

8. *Purdah,* which literally means curtain, refers to the system of seclusion of women prevalent in the Middle East and South Asia. For a fuller discussion of purdah see Hanna Papanek, "Purdah in Pakistan: Seclusion and Modern Occupation for Women," *Journal of Marriage and the Family,* August 1971.

9. We expected MPs to name a leftist leader more frequently, since socialism is one of the four guiding principles of state ideology in Bangladesh. For a fuller discussion on the making and breaking of consensus on socialism see Rounaq Jahan, "Bangladesh: Constitutional Experimentation in the Aftermath of Liberation," unpublished paper presented at the 1975 Annual Meeting of the American Political Science Association, San Francisco, 2–5 September 1975.

10. Sidney Verba and Norman H. Nie, *Participation in America* (New York: Harper and Row, 1972).

11. Ibid., p. 2.

12. Sheik Mujibur Rahman, founding father of Bangladesh and Mujibbad, was brutally assassinated in the August 1975 military coup d'etat that sought to overthrow Mujib's "autocratic" rule and to restore democracy. Most of the ideals, although not the name Mujibbad, survive. In a proclamation issued April 22, 1977, Major General Zaiur Rahman substituted the Muslim religion for secularism as one of the four "ideals" of the Bangladesh constitution. The three others—nationalism, socialism, and democracy—remain intact.

13. Verba and Nie, pp. 95–101.

14. For a detailed analysis of women in the purdah society of Bangladesh see Rounaq Jahan, "Women in Bangladesh," in Ruby R. Leavitt, ed., *Women Cross-Culturally* (The Hague: Mouton, 1976).

15. For a detailed discussion of the political movements in Bangladesh in the 1950s and 1960s see Rounaq Jahan, *Pakistan: Failure in National Integration* (New York: Columbia University Press, 1972), pp. 38–49, 167–177.

16. Adapted from Pakistan, Ministry of Economic Affairs, Central Statistical Office, *Twenty Years of Pakistan in Statistics, 1947–67,* pp. 170–173, 186, and from Bangladesh Bureau of Statistics, *Statistical Digest of Bangladesh,* 1972, pp. 252–253.

17. *Gherao,* an Indian word, literally means "to surround." Strikers surrounded the management and would not let them leave the office for days unless they came to some settlement. For a detailed discussion see Rounaq Jahan, *Pakistan,* pp. 174–175.

18. Anthony Mascarenhas, *The Rape of Bangladesh* (New Delhi: Vikar Publications, 1971).

19. See Rounaq Jahan, "Women in Bangladesh," for a detailed discussion of this point.

20. Ibid.

21. Lenin wrote some very moving pieces on women's subjugation in Tsarist Russia. See V. I. Lenin, *Collected Works* (Moscow: Progress Publishers, 1964), Vol. 23; on Vietnamese women see Le Duan's speech "Role and Tasks of the Vietnamese Women in the Revolutionary Stage," in *Alternatives* 1, nos. 2 and 3 (June/September 1975).

22. For an analysis of rape and political power see Susan Brownmiller, *Against Our Will: Men, Women and Rape* (New York: Simon and Schuster, 1975).

11   Indira Gandhi
as Head of Government

Manjulika Koshal[1]

Indira Gandhi became the prime minister of India on January 24, 1966, after the nation had come to a halt at the sudden death of Lal Bahadur Shastri on January 11. The country was not emotionally prepared to select a new prime minister after his short two-year tenure in office. Unlike Nehru, Shastri had never indicated his successor. As a result, every Congress leader deemed himself capable of the post. Mrs. Gandhi's selection at such a time was a compromise in the hope of avoiding a split of the Congress Party.

Furthermore, some hoped that she would serve as the puppet of the Congress Party. To others, it appeared that she could be easily influenced; to still others she was the strongest vote getter and the only person capable of leading the party into the 1967 elections. In addition, almost everyone agreed that she was needed to continue the Nehru tradition. As Marvin Zim pointed out in a *Life* magazine article, Indira was the choice of Congress Party chiefs who had been virtually suffocated by 17 years of her father Jawaharlal Nehru's autocratic rule.[2] They hoped that she would be reserved enough to stay out of their private realms of power. Hence the 1966 succession essentially was a party affair, and it was party interest and the desire to keep Morarji Desai out rather than national interest that accounted for Indira's victory. In this light one can state that while Shastri in 1964 had been a preeminent candidate, Mrs. Gandhi in 1966 emerged from a process of elimination. Elimination notwithstanding, she was thought to be the most suitable candidate.

According to some, Indira was elected because of her father's name only. However, this analysis is simplistic. Nowhere is there evidence that her father made any attempt to cultivate Party support for his daughter.

In the opinion of George A. Floris, the reason for Indira's victory was that 355 members of India's parliament, who had been handpicked for their candidacies mainly from the late Prime Minister Nehru's personal adherents and friends, chose his daughter.[3] (Only 169 voted against her.) But the question that comes to mind is why only one candidate, Morarji Desai, decided to stand against Indira. Did all the others think themselves less able than Indira, or was their friendship and loyalty to Nehru so great that they decided to forgo their own chances for a prime ministership by choosing Nehru's daughter? Or, what was more likely, were they intent on blocking the election of Desai, the leader of the Congress Party right wing?

The election of Shastri as prime minister, as well as the election of Kumaraswami Kamaraj as party president, were carefully orchestrated by the Syndicate, a small group of Congress Party leaders who had organized in 1963 for the purpose of controlling the Congress Party. The Syndicate had made sure that at the January 1964 All-India Congress Committee (AICC) session in Bhubaneshwar, none of the seven elected to the working committee of the Party (including Indira) supported Desai. Indira received the largest number of votes (347), indicating significant personal support within the party.

Upon the death of Shastri, however, there did not seem to be any candidate able to command the support Shastri had enjoyed. The Syndicate was less united, Kamaraj's position was less secure, and the pressures for unanimity were not so great as they had been in 1964. Desai refused to work with the Syndicate and others toward a unanimous choice for prime minister and instead ran himself in the hope of winning. Desai underestimated his support and Kamaraj managed to rally a large majority in support of Indira Gandhi.[4]

When one examines Indian history and finds that women have been playing active political roles for many years, it is not so surprising that India had a woman prime minister. Years ago Mahatma Gandhi (not related to Indira) often urged women to participate in politics. In 1917 Annie Besant was elected president of the Indian National Congress.[5] She also helped to establish the All-India Women's Congress, the first modern organization of women in India. This group was concerned initially with women's education and social welfare, but later expanded its concerns to social legislation, the legal status of women, and improvement of economic opportunities for women.

In 1937, when the Congress formed ministries in the provinces under the Government of India Act of 1935, women appeared in a new role as legislators and about 80 women entered the legislatures. The next landmark was the freedom struggle in which women fully participated, encouraged by the Mahatma. These women faced bullets, were beaten and arrested by British police, and spent time in jail.

Indira along with her father and grandfather likewise served her time in jail. After independence, the constitution gave unconditional universal franchise to all adult men and women and by 1966, when Indira assumed office, there were 59 women in the Indian parliament. At that time there were only 13 women in the U.S. House of Representatives, a body of comparable size. Presently about 10 percent of the members of parliament are women compared to a mere 4 percent of the U.S. House.

Beatrice Pitney Lamb reports that in recent years there has been a woman governor of a state, two women who served as chief ministers at the state level, and substantial numbers of women serving in every form of government-administered service.[6] A woman has served as head of the Bombay School system with responsibility for the education of 600,000 children. A woman has also served as head of a large university. There are numerous women serving as principals of colleges. But all of these women are part of a tiny minority of highly educated westernized women in a society where the vast majority of their sisters remain illiterate. In other words, like Indira herself, they are the exception, not the rule.

In India almost all of the political parties, even the conservative Jana Sangh Party, have women's organizations. This fact may well facilitate women's running for public office. The general elections of February 1962 give us such an example. Maharani Gayatri of Jaipur, although contesting under the opposition Swatantra Party, won her constituency with a majority larger than that of anyone else in the country. One could say that she won her election merely because she was a maharani. This may be true, but it may also indicate that the educated as well as the uneducated masses of India were ready to accept the political leadership of a woman.

Thus Indians are quite accustomed to seeing women in high office. One Indian remarked that having a woman boss does not take away one's manhood. On the other hand, Indian men marvel at the special treatment given to women in America, such as opening car doors, while women are kept out of all important affairs. The choice of Indira Gandhi was never criticized because of her gender. Whatever criticism was leveled at her choice was on the grounds that she was Nehru's child, *not* that she was his *female* child. In fact, another reason for Indira's selection may have been the brave and dignified example of the Ceylonese prime minister Mrs. Bandaranaike, who had led her country for several years of firm and stable administration. She had proved that a woman is not necessarily too weak or too strong to head a constitutional government.[7]

The selection of Indira was also influenced by her contacts with

foreign dignitaries, her excellent performance as Minister of Information and Broadcasting, her experience in listening to top-level
discussions about politics and government policies while accompanying her father, her education and sophisticated manner, her cordial
personality, her travel experience, her lack of serious enemies, her
ability as a conciliator, her respect for opposition, and her organizational ability. According to some, no prime minister ever entered
office with such prior training for the position.[8] Indira Gandhi, a
child of politics, was uniquely qualified.

Prime Minister in Action

Indira Gandhi's performance as prime minister can be reviewed in
two respects: the one, her handling of the immediate problems, the
other, her attempts toward economic, political, and social improvement of the country. She assumed office at a time when the government faced the most serious problems since the year her father took
office. Two leaders had recently been lost; the monsoons had failed
for the second year in a row, thus creating the worst drought conditions of the century. The resultant food shortages led to inflation and
consequent mass violence in many parts of the country. Also the
eastern border states of Assam, involving the Nagas and the Mizos,
actively sought independent status. Simultaneously, the Sikh demand
for Punjabi Suba on the basis of their language created yet another
problem.

Indira settled the Naga problem in just two meetings with them.
The settlement led to the formation of a committee to maintain
vigilance over hostile activities and to a declaration that Nagaland was
a part of India. The Mizos were overpowered by the Indian police
after a battle of six days. In their case Indira showed firmness, while
with the Nagas, she was cordial.

With regard to the food problem, Indira first tried to end the
violence. Her approach was through conciliation, by sending the
Central Food Minister and the Home Minister to the states and also by
making personal visits. She boldly and publicly admitted the problem
of food and the urgent need to solve it but tried to make people
realize that this would take some time. Her speeches appeared to have
a calming effect. All over the country business and communications
were restored and peace once again reigned, at least for a while. Her
visits and direct communication convinced the people that she sincerely wanted to solve their problems.

Indira solved the Punjab issue by conceding to the demand for the
Punjabi Suba, thus dividing the East Punjab area into Haryana

(Hindi-speaking) and Punjabi Suba (Punjabi-speaking), a just division on the basis of language. But both states demanded the inclusion of Chandigarh, mainly because it was a new, well-planned, and clean city. Indira ended up including Chandigarh in the Punjab and giving Haryana the area of Fazilka for the building of a new capital to be financed by a grant of Rs. 100 million and a loan of like amount. This action has been described as a masterpiece of diplomacy and successfully obliterated major stresses within Haryana's Congress Party.

However, there were some economic problems such as population, banking, and currency that would prove to be far more difficult. Some of the steps Indira took at that time perhaps foreshadowed her more recent actions.

Her first step was to devalue the rupee on June 5, 1966, in an attempt to improve India's foreign trade and foreign-exchange status. The nationalization on July 19, 1969, of the fourteen leading commercial banks, those with deposits exceeding Rs. 500 million, was her second major step. Banks with deposits less than Rs. 500 million and branches of banks incorporated outside India were exempted. Compensation to the erstwhile banks was made available either through a 10-year government bond at 4.5 percent interest or through a 30-year bond at 5.5 percent interest.[9] The main objectives of this measure were to eliminate bank credits for speculative and unproductive purposes, to mobilize resources to agriculture and small industrial sectors, to serve as a source of credit for the poor and as a custodian of savings for the wealthy, to provide professionalism for bank management, and to provide jobs for the young.

The other issues, such as higher income and corporate tax rates and an increased role for the public sector, were interpreted by some as a game of power politics rather than a fiscal program. The contention that Indira's budget was motivated by political rather than by economic considerations may have been true because after the split in Congress there appeared to be no organized opposition to the enlarged role of the public sector. The persons affected by the ceiling on property or wealth appeared to be mostly those in the middle income brackets, not a large voting bloc. Those affected by the corporate tax constituted an even smaller, although powerful, voting bloc. Indira's so-called game of power politics displayed not only her talents as an effective politician but also her strong belief in socialism.

The trend of economic growth that seemed to result from Indira's decisions may have been satisfying and the future may have been promising, yet if the population growth were not checked, all decisions would have proved useless. The Fourth Plan had assigned family planning the highest priority and had allotted Rs. 3 billion, which was almost 17 times more than the allotment of the Third Plan. Dr. S. Chandrasekhar, who was Minister of Health and Family Planning at that time, told the *Overseas Hindustan Times* that 12 million births had been prevented through the family-planning drives. He predicted that the target for reducing the birthrate in the Fourth Plan could be achieved. It was hoped that the growth rate would be reduced from 2.5 to 1.5 percent by 1980.

Indira Gandhi is credited with significant progress made in the field of education since she took office in 1966. India spent 2.9 percent of the national income on education in 1965–66, 3 percent in 1968–69; and in 1980–81 the government proposed to spend over 6 percent. This expected figure of 6 percent compares favorably with more highly developed countries.[10] In fact, the future investments in education, health, nutrition, and family planning were expected to grow by not less than 10 percent per year. Also, in social-welfare schemes alone, there has been an increase of Rs. 41.8 million under the revised Fourth Plan which Indira presented to the Parliament on March 24, 1970.

In her political life at home, Indira had some rough moments. But in the area of foreign policy her life was somewhat easier. She tried to follow in the footsteps of her predecessors by maintaining the policy of secularism, socialism, and nonalignment. At the same time, she was able to keep up cordial relations with almost all foreign countries. After Indira took office many foreign dignitaries visited India, and she was also invited to visit many countries. Her skills in foreign relations helped India to obtain foreign aid and loans for relieving India's food problem. For example, United States Vice President Hubert Humphrey visited India and announced a loan of $100 million on February 16, 1966. On February 20, 1966, the Hungarian Council of Ministers visited India and offered Rs. 250 million credit. The Japanese Foreign Office delegation and the Yugoslavian prime minister followed them. Indira herself represented India at all the peace talks, international conferences, and United Nations meetings.

In reply to a question in the Rajya Sabha (the upper house of Parliament) concerning the government's plan for nuclear testing, Indira stated on November 26, 1970, that India proposed neither to manufacture atom bombs nor to hold underground nuclear tests. This statement, however, became especially significant in light of the later developments that brought India into the ranks of those with nuclear capability. Furthermore, India's support on November 26, 1970, of the United Nations resolution on environmental problems and the attempts to study air pollution in India appeared to be another indication of India's concern with human security and human health.

When Vice President Humphrey visited India in 1966, he probably went to ask India's support for the United States intervention in Vietnam. But Indira startled Mr. Humphrey by her frank and outspoken enunciation of Indian policy on Vietnam, which could not be reconciled with the American armed presence in Southeast Asia. So when Mr. Humphrey returned home he reported to President Johnson that the "girl" who was coming to Washington was a stateswoman of considerable magnitude. Even so, President Johnson was charmed when he found, in addition to her elegance of manner and expression, a sophisticated mind that had been trained over years to deal with political problems and situations. She was polite, gracious, and soft-spoken, but she would not yield on any basic issues of India's national policies.

According to an Indian correspondent in London, "politicians in both parties in the U.K. have said privately that in Indira Gandhi there has emerged a first class political tactician able to manipulate and manage people and situations in contrast to past leaders who were frequently lost in the clouds of the doctrine."[11] This remark was probably made in reference to Indira's bold performance in solving the internal political problems that surfaced soon after she had taken office. But with the general elections of February 1967, everyone became aware that the country no longer believed in one-party democracy. More than half of the states did not poll a majority for the Congress Party. On November 22, 1969, the Indian National Congress (84 years old) finally split, after contesting Indira's leadership.

But Indira Gandhi seemed to have won these fierce battles with remarkable courage, determination, boldness of purpose, and independence of personality.[12] She called a separate A.I.C.C. session at which 445 out of 705 elected members were present. This group removed Mr. Nijalingappa from the Congress presidency and declared invalid Indira's expulsion from the Congress Party. Then Indira reshuffled the Cabinet and was successful in seeing her own candidate, V. V. Giri, elected President of India. Presumably she now had no enemies in her Cabinet. For a time, she commanded overwhelming support from the opposition parties, such as the Dravida Munnetra Ḳazhagam (a Tamil-oriented antinorthern party), the Communists, and some independents.

By a random sample survey conducted in August 1969, Indira was found to be the only member of the Congress Party who commanded all-India support. This survey was conducted by the Indian Institute of Public Opinion to measure the popularity of the important leaders. The findings disproved the allegations that Indira's major appeal was only to the young voters, the uneducated, and the lowest income groups. Moreover, she was the only leader who commanded not only reverence but also affection.

Her popularity and her performance in office lead one to conclude that women not only can head their government but can also prove successful. This statement could be made with even greater confidence after the fifth general elections of March 1971. Over 275 million voters exercised their right to vote, electing 518 members of Lok Sabha (the lower house of the Parliament). Indira and the New Congress won a sizable majority. In fact, the New Congress captured all seven seats in the Delhi area, formerly a Jana Sangh (conservative Hindu party) stronghold. Significantly, every minister of Indira's cabinet was returned, indicating support for her policies. This victory was not only a surprise to all but also appeared to be a clear indication of the people's faith in Indira's abilities and future performance. A few years afterwards, however, she faced charges of corruption in election campaigns and eventually was defeated at the polls, perhaps indicating that the enchantment was wearing off in some quarters.

After the Peak

It seems appropriate to add a few more points about Indira as head of the government, especially in view of her controversial enforcement of emergency powers beginning in June 1975 and her subsequent defeat at the polls.

The country made definite progress in economic growth during 1975–76. A World Bank report highlighted some of the more significant and favorable developments in the economy during Indira's final years: a bumper harvest at record level; control of the high rate of inflation; a significant decrease in the deficiencies in the supply of electricity; an increase in coal production by more than 10 percent over previous years; a great reduction in the man-hours lost by strikes in the industrial sector; a reduction in smuggling and black-market activities; achievement of a high level of efficiency by public enterprises and administration services; great improvement in the balance-of-payments position (with the accumulation of about $800 million in reserves) in spite of the continuing high trade deficit of about $1500 million; and a dramatic reduction in wholesale prices. At the end of January 1976, wholesale prices were 8 percent below the level of the previous year and were still declining.[13] In addition, it is estimated that between 1952 and 1975, 22.5 million births were prevented through the IUD (intra-uterine device) and sterilization.[14] A target of zero population growth was projected by 1984.

These improvements resulted from some changes in basic policies of the government which were based on careful thought and planning. For example, the government's efforts to increase supplies of scarce goods, on the one hand, and to curb demand, on the other, along with the bumper harvest, made India's anti-inflationary program one of the most successful. Similarly, an increase in food production was possible due to the government's policy of stopping the genetic deterioration of high-yielding varieties of wheat and reducing fertilizer prices. Such problems as overriding unemployment, corruption, and explosive population growth have been greatly reduced as a result of the drastic measures taken by the government. Specific measures were taken to deal with what Indira believed to be a crisis situation.

Most of these measures were part of the twenty-point economic program initiated just after the Emergency was declared on June 26, 1975. In the world reaction to her use of power, almost every nation seemed to favor the twenty-point economic program. However, opinion varied in regard to the purpose of these measures. Some circles believed that these changes were temporary and were politically motivated to win public support for the Congress Party. Some even thought that these measures were adopted under the garb of the Emergency so that Indira could remain in office. Those who charged Indira with such self-serving motivation point to the reports that tens of thousands of her political opponents were arrested; civil rights were suspended and the press was censored. In late October of 1976, the government postponed national elections for the second successive year because "disruptive forces" were an even more dangerous threat than when the Prime Minister had imposed the Emergency 16 months earlier.

Nevertheless, some very important facts need consideration. First, in any assessment of the Emergency it could be argued that the government needed to use emergency powers when the political and economic situation of the country became uncontrollable and the peace and liberty of the people were in danger. In recent years there had been signs of political disintegration. Civil servants appeared indifferent to the public welfare. Corruption was rampant, and there was discontent among workers. The opposition attempted to incite not only workers but even the army and the police. As a result, the functioning of the government appeared to be paralyzed.

The second relevant point is an assessment of the results of the Emergency. After reviewing the list of measures adopted and the policies implemented by the government during the Emergency, one would have to agree that a number of benefits for the public followed after the Emergency was declared in 1975.

Third, one should review the allegations Indira faced and her reaction to them. These allegations originated in 1971 when in her home state (Uttar Pradesh) her opponent Raj Narian (a Socialist Party candidate) charged her with fourteen violations of the election laws. The case dragged on and in 1975 Indira finally testified in her own defense. On June 12, 1975, she was found guilty of two of the fourteen charges. One charge involved the use of a government officer to work in her campaign, and the other dealt with the use of local officers to prepare for two campaign rallies. Accordingly, she was asked to give up her seat in Parliament and to hold no elective office for six years. She immediately appealed to the Supreme Court in New Delhi.

On the face of it, both violations were trivial, but the opposition party clamored for her resignation, dramatizing the issue of corruption to win popular support. On June 24, 1975, Indira received a conditional stay of her sentence from the Supreme Court. She was allowed to remain as Prime Minister provisionally but not as a paid or voting member of the Parliament.

After this decision, Raj Narian and his party announced a week-long civil disobedience movement. It was the resulting disruption that prompted Indira to impose Emergency rule two days later. A constitutional amendment was enacted that granted the prime minister and the president of India immunity from criminal and civil charges stemming from offenses committed before they assumed office and while they held office. This amendment thus nullified the specific charges of which Indira had been found guilty.

Some critics questioned the ethical grounds for such an amendment. Some attacked Indira for thus opposing basic principles of democracy. However, she evidently believed that if she had not proclaimed the Emergency, the opposition would have destroyed Indian democracy by extraconstitutional means. She argued that democracy meant responsibility and discipline, not license. Democracy comprises two obligations—the obligation of the government to protect freedom of the press, freedom of speech, and freedom of association and the obligation of citizens not to paralyze the functioning of the government. But according to Indira, democracy was being destroyed by abuse of the very freedoms democracy is intended to protect. Thus she argued that it was necessary for the government to enforce discipline by suspending fundamental rights as well as the national elections.

National elections had never before been postponed in the history of independent India. But under the emergency powers spelled out in the Indian Constitution, elections could be postponed one year at a time for as long as the Emergency lasted. And the Emergency, with its suspension of civil liberties and its assumption of broad police powers, could last as long as the government wanted it to.

One Indian observer suggested in the *New York Times* that "to protest now that Mrs. Gandhi is using means that are too drastic is the height of hypocrisy." India, he observed, "cannot, at this stage, afford the luxury of American-style 'politics-as-usual' when people are crying for the bare necessities of life." He asked, "What is the value of freedom of dissent or a free press to an illiterate farmer or a grossly underpaid teacher in an Indian village?"

But there were also grave misgivings. In the words of an opposition member of Parliament, also quoted in the *New York Times:* "Let the trains run on time and the students stop rioting. It's good, and I'm all for it, and I will say I am. But why did we need an Emergency for that? Why must we achieve these gains at such enormous cost to Indian democracy?"

Charges of dictatorship aimed at Indira stemmed in part from limitations placed on the jurisdiction of the court system over federal laws and constitutional amendments. These limitations were designed to give the President (generally believed to be a figurehead taking his orders from the Prime Minister) a free hand to make changes in the constitution during the following two years without parliamentary approval. Bitter opposition also resulted from the fact that thousands of Indira's political enemies, including some members of Parliament, found themselves in jail. On the whole, however, it is more likely that the government's program of forced sterilization rather than such civil-liberties issues was responsible for Indira's overwhelming defeat at the polls in the March 1977 general elections. In the rural constituency that Indira had carried by 110,000 votes in the 1971 election, she lost by 55,000 in 1977. Her son Sanjay, in his first venture into elective politics, was defeated by 75,000 votes in a neighboring district.

There is a certain irony in the fact that Morarji R. Desai, with whom Indira had done battle in the 1969 Congress Party split, became the new Prime Minister on the Janata Party ticket at the advanced age of 82. He thus led the first change in party rule at the national level since Independence. Desai and most of his cabinet had spent part of the Emergency period in jail, an interesting parallel with Indira and her father and grandfather under the British. In fact, the press, severely censored during the Emergency, almost universally hailed Indira Gandhi's defeat as "a second liberation struggle" for India.

However, Indira's "retirement" from politics was short-lived. In the parliamentary by-election of November 5, 1978, she made a successful comeback, showing characteristic resilience, and no doubt embarrassing Prime Minister Desai. She defeated the Janata Party candidate, 60-year-old Verendra Patil, by 249,376 to 172,043 in Chikmagalur, a district 1100 miles south of New Delhi. It remains to be seen whether she can work her way back into national leadership from her newly won position as opposition leader. The world has certainly not heard the last from Indira Gandhi, but there is little reason to believe that her achievement as India's first woman Prime Minister has contributed to any significant increase of women in high places in Indian government and politics.

Notes

1. The author is thankful to Professor Usha Mahajani for her comments and suggestions on the earlier draft of this paper, which was originally prepared for the 23rd annual meeting of the Association for Asian Studies in Washington, D.C. 29–31 March 1971.
2. Marvin Zim, "The Lady Who Now Leads India," *Life,* 28 January 1966, p. 27.
3. George A. Floris, "India Under Indira," *Contemporary Review,* October 1966, p. 176.
4. For a detailed discussion see Stanley A. Kochanek, "Post Nehru India: The Emergence of the New Leadership," *Asian Survey* 6, no. 5 (May 1966).
5. Mrs. Annie Besant was of European ancestry, yet she could emerge as an Indian lady; no one ever questioned her bona fides. She was an Indian woman because she felt and behaved like one. Moreover, there is something like an idealized, or cultural, as against racial ethnic concept of Indian womanhood in India. Moreover still, she was born in Madras.
6. Beatrice Pitney Lamb, *India: A World in Transition,* 4th ed. (New York: Praeger, 1975), p. 164.
7. Floris, p. 176. Mrs. Bandaranaike lost her bid for reelection in July 1977.
8. Michael Brecher, *Nehru's Mantle: The Politics of Succession in India* (New York: Frederick A. Praeger, 1966), p. 106. See also S. Vijayanand Bharati, *Can Indira Accept This Challenge?* (Bombay: Vora & Co., 1966), p. 250.
9. Provision for interim payment also existed, to the amount of half their paid-up capital, in cash on the condition that the amount should be distributed among the shareholders.
10. The United Kingdom spends 4 percent of its national income; the United States, 5.1 percent; Japan, 5.2 percent; and the USSR, 7 percent.
11. *The Overseas Hindustan Times* 20, no. 18 (29 November 1969), p. 3, col. 4.
12. Indian people unaware of her determination, and seeing only her fragile and delicate figure, also suffered anxiety when she was visiting the West for the first time after becoming Prime Minister. They thought that the big, bad wolves of the Big Powers jungle would frighten the Little Red Riding Hood from India out of her wits.
13. *The Overseas Hindustan Times* 27, no. 22 (27 May 1976), p. 16, cols. 1–2.
14. *The Overseas Hindustan Times* 27, no. 1 (1 January 1976), p. 3, col. 4.